# THE WAR OF 1812 IN THE AGE OF NAPOLEON

CAMPAIGNS & COMMANDERS

GREGORY J. W. URWIN, SERIES EDITOR

# THE WAR OF 1812 IN THE AGE OF NAPOLEON

Jeremy Black

University of Oklahoma Press : Norman

Library of Congress Cataloging-in-Publication Data

Black, Jeremy.
The War of 1812 in the age of Napoleon / Jeremy Black.
p. cm. — (Campaigns and commanders ; v. 21)
Includes bibliographical references and index.
ISBN 978-0-8061-4078-0 (hardcover : alk. paper) 1. United States—
History—War of 1812. 2. United States—History—War of 1812—
Causes. 3. United States—History—War of 1812—Influence.
4. Great Britain. Army—History—War of 1812. 5. Great Britain.
Navy—History—War of 1812. 6. Great Britain—History, Military—
1789–1820. 7. Great Britain—Foreign relations—1800–1837.
8. Napoleonic Wars, 1800–1815. 9. World politics—To 1900.
I. Title.
E354.B55 2009
973.5'2—dc22

2009013810

The War of 1812 in the Age of Napoleon is Volume 21 in the
Campaigns and Commanders series.

The paper in this book meets the guidelines for permanence and
durability of the Committee on Production Guidelines for Book
Longevity of the Council on Library Resources, Inc. ∞

1  2  3  4  5  6  7  8  9  10

TO WILLIAM HAGUE

William Steeple Davis, *Victory of Frigate United States Over the Mace-donian* (ca. 1911). Glass negative, 8 in. × 10 in. A gift of the State Historical Society of Colorado. Library of Congress, Prints & Photographs Division, Detroit Publishing Company Collection, LC-D416-22696.

# Contents

# Maps

# Preface

"We went to Washington. . . .
And burned down all his stuff."

"The War of 1812," a song from the Canadian play *The War of 1812* by "Three Dead Trolls in a Baggie,"[1] is not the greatest music. Moreover, its presentation of the Canadians punishing a mad President Madison by burning the White House is wrong, although the lyrics have more edge than Jimmie Driftwood's folksy song "The Battle of New Orleans," which, in turn, was a hit for the British singer Lonnie Donegan.[2] The lyrics from the Canadian play also capture a violence commented on by Thomas Jefferson, the former President, in 1816, when he wrote of

> the different degrees in which the war has acted on us. To your people [the British] it has been a matter of distant history only, a mere war in the Carnatic [south-eastern part of India], with us it has reached the bosom of every man, woman and child. The maritime parts have felt it in the conflagration of their houses and towns, and desolation of their farms; the borderers in the massacres, and scalping of their husbands, wives and children, and the middle parts in their personal labours and losses in defence of both frontiers, and the revolting scenes they have there witnessed.[3]

Flames and water. These are abiding images of the War of 1812, a war that lasted until 1815 and was crucial to the destiny of North America. Flames most famously with the burning of much of the new capital of Washington by British troops in 1814. Water because many prominent clashes occurred at sea; because the naval struggle on the Great Lakes and on Lake Champlain was crucial to the fate of Canada and the war between the British forces based there and the Americans; and because it was by sea that the British came to attack America's cities, successfully at Washington, but unsuccessfully at Baltimore and New Orleans.[4]

1812 is most remembered in history as the year of Napoleon's disastrous and fatal invasion of Russia, but, as Moscow was in flames, another crucial struggle was being waged across the world in North America. The War of 1812, between the world's leading empire, Britain, and the first of the states that won independence in the New World, the USA, was to be of great importance to the fate of North America. Crucially, this war ensured that the USA was not to conquer Canada. This was fundamental not only to Canada, for which the conflict was the first stage to confederation in 1867, but also to the USA. Indeed the war was a war of survival for Canada and the cornerstone of Canadian national identity, or at least of the country's creation myth. The attempt to "liberate" Canada was also central to Americans' understanding of the regional and global role of the USA, as well as their understanding of the nature of the American Revolution, with the "liberation" of Canada presented as unfinished business from the previous conflict.

The history of the USA, however, would have been very different had it included Canada and the Canadians, not least because the slave states of the South would have been in a decided minority. Moreover, the public culture of the USA would have had to adapt to the fact that Canada, at least initially, would have been occupied territory, and, moreover, territory that Britain would probably have sought to reconquer. The role of an ethnically French Québec in a greater USA might also have been very interesting, as would that of Ontario with its former American Loyalists who had taken refuge there. Their inclusion in the Union might have led to the strengthening of a certain kind of conservatism. The war also saw the crippling of Native American (known as "Red Indian" in my childhood) resistance east of the Mississippi, both in the Old Northwest and in the Southeast, as well as the end of British-Native American cooperation; and this was crucial to the eventual American advance to the Pacific.

In turn, the War of 1812 led to monumental changes in the political map of the USA and to the enshrinement of Jeffersonian Republicanism as the dominant interpretation of the Revolution. Indeed the political consequences of the war, its impact on America's politics, public culture, economy, and territorial expansion, were more important than its military results. The war buried the Federalist Party, with significant consequences for the political development of the country and for American public culture. The conflict, moreover, encouraged the economic transformation of the USA, so that it focused on industrial production, rather than on importing manufactured goods from Britain. This was to be of crucial importance to America's development. Britain's failure in 1814–15 to inflict serious defeat on the USA helped ensure an eventual transformation in the relationship between the two countries toward a less hostile situation. It was indeed to be the last war between the two powers, and this helps underline its importance both to their histories and in world history, while more specifically, this book indicates the relevance of the international context to American experience of this war.

Lastly, as an unwanted war from the British perspective and an unsuccessful one from that of the USA, this conflict shows how easily wars can break out and how they can fail to fullfil expectations. Both points are worth pondering today, and the book indicates the limitations of expeditionary warfare, as well as of other specific problems encountered by engaging in warfare in that period.

Discussion of war can lead us to forget its horror. It is salutary to note from the account by Shadrach Byfield of the 41st Foot, a regiment in the British army, in particular his description of the aftermath of the battle at Frenchtown in January 1813, in which he was badly wounded:

> While in the barn I was much affected by seeing and hearing a lad of about eleven or twelve years of age, who was wounded in one of his knees. The little fellow's cries, from the pain of his wound, his crying after his dead mother, and saying that he should die, was so affecting that it was not soon forgotten by me. He was a midshipman belonging to one of the gunboats.[5]

Joseph Hutchinson of the Royal Fusiliers, a young but experienced veteran, provided another insight when writing of his return to the safety of a frigate after the New Orleans campaign:

It is quite impossible to describe my feelings in finding myself in comparative comfort, for on disembarking 20 days before we were desired only to take what we had on our backs and in consequence for those days we never had our clothes off. I now found my baggage on board . . . and after a good dinner and a glass of comfortable grog [rum and water] turned in to bed and got a comfortable sleep without the dread of having a shell tumble on us every instance."[6]

This book is a product of an Atlantic vantage point, which accounts for its contribution to the academic coverage of the war as the latter tend to reflect national perspectives, mostly American, but also Canadian. The book offers a dramatic war narrative, but it is framed within a political and economic account that makes sense of the struggle.

It is my great pleasure to record my enjoyment of my visits to North America, both Canada and the USA, the two countries whose separate paths were secured by this war. In the period when I was writing this book, I was fortunate to be invited to speak at Monticello, Adelphi, Auburn, Sam Houston State, and Mary Washington Universities, the Universities of West Florida, North Georgia, West Georgia, and Southern Mississippi, Wabash College, and for the Strategy and Policy Division of the US Navy's Division of Distance Education. Katherine Braund, Guy Chet, David Gates, Jeanne Heidler, Wayne Lee, Kevin McCranie, Peter Onuf, Thomas Otte, John Stagg, Armstrong Starkey, Neville Thompson, Neil York and four anonymous readers kindly commented on an earlier draft and Wade Dudley, Richard Harding, Andrew Lambert, James Lewis, and Sam Willis on sections of the draft. I have also benefited from the advice of Kenneth Baker, Rafe Blaufarb, Jay Buckley, James Chapman, Frank Hamilton, Peter Hoffenberg, Michael Leggiere, Naomi Nelson, Nicholas Rodger, and Harvey Sicherman. William Clifton was most helpful on a visit to Pensacola and Annette Bonacquisti on another to Philadelphia. I am also grateful to the staffs of the Special Collections section of the libraries of Auburn University and the University of West Florida, the Pennsylvania Historical Society, the British and Bodleian Libraries, the National Archives, and to John Draisey, the county archivist at Devon Record Office. I would like to thank Charles Rankin, editor in chief of the University of Oklahoma Press, and Gregory Urwin, general editor of the Campaign and Commander's Series, for their support, and Steven Weingartner, for proving an exemplary copyeditor. Finally, Jon Latimer, who wrote a good book on the war, encouraged me in this project, not least to offer a different perspective, and I much regret his early death.

Looking back, I recall with pleasure the company of Harry Coles, a noted historian of the conflict, when he was a visiting fellow at the University of Durham, and would like to thank Stan Carpenter for showing me some of the campaigning sites of the war on several trips to the USA, including Fort McHenry. Finally, it is a great pleasure to dedicate this book to William Hague, a distinguished historian of this period as well as a noted parliamentarian.

# Note on Terms

As in any conflict in which there were a number of participants, there are different terms that may be used, and discussion with other scholars reveals that these terms are employed with cause. For example, to use Native Americans, as in this book, neglects the extent to which some lived in modern Canada, where they are known as First Nations, a term not generally employed in the USA. As a result, some scholars favor Indians. Yet, in a book that deals with British military commitments as a whole, and therefore discusses warfare in India, such a term is confusing. Native Americans is the preferred term here, not least because most of those considered lived in what is now the USA, while Canada is also part of North America.

There has been confusion about proper names, an issue profitably addressed by Donald Hickey, the leading American scholar on the war, in his excellent survey of misunderstandings and myths, *Don't Give Up the Ship!* (Urbana, 2006). For example, he underlines that Fort Michilimackinac should really be termed Mackinac; the island, in contrast, is shown on maps of the period as Michilimackinac and some authors refer to it by that name as well as Mackinac. Hickey also points out that Malden has been misapplied and is the name of the township not the fort, which should be called Fort Amherstburg.

# THE WAR OF 1812 IN THE AGE OF NAPOLEON

# INTRODUCTION

The War of 1812 is etched into the American memory, with the heroic defense of Baltimore in 1814 and New Orleans in 1815 fitting symbols of national fortitude. The first indeed is remembered in the lines of the national anthem, "The Star-Spangled Banner." The achievements of frigates such as the *Constitution* against the mighty British navy in 1812 also serve as a powerful example of valor and resolution, as does Oliver Hazard Perry's total victory over a British squadron on Lake Erie in 1813.

The war is even more important for Canada, as Canadian regulars, militia, and volunteers played a central role, alongside British regulars, in ensuring that the USA would not spread north. Canada's survival was the product of the War of 1812, and there is a direct path, from the major Canadian military effort in the war to confederation in 1867, the key step in the creation of an independent Canada.

In leading to the creation of an independent Canada, the War of 1812 is also a reminder of the role of contingent factors and chance events in the shaping of America's frontiers, with all the consequences that that shaping had for the domestic political development of the USA. Although the major cause of the conflict was American maritime grievances against Britain, the War of 1812 might have led to the annexation of part or all of Canada, or to a peace treaty, or subsequent settlement, that drew the unsettled border of Canada and the USA farther north than was to be the case. If so, the consequences would have included a greater number of free states within the USA, which might well have affected the dynamic between free and slave states. Equally, the war could have led to a Canadian border that was farther south, with future states like Washington becoming part of Canada. Moreover, as a reminder of the uncertainty of frontiers, cooperation between Britain and the Native Americans was a challenge to the expansionism of the USA.

Yet the war is also widely forgotten. This is particularly so in Britain, let alone Continental Europe, in both of which it is totally overshadowed by the Napoleonic Wars. Thus, accessible and commercially successful studies of the British army have included no mention of the conflict,[1] while it is not taught in British schools, and scarcely, if at all, covered in university courses. Nor does it feature extensively in fiction.

There are also key aspects of the struggle that are neglected in the USA, not of course among scholars, who have produced excellent work,[2] but as far as the wider public is concerned. Most of the latter are unfamiliar with the repeated American military failures during the war, with American political divisions, and with the fate of the Native Americans. This book directs attention to all these facets. It treats the War of 1812 as important for the history of North America, but also as instructive about the limitations of expeditionary warfare, both American and British. The last is directly topical today in what has become, since the end of the Cold War, an age of American-British (rather than Anglo-American) expeditionary warfare. The consequences, in the War of 1812, both of engaging in an indecisive war and of command faults, were drawn out at the time of the Vietnam War,[3] and their relevance remains.

The USA was a state born in war, and its early decades as an independent country involved the assertion of power through force, against both foreign and domestic challenges. Indeed, national needs and debates focused on force, and on how best to secure, sustain, and use it, were crucial in the political and governmental history of these decades. The subject of force, however, is generally neglected these days, because of a preference, in accounts of the American Revolution and of subsequent decades, for social themes, especially currently topical ones of gender, sexuality, and race. Furthermore, among political historians—and, here again, American scholars are not alone—

there has traditionally been a disinclination to come to terms with the formative context of international competition and military need for the character and development of countries. Under this head, the hostility to the teaching of military history in many American university history departments, and the marginalization of the subject there, are richly suggestive.[4]

In seeking as a foreigner to discuss the subject, there is, of course, a danger that the opposite approach is taken. This entails an excessive focus on this international context to the early republican period of American history at the expense, in particular, of the role of domestic political debate in not only framing but also determining the understanding of this context, and therefore in providing the essential narrative. Yet, this international context is a necessary perspective, and, moreover, it is one that is generally underplayed in the standard accounts of the War of 1812—a conflict that, in fact, was very much set within a wider context of international conflict.

If contexts are the order of discussion at the outset, then the interpretative one also requires understanding. Here the key problem is posed by American exceptionalism, the conviction that America was, and is, different, that there is, for example, a distinctive American way of war.[5] This is an approach that discourages American scholars from looking for parallels that might add comparative insights, and foreign scholars from doing the same. In contrast to this emphasis, America was not in fact alone between 1775 and 1815 in having to define itself as a new state in an acutely threatening international order, for this was also true of a host of states and would-be states across the Western world. The usual comparison for the American Revolution is with the French Revolution that began in 1789, which, in fact, was only one among a number of European, and indeed Western, revolutionary or radical movements. In several countries in the 1780s, shortlived radical governments were established. These included Geneva, the United Provinces (modern Netherlands), and the Austrian Netherlands (modern Belgium), in all of which, unlike in the USA and France, the new order was suppressed by counter-revolutionary force.

The destruction of Polish independence can also be located in this context, as the reform movement that had drawn up a new Polish constitution in 1791 was a particular issue for Catherine the Great of neighbouring Russia. Initially successful in maintaining their independence in 1794, the Poles were crushed later that year and their country partitioned out of existence in 1795 by the neighboring empires. This fate was a chilling threat to the USA, not least because the willingness and ability of Austria, Prussia, and Russia, despite their differences, to combine to destroy Poland underlined the challenge potentially posed by British, French, and Spanish power in the New World. And indeed, this was an issue for the USA, with, from 1783, Britain still controlling Canada; Spain the colonial power in Florida (which then stretched to the Mississippi) and Louisiana; and France allied to Spain and strong in the West Indies. The world's three strongest naval powers were, in order, Britain, France, and Spain. The USA could not compare, and it was unclear that it could compete. The fate of Poland was also a reminder that the price of liberty was eternal vigilance, a theme with which American leaders, anyway, would have been familiar from their reading of the classics and also from the history of Israel in the Old Testament. The classics and the Old Testament also taught that the danger could come from within, as it fatally did to the Roman Republic, as much as from without.

Across the Western world, the issues were similar. In particular, as with all revolutionary periods, irrespective of the goals of policy, there was the question of how to secure the survival of the revolution, how to ensure the availability of the necessary military forces, and how best to control them. The last involved both the specific issue of their loyalty, and the more general one of long-term political and social impact. The issue of loyalty was most acute if the new political system was felt to be under threat. A sense of danger led, for example, to the execution of French Revolutionary generals for being unsuccessful, as Dillon was in 1792, and Custine in 1793, because a lack of success was held to betoken an absence of zeal, if not worse.

Such an approach would have played havoc with American commanders in 1775–83 and 1812–15: Schuyler, Lincoln, and Gates would have been prominent victims in the former, and Washington could have been executed for failing to save New York City in 1776 and Philadelphia in 1777, or for not crushing Clinton at Monmouth Court House in 1778. Many American generals in the War of 1812 would also have been executed, notably Hull, Wilkinson, Smyth, Chandler, Winder, Hampton, McClure, and the secretary of war, Armstrong. As it was, a number of generals were dismissed and court-martialed, and more deserved to be so.

Alongside ensuring effectiveness, a failure to control the military was clearly a serious problem for new governments and states. Napoleon's coup in 1799 revealed this in France, while successive *caudillos* were to make it apparent in Spanish America. Haiti, which won independence from France in 1804 after a struggle that had begun in 1791, suffered greatly from the same problem. Despite the subsequent tendency to see the American military as apolitical, the USA was also affected by the problems of controlling the military. Brigadier General James Wilkinson, governor of the Louisiana Territory after it had been purchased from France in 1803, and later an important if eventually unsuccessful figure in the War of 1812, was heavily involved with the plans associated with Vice President Aaron Burr in 1804–6. These included the secession of New York and New England (1804),[6] and, subsequently, the "Spanish Conspiracy," which appears to have included plans for a Western secession. Wilkinson, indeed, hoped to seize Santa Fe from the Spaniards for his own ends, and his self-serving treason was not dependent on Burr, nor restricted to Burr's schemes. Furthermore, those schemes nearly put paid to the career of the best American general prior to the Civil War, Winfield Scott. A key commander during the War of 1812, who trained and led his regulars to take on the British, Scott was court-martialed in 1810 and suspended from active duty for a year for saying that Wilkinson was as culpable of treason as Burr.[7]

There was a strong fear of military force subverting the republic: of a Benedict Arnold, Oliver Cromwell, or Napoleon Bonaparte, or their equivalent; indeed, in religious terms, of an ungodly "Man of Blood" acting as an un-Christian tyrant. There was also a profound anxiety about the problems for American public life that could come from the military, irrespective of the intentions of its commanders. In part, this anxiety stemmed from the origins of the American state (the federal entity as well as the individual states), for it was a product of British political culture which included a strong critique of army power.[8] America, in its origins, was also a reaction against the supposed authoritarian practices of the British metropole, not least in its use of military force, in its expectations of financial support for the military, and in its readiness to rely on military governance, as in Massachusetts in 1775.

The political culture was that of opposition to a standing (permanent) army, or, more realistically, to a large one that was not under the law. This opposition was the product of a seventeenth-century English tradition, directed against Stuart and Cromwellian autocracy, that had been revivified in the "Commonwealth" and Country-Party critique of supposed "Old Corps" Whig governmental practices and intentions during the reigns of George I (1714–27) and George II (1727–60). From the North American perspective, taking up this view might appear surprising, as British regulars had played a key role in the conquest of French Canada in 1758–60, thus ending the challenge to British North America's most vulnerable borders. As a result, American colonists, indeed, initially lauded the British soldiers, but their mood quickly changed, and notably so when the ministry appeared to be positioning troops to enforce postwar taxes.[9]

The British military was soon widely seen, particularly by self-conscious local politicians, as autocratic in intention and manner. Some British officers indeed loathed the American troops and thought them incompetent, a judgement that the French and Indian War (1754–63)[10] did not bear out, but one that reflected not so much a hostile response to an American proto-nationalism as the negative view that many regulars held of militia and, indeed, of civil society.[11] Under George III (r. 1760–1820), the king of Britain during both America's War of Independence and the War of 1812, American hostility to the British military rose when it had been associated, first as cause and, subsequently, as support, for an unpopular process of taxation. This hostility was to be accentuated by the experience of war and British occupation during the subsequent independence struggle.

These attitudes were not the best background for any attempt to create a standing force to fight for and maintain American independence. This problem was exacerbated by the extent to which assumptions and practices about military goals and activity were not federal-based and focused on a standing army, but, instead, state-based and militia-orientated.[12] The USA therefore represented an accentuation of the commonplace habit in the British world of seeing regular forces in a critical light, as potential supporters of centralisation and arbitrary government. In forming this attitude, moreover, the acceptance of the theory of natural rights or natural law in the Declaration of Independence questioning the legitimacy of all authority, especially central authority, and the discrediting of executive power were particularly important.

During both the American Revolution and the War of 1812, this uneasiness about a powerful executive and strong army was the key political context for the problems facing the American military effort. These political issues are the crucial introduction to American effectiveness in the War of 1812, or, rather, to the limited effectiveness that was to be shown; and the central linkage between politics and conflict, both domestically and internationally, is a major theme of this book.[13]

# 1

# PATHS TO WAR

"The World Turned Upside Down" was the tune reportedly played[1] on 19 October 1781, when British troops marched out of their ruined positions at Yorktown, Virginia, in order to surrender to the victorious American and French forces. Yet thirty-two years later, in 1813, British warships were in the Chesapeake and, the following year, troops landed, defeated the Americans at Bladensburg, and burned the public buildings in Washington, the city named after the victor at Yorktown.

What were the British and Americans doing going to war in 1812, and what were the characteristics of the two military systems that competed? This chapter assesses what was at stake, but does so in a dynamic fashion that reflects the changing domestic and international pressures and developments of the period. In particular, it is necessary to look at the character of American society and public culture, because these explain much about the drive to war and about the nature of the conflict that could be waged by the Americans.

The siege of Yorktown was the key clash in ensuring British defeat in what became known as the War of American Independence or, simply, the War of Independence (1775–83). This defeat was indeed an epic episode in world history, but, like many such episodes, it left many aspects and consequences unclear, and the War of 1812 was, in part, one such consequence and was explicitly seen as such by American supporters of the conflict. In particular, major topics in Anglo-

American relations remained at issue, while the very nature of the new American state was also unsettled.

Rather than beginning with the rundown to war, however, I deliberately want to start with American debates about how to organize the country for conflict. These help to explain how the USA fought the war as it did, a key aspect of the conflict, and therefore why the Americans failed to mobilize the resources of their society and achieve their goals despite the fact that, for most of the war, Britain was already heavily committed in a life-and-death struggle with Napoleon's France. Those who wish to move at once to the campaigning should turn to chapter two, but this chapter will provide significant background, not least to the politics of American warmaking, before turning to Anglo-American relations and the causes of the War of 1812. The last have to be explained both with reference to the wider international context of the world war then being waged by Britain and France, and with regard to the particular factors that led the USA to declare war on Britain.

## America as a Military Power

For the USA, the War of 1812 was problematic, indeed poorly-advised, for political and military reasons. Division over goals was crucial to the first. The problems of transition from a military and a military ethos based on a war of independence to those of a state engaged in international conflict were crucial to the second. The character of American warmaking owed much to the nature of the new society and, in particular, its origins in a revolution against imperial Britain. America was created as a society believing in small government and with a suspicion of and, in many cases, hostility to, a permanent military. This hostility reflected longstanding ideas about the dangers of a standing (permanent) army, as well as the way in which the imperial link with Britain had been broken, and therefore the foundation myth of the new country. Ironically, this was a myth that underplayed the major role of the regular soldiers of the American Continental Army in resisting and, eventually, defeating the British.[2] The resulting failure to appreciate the role of regulars was a constraint on postwar American military effectiveness as it discouraged attempts to build up the army.

The anti-authoritarian nature of American public life instead led to an emphasis on voluntary military service by citizens in the shape of a militia, with the civilians presumably possessing skill and weapons as a consequence of the right to bear arms, a right linked to militia service.[3] Events, however, rarely conform to hopes, and more than a militia would be required if the USA was to fight the battle-hardened British regulars successfully. This need was a key issue in the War of 1812, where the militia were handicapped not only by their own limitations, especially limited training, restricted enlistment periods and, in many cases, a reluctance to serve outside the USA, but also by the inadequate military infrastructure, particularly in the shape of poor logistics. Adequate structures had not been defined to integrate militia and regular forces, nor to deal with the supply, pay, and financing of militia forces operating outside the country. These deficiencies greatly handicapped operations against Canada and were a particular problem in ensuring that the use that could have been gained from the militia, for example the large Pennsylvania militia, was not realized. Political opposition in New England to the war also posed serious limitations on the use of the militia from its states.

The problems of American land power had also been urgent from the outset of the War of Independence in 1775, because the British then had a substantial force of regular troops in Boston, and also as a result of the major and continuing cause of American vulnerability: its lack of a battle fleet. Whatever the strength of individual American warships, as seen in 1812 when three British frigates were captured (see Chapter 4), and whatever the potential of American privateers, the Americans lacked a fleet able to block the use of the Atlantic Ocean by the British. The War of Independence had already made these factors clear. And, in the War of 1812, the British did use their naval superiority, both as a means of supply and communication, which enabled them at least in part to solve the logistical issues of operating in North America, and also as the basis for a strategic dimension of attack on the USA. In the nineteenth century, this British naval capability was to lead to a heavy emphasis in the USA on coastal fortifications, in military doctrine, force structure, and expenditure. This was a policy that was clearly directed against Britain, the leading world naval power through the century,[4] but it was not a viable solution during the War of Independence, nor really during the War of 1812. The relevant forts were lacking at the strategic level and, operationally, garrisons in positions such as Fort Washington and Ticonderoga were unable to prevent British advances, as the campaigns of 1776 and 1777 respectively showed. Instead, by fixing troops as garrisons and exposing them to attack, forts were actually a source of vulnerability, which the fall of Fort Washington in 1776 demonstrated. Similarly, the forts that blocked the river approaches to Philadelphia were captured by the British in 1777.

The War of 1812 indicated that forts could play a key role, the defense of Fort McHenry helping to save Baltimore in 1814. Indeed, no fort designed by an engineer trained at West Point was lost. Washington and New Orleans, however, were not adequately protected by forts. Instead, the British had to be opposed in the field by forces hastily throwing up whatever field fortifications they could, as at Bladensburg and Plattsburg in 1814, and outside New Orleans in 1815.

America, therefore, was vulnerable to attack, and it was understandable that the success of the American Revolution did not end disputes over how best to organize the military. Instead, it encouraged them, as there was room for political debate, without the immediate needs of war lessening the range of options. Moreover, the degree of federal responsibility for defense proved a particular issue of controversy, which looked back to colonial-era disputes over the control and financing of military force.

Yet, as far as both military organization and foreign policy were concerned, the Americans largely avoided the fissiparous and institutionally divisive consequences of a federal system. They did so by giving the key power to the federal government rather than the states. But this was resented at the state level. Individual states lacked the right to negotiate foreign treaties or to make war, although their relations with Native Americans initially threatened to permit both points. Thus, in the mid-1780s, Georgia raised state forces for duty against the Cherokees. During the War of 1812, Benjamin Hawkins, the government's agent with the Creeks, commented on Georgia raising its own troops in an inappropriate fashion. At any event, the states controlled their militia, and this was a central element in American military organization.

Given the unsettled nature of relations between federal and state agencies and aspirations, the nature and size of the national army was particularly controversial. While heading the War Department in 1785–94, Henry Knox, a keen Federalist, pressed hard for a stronger federal government and a national military establishment. In 1783, he had aroused concern by founding the Society of Cincinnati as a body for officers from the War of Independence and their descendants. The society and his policies in general were seen as a threat to the confederation government. Although there have been suggestions that it has been exaggerated,[5] Knox faced opposition to a permanent force,[6] as well as the limiting consequences of the financial weakness of the federal government.

On 3 June 1784, the day after decreeing that the last units of the Continental Army be disbanded, the confederation Congress nevertheless voted to establish a seven hundred-strong regiment of one-year volunteers in order to strengthen America's presence in the Ohio Valley. This was a region where, behind sensitive relations with Native Americans, there was concern about British intentions, as the British were seen as the sponsors of their opposition, although this fear underrated the capacity of the Native Americans to make their own decisions.

To many Americans, the fate of the Ohio Valley was a key test not only for national expansion, but also of national vitality; and this feeling helped provoke the War of 1812. Looking back, competing ambitions over the Ohio Valley had been the cause of conflict between Britain and France in 1754, while, during the War of Independence, Native Americans allied to the British had pressed on the borders of European-American settlement, diverting troops from fighting the British, especially in 1779. Moreover, after 1783, the region appeared crucial to the future of the United States, as well as a site of strategic competition with Britain.

Like the 1748 Peace of Aix-la-Chapelle between Britain and France, the Treaty of Paris of 1783 had not clearly settled the boundaries of North America nor, more seriously, the issue of power there. Just as the first peace had thus laid the foundations for the resumption of conflict in 1754, a conflict known as the French and Indian War in the United States and as the Seven Years' War in Britain, so the seeds of war in 1812 owed much to the failure of 1783. Moreover, whatever the nature of the agreement between Britain and its former colonies, such an agreement did not include the Native Americans, and the position and views of the latter became more prominent as a result of expansion by the European Americans (Americans for short), and the prospect of yet more expansion.

Indeed, this dynamic element of the situation in North America could not be adequately captured in any peace treaty between Britain and the United States, or between the latter and Native Americans. US expansion in accordance with treaties suggested the purchase of land by the Americans and agreement by the Native Americans, but there was also incessant American pressure, including conflict, which helped lead to rejectionist religious revival among the Native Americans. From this perspective, the War of 1812 emerges not, as it can be presented, as an interlude in improving Anglo-American relations looking toward later cooperation between the two powers, but instead as the culmination of bitter relations and conflict between Native Americans and European Americans that helped result in the subjugation of the former to the east of the Mississippi. In turn, this subjugation paved the way for the subjugating of those farther west.

In 1784–86, three treaties with Native Americans ceded much of southern and eastern Ohio to American settlement. This settlement was seen by most Americans as a rightful response to the God-given opportunities for expansion, and this expansion as a recompense for their struggle for independence from Britain. In July 1787, Congress went on to pass the Northwest Ordinance. This not only reasserted American sovereignty over the region, but also made it clear that this sovereignty was to be the prelude to settlement. The ordinance provided for the establishment of new states there, and thus for an advancing frontier of American settlement combined with a dynamic political structure capable of organizing these acquisitions. This structure included the prospect of new militia forces that would support further expansion.

The ordinance declared that Native American rights would only be infringed "in just and lawful wars authorized by Congress," and that Native American lands would only be acquired with their consent. This, however, was a policy that was to be widely honoured in the breach, helping to lead to conflict with the Native Americans. Such warfare, in turn, was used to justify renewed expansion by the new country and the development of its military strength, while this conflict also encouraged suspicion of Britain, which was seen as the sponsor of Native American opposition.

The absence, until the Constitution was settled and established, of a well-organized government or a system of direct taxation, was a fundamental limit to American military capability at the federal level. By the end of 1786 the regiment established in 1784 consisted of only 565 officers and men. The army, however, was subsequently expanded as relations slipped into an initially unsuccessful war with Native Americans, with American defeats in 1790 and 1791. Nevertheless, after Anthony Wayne's conclusive victory over Blue Jacket at Fallen Timbers on 20 August 1794, and the resulting Treaty of Greenville of 1795, the army was cut to 3,359 men in 1796. The army was then expanded anew by the governing Federalists in 1798, during the Quasi War with France, with Washington as commander in chief and Alexander Hamilton (1757–1804), a key Federalist leader, as senior ranking major general.[7] The latter sought to develop the force as a powerful permanent body able to unite America against internal subversion and foreign threat, but his intentions were suspect to many and he was accused of authoritarian aspirations.

Opposed to France in the late-1790s, the Federalists linked foreign and domestic policies closely to military preparedness, and built up both the army and the navy. "Millions for defence, but not one cent for tribute" [to a foreign state] became their slogan, after the "XYZ" affair, a supposed French attempt to buy off the Americans. The limiting consequences of federal financial weaknesses ensured, however, that the construction of ten frigates during the Quasi War was financed by subscriptions raised in 1798 in the major ports, such as Philadelphia.[8] The Federalist government also passed the Alien and Sedition Acts in order to strengthen it against internal opposition. This was a divisive step. In response, while asserting states' rights in their resolutions, Kentucky and Virginia denounced the acts as violations of the U.S. Constitution and thus, in effect, pressed the role of state governments in deciding the constitutional character of federal actions. Regional and other tensions led to continuing reports of the imminent dissolution of the Union, such as that sent Robert, Viscount Castlereagh, the British secretary of war, by Francisco de Miranda, the Venezuelan revolutionary, in 1807.[9]

Differences over the size and organization of the military in part rested on contrasting conceptions of the international system. Whereas Hamilton advanced a pessimistic interpretation of competing states and of the need, in response, for governmental and military preparedness,[10] critics felt that a benign international system was possible. Indeed, Thomas Jefferson (1743–1826) and the Democratic-Republicans, who gained power after the bitterly contested election of 1800, limited the peacetime army establishment to 3,284 men. They were not interested in a European-style military nor in what they saw as an authoritarian army of imperial size, being opposed to the taxes maintaining such an army entailed and suspicious of the existing army, not least because most of the senior officers were Federalists.[11] Jefferson, president from 1801 to 1809, preferred to rely on national unity, which was an example of the comforting illusion that virtue would necessarily prevail. This view led him, in his inaugural address in 1801, to claim that America was the strongest country in the world.

The contrast with the French Revolution was dramatic. Plunged into war in 1792 with Austria and Prussia, with Britain, Spain, and the Dutch joining against them the following year, the Revolutionaries had sought to mobilize the resources of society. The *levée en masse* of 1793 stipulated a general conscription for all single Frenchmen aged between eighteen and twenty-five. In 1798, under the Jourdan-Delbrel law, the obligatory nature of military service in France was extended. French forces held off and then defeated those of much of Europe, ensuring that by 1802, when peace temporarily came to the Continent, France, by then under Napoleon, was the dominant power in Western Europe.

In the USA keeping a large military establishment, such as that in France, at a distance had benign consequences from the Jeffersonian perspective but, nevertheless, was related to military practices that were not conducive to professionalism, and therefore effectiveness. In the early republican period, the habit of commissioning men directly from civil life, rather than promoting from the ranks in peacetime, led to a stress in appointments on political affiliation, social connections, and appropriate conduct. All of these brought the military close to civil society, but with deleterious consequences for military effectiveness. This was amply seen in the War of 1812, especially its early stages when much of the senior officer corps proved inadequate. Moreover, the decentralized nature of the armies' command system, with the generals in the nine (later ten) military districts reporting directly to the secretary of war,[12] lacked coherence and could not provide integrated operational planning or activity. More generally, the political atmosphere was not one that identified professionalism with effectiveness. This was true of the regulars but even more the militia and volunteers.

Yet, on a less critical note, the American system of officer procurement through political appointments served much the same purpose as the British purchase system, namely obtaining officers who would support the political and social status quo. It was therefore a way for the young republic to control its military. In addition, aside from the small size of the army, very few rank-and-file American regulars were qualified to become officers, as they lacked the education and status to lead. This problem made political appointments less pernicious than would otherwise have been the case. Richard Rush, the comptroller of the treasury, was told in 1813 that out of the seven hundred soldiers that General Alexander Smythe had joined together to form a regiment, "There was not a man fit to make a sergeant or corporal. . . . And every officer . . . was as ignorant, and unable to give any just instruction."[13]

As with the army, the Federalist plan to build up the navy was stopped when the Jeffersonians took power. Albeit within what he sought as a balanced navy, including ships of the line, frigates, and floating batteries,[14] Jefferson favored coastal gunboats rather than the more expensive frigates with their oceanic range, and timber stockpiled for the construction of ocean-going ships was used for other purposes.[15] This emphasis on gunboats conformed to the militia tradition of American republicanism. Militia, moreover, could use gunboats to defend the fortifications being built. Again, there was a stark contrast to the determination of the French Revolutionaries and, later, Napoleon to use their ships the line against Britain.[16]

The overall American emphasis on the defensive, on land and at sea, was not the best preparation for an effective operational army, nor, specifically, for an invasion of Canada. Yet, far from political differences over the military being an aspect of American exceptionalism, they were also reflected in serious divisions over foreign policy and defense in other states with a public politics, such as Britain, the United Provinces (Netherlands) in the 1780s, and France in the early-1790s.

## Anglo-American Relations

Number 8 of *The Federalist* claimed, "Safety from external danger is the most powerful director of national conduct." Within the USA these political divisions focused heavily on relations with, and fears about, Britain, which very much dominated American political consciousness after, as well as before, independence; but the situation was very different on the other side of the Atlantic. The American Revolution had indeed proved a traumatic civil war within the British empire. A sense of doom had become attached to the crisis, and British readers turned to the *Decline and Fall of the Roman Empire* (1776–88) by Edward Gibbon (a member of Parliament who wrote a pamphlet in support of the war), in order to look for an historical echo of their current plight. Yet, once the struggle was lost, there was singularly little effort devoted to dreaming of *revanche*, and neither domestic political divisions nor fears of international developments focused on the USA. Although the loss of the colonies was a blow to the national psyche, there were long-term advantages. Britain was now able to pursue imperial growth without the complications presented by these populous white settler colonies. Canada, and, later also, Australia and New Zealand, were to provide sufficient space for emigrating Britons (as did the USA), but they did not create the same problems of governance posed by the more populous thirteen colonies. Moreover, Britain effectively retained the American market, which proved a key help to the expanding British economy.

In the short term, despite the peace treaty in 1783, a range of issues remained in dispute with the former colonies, but the theme was of reconciliation. The leading exponent of opposition to the American Revolution, George III, had been pleased to be away from London when the humiliating peace that acknowledged American independence was proclaimed in 1783, but he struck an appropriate note of wise and honest courtesy, on 1 June 1785, when he received John Adams as the first American envoy to the Court of St. James. A delighted Adams recorded George as saying:

> I have done nothing by the late contest but what I thought myself indispensably bound to do, by the duty which I owed to my people. . . . I was the last to consent to the separation; but the separation having been made, and having become inevitable, I have always said, as I say now, that I would be the first to meet the friendship of the United States as an independent power. . . . let the circumstances of language, religion, and blood have their natural and full effect."[17]

Adams was to go on to succeed Washington as president, serving from 1797 to 1801. Not everything, however, was so benign. The following March, Jefferson, on a visit from his embassy in Paris, was received by George. There are no detailed contemporary accounts of the meeting, although in his autobiography, written thirty-five years later, Jefferson was very critical. Claiming, probably inaccurately, that he had been ungraciously received, Jefferson added, "I saw, at once, that the ulcerations in the narrow mind of that mulish being [George III] left nothing to be expected on the subject of my attendance."[18] Ironically, the two men in fact had much in common, from an interest in architecture and applied science to a disdain for luxury.

Relations in America, however, did not bulk large in British governmental concern, and unsurprisingly so, as there were far more contentious issues with other European states. Indeed, Britain, which saw a major postwar recovery in stability and prosperity, came near to war with France in 1787, with France and Spain in 1790, and with Russia in 1791. It was also at war with France from 1793 until 1802, and from 1803 to 1814, as well as in 1815. These wars involved France's allies, which, as a result of French military successes, swelled to include the Netherlands and, from 1796 until 1808, Spain. In 1800, Spain was obliged to cede Louisiana to France, reversing the transfer of power over the colony in 1763.

Concern about European power politics was not the sole factor in ensuring that the British government did not devote more attention to the USA. In addition, American independence had little immediate consequence for European power politics. America did not develop as a major naval power until the late nineteenth century,[19] and the Americans did not see their revolution as for export throughout the European world. Instead, within the USA, there was a powerful sense of American exceptionalism: of a culture and society separate from those of Europe.[20] This disengagement was further encouraged by the turmoil of the French Revolutionary period.[21] The sense of distance helped ease relations with European powers, although it also fostered a degree of unreality in responding to their policies.

On the British side, George III himself, from 1783, devoted little attention to the USA, although he played an indirect role thanks to his personal commitment to the many Loyalists who had fled America, and whose claims to compensation were largely ignored there. In the peace treaty, the American government only agreed to recommend to the individual states that the Loyalists be treated fairly. In practice, their claims were generally neglected. Although some Loyalists returned to the USA, and others had taken refuge in Bermuda and Britain, many had fled to the British colonies in what is now Canada, and George supported schemes to provide them with land there.[22]

Canada was envisaged as a very different society to that in the USA. An Act of Parliament of 1791, the Constitutional or Canada Act, contained a provision for land grants to support Church of England rectories or parsonages, while in other sections it provided for land grants to support "a Protestant clergy," a wording that led later to great controversy. The act's provision for a hereditary aristocracy, which was seen as a way to safeguard loyalty, never came into effect, but that did not deter some officials from trying to act like British aristocrats. The act sought to limit the powers of the elected House of Assembly and buttress the authority of the appointed Legislative Council. The system of land granting and the creation of crown reserves came later, but also contributed to divisions and discontent. As all these various terms were being worked out amid other government policies, the colony of Upper Canada (Ontario) experienced divisions and a degree of hostility to its rulers. This hostility is the context for the concerns of British administrators and commanders such as Francis Gore, Prevost and Isaac Brock about the dependability of the militia if the Americans invaded Upper Canada.

Meanwhile, aside from over the Loyalists, there were other issues at dispute between Britain and the USA. Relations were complicated by disputes over the drawing of the frontier and over the American wish to participate in the profitable Newfoundland fishing rights. Furthermore, the activities of British officials, officers, and traders on the frontier aroused American suspicion for many years.[23] More generally, the British secretary of legation, Edward Thornton, claimed "the malignity against England though less violent, is not less fixed."[24] Aside from anger and suspicion, a political practice and national culture different from, and often in opposition to, that of the former mother country was developing; although such a contrast had already preceded independence. In 1813, John Jay, an anglophile, who had been secretary for foreign affairs under the Articles of Confederation, expressed his concern to Noah Webster, the compiler of the *American Dictionary of the English Language* (1828), that his work would "impair" the sameness of the language in the two countries. To underline the complexity in relations, however, British traditions also influenced the new national culture.[25]

Moreover, America had cut free from the French alliance which had been so threatening to Britain. The *Public Advertiser*, a prominent London newspaper, had carried a letter from a "Bostonian" (newspaper letters were pseudonymous) in its issue of 15 January 1783, claiming that "the French and our States [the USA] will rear such a navy in America, that England will not hold an inch of territory on the face of the Earth in a very few years." However, despite the rhetoric of shared struggle and common goals, the French found the Americans unwilling to help, ungrateful, and opposed to accepting a commercial relationship on French terms. French officials thought the Americans self-interested and unprepared to translate declarations of gratitude into action, and that at a time when the financial burdens of French intervention in the recent war were felt all too keenly. Indeed, these burdens helped contribute to the political crisis that led to the French Revolution. No lasting political or economic entente had been created between America and France as a result of wartime cooperation.

Peace from 1783, indeed, allowed British competitors to reestablish their commercial position, and caused a precipitate decline in Franco-American trade. British trade, in contrast, boomed, and this, combined with the negative balance of trade between France and the United States, ensured that trade with America moved French capital into the British economy. American success in overcoming French efforts to keep them out of the trade of the French West Indies (principally Martinique, Guadeloupe, and Saint Dominique) was an added cause of tension between France and America, while the Americans also competed in traditional French markets, such as the Ottoman (Turkish) Empire. Moreover, French officials complained about indifference on the part of American political leaders to their commercial aspirations. A consular convention signed in 1783 was not ratified by the Americans for five years and, in contrast to Britain, the Americans did not respond positively to French approaches for a trade treaty.[26] An Anglo-French trade treaty was signed in 1786, although it did not prevent the two powers from coming close to conflict in the Dutch Crisis of 1787 nor from going to war in 1793.

Commercial links between Britain and America revived strongly after the War of Independence. In defiance of traditional mercantilist assumptions, which linked commerce to politically-controlled markets, American trade with Britain rose greatly after independence.

America was populous, lacked the range of British industrial production, and was short of liquidity and thus still needed access to
Britain's credit which was often generously supplied. This need for
British credit and products was fortunate for Britain as she also faced
growing export problems in American markets. The continued influence of Britain on the eastern seaboard led to New York being described by the French envoy, Louis-Guillaume Otto, in July 1790, as
more like a suburb of London than an American town.[27]

Nevertheless, although there had been a willingness on the part
of Britain to concede or shelve contentious issues in order to bring the
War of Independence to a close, and (successfully) to divide the opposing coalition of the Americans, France, Spain, and the Netherlands,
there were limits to the British willingness to make compromises.
Sensitivity over the protectionist trading system of the British Empire led in March 1782 to the failure of an "American Intercourse Bill"
designed, at least for a while, to give American ships the right to carry
American goods to British possessions, and also to export from them,
and both at the preferential tariffs of British-owned goods in British
ships. Instead, protectionist principles were entrenched by Orders in
Council of May and July 1782, which respectively allowed free access
to Britain for American raw materials only and banned American
ships from carrying goods from the British colonies in the West Indies
to America. This protectionism blocked what had been a major
American trade route prior to the Revolution.

This prohibition was unpopular among Britain's West Indies
colonists, but the active lobbying of Parliament against it in 1783–85,
both by the Society of West Indies Merchants and Planters in London
and from the West Indies, was unsuccessful. Instead, the ban on
American ships carrying goods from the West Indies was strengthened by an Act in 1788, and Charles, Lord Hawkesbury, from 1796 1st
Earl of Liverpool, the president of the Board of Trade from 1786 to
1804, was a keen advocate of banning American trade with the West
Indies.[28] Liverpool, whose son, the 2nd Earl, was to be prime minister
throughout the War of 1812, was also angered by American restrictions on British shipping, and saw the limitations on American trade
in part in political terms, and America as a threat: "Our West Indies
islands will never be safe if the subjects of the United States are allowed to have a free intercourse with them, and to import, among
other articles, their democratic principles."[29]

Liverpool also saw shipping as crucial. In 1797, he responded to the argument that imposing a tonnage duty on American shipping might damage Britain's role as an entrepot for rice and tobacco, both of which were exported from America. He claimed, instead, that imposing a duty would be an appropriate response to American duties on British ships, as Britain had lost this trade since America became independent, and that "the extent of our navigation is to be preferred in general to the extent of our commerce, for on the first depends the security of everything."[30]

This attitude looked toward British action against American shipping in the 1800s, particularly the impressment (forcible recruitment) of sailors. Moreover, British trade policy hit America hard, for British conquests, during the French Revolutionary and Napoleonic Wars, of the colonies of other states—France, and her allies, Spain, the Dutch, and Denmark—ended the right of the Americans to trade there. Examples included Surinam in South America, captured from the Dutch in 1799 and (after it had been returned under the Peace of Amiens of 1802) again in 1804.

Whatever their differences with Britain, Americans had to be aware of a more complex context of international competition. In November 1790, Otto reported that the Americans, far from still being linked to France, were unlikely to take a role in the apparently imminent war between Britain and, on the other side, France and Spain (in the Nootka Sound Crisis over competing claims of the Pacific coast of North America), as they needed ten years of peace in order to settle their government.[31] In this crisis, George Beckwith, a British agent in New York, although not an accredited envoy, even explored, in discussions with Alexander Hamilton, then secretary of the treasury, possibilities for Anglo-American co-operation against Spain, although different views about the fate of any conquests from Spain prevented these talks from being taken further. Looking toward its future importance in the War of 1812, the future of New Orleans, then under Spanish rule, was particularly controversial in these discussions.[32]

There were also serious issues still in dispute. In American eyes, British recognition of American sovereignty was qualified by the British encouragement of frontier separatists in Vermont, and by continued support for Native Americans. George Hammond, the first British minister plenipotentiary to the United States, who arrived in Philadelphia in October 1791, found that the suspicions, indeed hostility towards British policy, of Jefferson, then secretary of state, hindered the progress of negotiations,[33] and he was harshly handled by Jefferson in 1792–93. The latter was more favorable then to the French envoy. More specifically, in 1793, concerned about the security of the major port of Baltimore from possible British attack, the Maryland House of Delegates authorized the construction of a fort at Whetstone Point, where Fort McHenry was to be established. It played a key role in the 1814 campaign (see Chapter 5). In March 1794, Congress passed an act to fortify America's major seaports.

Helped by Hamilton, relations with Britain, however, improved in 1794–95, with the negotiation of Jay's Treaty (1794), which settled, or at least eased, commercial and territorial disputes, thus improving American access to trade with the British West Indies. It also led to the abandonment of Britain's Native American allies. As a result both of defeat at the hands of the Americans and of this abandonment, the Native Americans agreed to the Treaty of Greenville with the USA in 1795, underlining the extent to which relations between the USA and the Native Americans could not be separated from the real, or possible, role of Britain. In 1796, Britain handed over the seven bases, including Detroit and Fort Niagara, in the USA that it had retained after the 1783 treaty. Jay himself was to be opposed to the War of 1812.[34]

The focus for America instead became animosity with France. In 1798–1800, in the Quasi War, France sank or captured over three hundred American merchantmen in response to the American part in maintaining British trade routes. France did not accept that neutral ships (among which American merchantmen were very important) could carry British goods, and thus sought to match Britain's blockade of trade with France.[35] Even Liverpool warmed to the Americans as a result, seeing the crisis as an opportunity to reknit relations, with the British navy playing a key role: "[T]hey must depend on our fleet for the general protection of their commerce, and this circumstance will tend, I think, to unite the two countries in a closer bond of union: their armed vessels however will afford us a considerable degree of assistance in destroying the small French privateers."[36]

Such an argument looked toward the language used about German submarines prior to America's entry into war against Germany in 1917 and 1941, and indeed neutral rights was an issue with a long legacy in international relations, not least affecting Anglo-American relations at the time of the Civil War. In practice, during the Quasi War, there was considerable naval cooperation between Britain and the USA against French attacks on trade: the Americans focused on trade protection in nearby waters and the British in the Caribbean. In 1796, Edward Thornton noted American support for Britain, but added "an opinion so fickle and inconstant is scarcely to be relied upon for any length of time."[37] Indeed, but Jay's Treaty kept relations pretty calm until the mid-1800s.[38]

Crucial clauses of Jay's Treaty, however, expired in 1803 and were not renewed by the Americans. Jefferson, now president, was unhappy with attempts to replace the treaty. Indeed, he rejected the Monroe-Pinckney treaty of 1806 because it did not end impressments: the forcible enlistment of British citizens serving on American ships. As far as the Americans were concerned, these were former subjects who had legally acquired American citizenship. Americans believed that individuals could select their own citizenship and legally renounce their former citizenship, a concept rejected by the British who believed that one acquired citizenship *jus soli* or *jus sanguine* and that one could never change that. The British government viewed those who rejected British citizenship and served in the American merchant marine as traitorous underminers of the war effort against France.

Trade and neutrality were the issues anew, when, in 1806–1807, in turn, Anglo-American relations markedly deteriorated, not least as a result of British warships enforcing the blockade with France and also using impressments. What the Americans with reason saw as the arrogant nature of British naval officers did not help.[39] On 25 April 1806, HMS *Leander* fired a shot at the American merchantman *Richard* which had refused to lay to for the examination of its cargo. This shot killed a sailor, leading to an outcry in New York where his corpse was paraded. In the *Chesapeake-Leopard* clash on 22 June 1807, an attempt by HMS *Leopard* to take a prominent deserter from the USS *Chesapeake* led to a ten-minute action, the surrender of the *Chesapeake*, and the seizure of four sailors seen as deserters. That July, Jefferson and his cabinet drew up a plan for an invasion of Canada and, also in 1807, the state of New York began constructing Castle Clinton in order to protect the island of Manhattan from British attack.

Trade was both the source of disputes and also a means of pursuing them. In the latter case, prohibitions and restrictions were seen as ways to lead European powers to be more sympathetic to American interests. In this respect, the key European power was Britain, which dominated Atlantic trade and insisted that it could control neutral trade with France. Britain was primarily concerned with preventing the neutral Americans from trading with France, and thus circumventing the British blockade, which was designed to weaken the French economy. As against Germany in 1940–41, this was seen as a crucial way to strike at a power that dominated the Continent of Europe. As a key context, British officials felt that the American government was pro-French.

On 11 November 1807, Britain issued Orders in Council prohibiting the indirect trade which neutral ships (mostly American) had been carrying between enemy countries and their colonies. It was no longer permissible to call at some American port *en route*. These were more onerous than the orders issued that January which had prohibited neutrals from trading between enemy ports.[40] The British attitude toward America was also one of possibly making allowances "in the shape of regulation" rather than accepting American claims.[41] In April 1809, a new set of Orders in Council declared a firm blockade. This control over their trade was increasingly unacceptable to the Americans, and helped to lead to the declaration of war by the US Congress on 18 June 1812. Neutral trade had for long been an issue in British relations with other powers, for example with the Dutch during the Seven Years' War (the French and Indian War) and the War of Independence, and with Russia during the latter;[42] and the USA joined this group once it became independent. The vigorous British response to Denmark when it pushed anew the idea of a League of Armed Neutrality, Nelson's 1801 attack on Copenhagen, indicated the firm British attitude,[43] and policy toward the USA can be set in this context.

The slave trade was an additional, albeit minor, issue. In 1807, with effect from 1 January 1808, the USA followed Britain in banning participation in the international slave trade by its subjects. There was scant effort by the American government, however, to enforce the ban. In contrast, Orders in Council were used by the British to justify seizing American slavers. The High Court in 1810 accepted the argument of the barrister James Stephens, who had become convinced of the horrors of slavery during his time in the West Indies. Stephens argued that slave trading was a violation of the law of nations, the laws of humanity, and Anglo-American law, and that, therefore, neutral slave ships could be legitimately seized.[44]

American legislation in response to British moves was primarily designed to ensure a change in British policy without going to war. It was also a determined effort to force American economic and sectional interests to heed the wishes of the federal government, and thus involved contentious and divisive issues of enforcement within the USA. Moreover, trade was intertwined with domestic politics, not only in terms of policy, but also with reference to political ideology.[45] In 1805, Jefferson had complained about "the influence gained by the commercial towns on public opinion, and their exclusive possession of the press."[46]

In 1806, a non-importation law was passed. In December 1807, Congress followed with the Embargo Act, designed to settle the trade issue by ending most of it: as well as blocking imports, American ships were banned from trading with Europe and the export of American goods there was also prohibited. This legislation reflected Jefferson's mistaken conviction that Europe was dependent on American agricultural exports, and thus that the USA could use the economic weapon to force compliance to its will. The embargo hit the growth of British exports to the USA, but it also caused great damage to the American economy (and public finances which were dependent on import duties) as well, in consequence, as a marked revival in support for the Federalists, support that was to be shown in the congressional elections of 1808.

As a result, after the end of Jefferson's presidency a Non-Intercourse Act, which banned trade with Britain and France (rather than Europe as a whole), replaced the Embargo Act in March 1809. This new act, however, led to large-scale evasion and also encouraged the West Indies to turn to Canada for supplies, which was not the American intention. Non-intercourse, indeed, proved damaging economically and was abandoned in 1810. Instead, an act of 1 May 1810 (often referred to, after its reluctant sponsor Nathaniel Macon, as Macon's Bill No. 2) established restrictions on Britain or France if the other agreed to respect America's rights. This was cleverly manipulated by Napoleon in order to turn American anger against Britain. An ambiguous response by Napoleon that summer was seen as favorable by Madison and, as a result, another non-importation act was passed in February 1811: it prohibited British goods and ships, while permitting continued exports.[47] The British government correctly argued that the French repeal of measures against American trade was fraudulent and that Britain was being treated unfairly.

American pressure had an influence on Britain, not least due to the serious economic problems there of the early-1810s in both trade and industry. Britain's economic options moreover were reduced by the partially successful French attempt to close Continental Europe to British trade: the Continental System, decreed in 1806–1807 and enforced thereafter. This system increased the significance of British trade with America. Yet, while noting these problems, it is important not to exaggerate the responsiveness of the British government to pressures from its merchants. In 1797, Liverpool caustically claimed that British merchants involved in trade with the USA were "better friends to the commerce and navigation of the United States, than to those of Great Britain,"[48] and the ministry focused on the latter. In the winter of 1811–12, however, pressure in Parliament on the government to settle disputes with America grew.

Trade was also important in the deterioration of French relations with Russia, the other key estrangement of the period, and one that was to be important to the geopolitics of the War of 1812. There were other tensions between the two powers, not least competing interests in north Germany, Poland, and the Balkans, and Tsar Alexander I's anger with Napoleon's bullying intentions and manner, but Russia's unhappiness with the prohibition on trade with Britain that was central to Napoleon's Continental System was also crucial. There were longstanding and important commercial links between Britain and Russia.

In December 1810, Russia left the French economic camp when it abandoned the Continental System, which was proving ruinous to the Russian economy. New Russian regulations were announced for neutral shipping, which included that of Britain with which Russia was not at war. Such a unilateral step threatened the cohesion of the French economic and international system, particularly in the Baltic Sea, a key trading area for Britain as well as northern Europe. Alexander's move also challenged Napoleon's insistence on obedience and his treatment of allies as servants. He responded with bluster, but also by stepping up the military preparations for possible war with Russia, a process that accelerated from October 1811.

The American army, meanwhile, was built up as relations deteriorated with Britain, and also as an internal police force to enforce the trade embargo. In November 1811, in his annual address to Congress, Jefferson's successor as president, his former secretary of state and a fellow Virginian, James Madison (1751–1836), proposed increasing the army and recruiting a large number of volunteers. In 1812, the army establishment was still only 6,686 officers and men, while the navy had seven frigates, nine sloops and sixty-two gunboats, but no ships of the line. This was not the sort of force that could mount transoceanic amphibious operations and, indeed, this crucial lack of capability helped ensure that American power was restricted to "near America." There could be no intervention, for example, in the Latin American Wars of Independence: not, for example, in the rebellions in Venezuela launched in 1806 and 1811, nor that in Mexico beginning in 1810, nor that in Texas which started in 1812. Sending three frigates and a schooner to the Mediterranean in 1801 against the Barbary Pirates was scarcely sufficient for any major scheme, and anyway depended on the tolerance of Britain, France and Spain for a neutral USA. Similarly, the overland force under William Eaton that marched from Alexandria in Egypt to help capture Derna during the war with the Bashaw of Tripoli contained only ten American marines, alongside thirty-eight Greeks and about three hundred Arabs.

This scarcely compared with the overseas forces that Britain deployed: in 1807, six thousand troops were sent to capture Alexandria in Egypt, while a force of forty-eight hundred troops stormed Spanish-ruled Montevideo (in modern Uruguay), and was subsequently increased to eight thousand before conducting an unsuccessful attack on Spanish-ruled Buenos Aires later that same year. In 1809, ten thousand British troops captured the Caribbean island of Martinique from the French, while in 1814 (during the War of 1812) forty-seven hundred troops landed in Chesapeake Bay. The Martinique attack showed the sort of numbers that Britain could deploy on individual expeditions, and the Americans were fortunate that such numbers were not sent to the Chesapeake.

After war with Napoleon had resumed in 1803, the British used their naval power, amphibious capability, and transoceanic power projection to enhance their position in the New World. They seized St. Lucia, Tobago, Demarara, Essequibo (now both in Guyana), and Surinam in 1803–1804, following with the Danish West Indies—St. Croix, St. Thomas and St. Johns—in 1807, Martinique and Cayenne (now Guyane Française) in 1809, and the Caribbean islands of Guadeloupe, St. Eustatius, and St. Martin in 1810. Britain appeared all too powerful and menacing to American commentators.

Moreover, Britain dominated the European New World. Portugal, with its colony of Brazil, was very much a dependent ally of Britain. Invaded in 1807 by Napoleon, who wanted to seize the Portuguese navy and to expand his Continental System, Portugal was reliant for its survival on British military assistance. Spain, now, was also a British ally, or at least the many Spaniards who resisted Napoleon's conquest of the country in 1808 were supported by Britain. The Spanish empire (which comprised most of South America bar Brazil, as well as Central America, much of the south and southwest of the modern USA, Cuba, Puerto Rico, and the Philippines), was ruled in the name of Ferdinand VII, who had been imprisoned by Napoleon, and not in the name of Napoleon's brother Joseph, whom the French had placed on the throne. Britain was fighting on behalf of Ferdinand. Had the Americans been able to help the revolutionaries in the Latin American wars of Independence, they would therefore have hit at the British alliance system.

Aside from the small size of the US army, American military capacity suffered from the lack of any equivalent to the ancillary forces that greatly enhanced British capability. This capability was particularly seen around the Indian Ocean. The mostly native British East India Company army was 18,200 strong in 1763, 115,400, in 1782, and 154,000 in 1805. Indian troops played a major role in operations outside India: in Ceylon (Sri Lanka), the East Indies, Egypt, and Mauritius, although the Americas were too distant for such a deployment of Indian forces. The successful Mauritius expedition in 1810 included 3,000 Indian troops, and there were 5,770 Indian as well as 5,344 British troops in the expedition that took Batavia (modern Djkarka), the leading Dutch position in the East Indies, in 1811; and there were 1,800 Indian troops, as well as 900 British, in the force that conquered the inland Sri Lankan kingdom of Kandy in 1815. The earlier British attack on Kandy in 1803 had failed, and their success in 1815 reflected the British learning curve and the professionalism of a military that was far from anachronistic or rigid. This needs to be set alongside British failure at New Orleans that year. Kandy was an environment that was as difficult as that encountered by British troops earlier that year in Louisiana.

Indeed, during the War of 1812 with the USA, the British, very much the world power, continued to extend their control elsewhere. In 1812, on Sumatra in the East Indies, Brigadier General Robert Gillespie deposed the Sultan of Palembang and stormed the Sultan of Yoyzakarta's *kraton* (royal residence), despite its far larger garrison and numerous cannon. Pangeran Arya Panular, a Sumatran whose diary covered the assault, was impressed by the British combination of discipline, bravery, and determination.[49] Bandjarmasin (on Borneo), Bangka, Billiton and Makassar, all in the East Indies, were captured from the Dutch in 1812, and Bali from them in 1814. This activity underlines the range of British military commitments, and also the need to place the American war in perspective. In hindsight, relations with the USA appear more important than they did to the British and other Europeans at the time. To Britain, the war was an aggravating sideshow to the much larger conflict in Europe.

The Americans had no equivalent to the Indians employed by the British. There was a use of Native American allies, for example, Andrew Jackson benefiting from the support of about six hundred Cherokees and Creeks when he stormed the Creek camp at Horseshoe Bend in March 1814. Jackson indeed profited from the debilitating Creek civil war, which arose from Red Stick insurgents rising up against the Creek establishment. The latter sided for the most part with the Americans, as again in 1818 when Jackson successfully invaded Florida in the First Seminole War. However, the number of Native American allies was small, and they did not represent an appreciable offensive capability, other than against nearby areas. As friendly Shawnees, moreover, discovered during and after the war, fighting for the United States did not prevent harsh treatment, both from settlers and, after the war, from the government.[50] This treatment helped ensure that, both in the Southeast and in the Northwest, more Native Americans fought with the British than against them.

Slave troops had been used with some success in the West Indies by both Britain and France in the 1790s, the British raising twelve regiments in 1798, and the success of the Haitian Revolution in what had been the leading French slave economy—Saint Dominique—underlined the military proficiency of slaves and their suitability for campaigning in the West Indies. Yet, this very revolution, and indeed the Aponte Rebellion on Cuba in 1812, underlined the American revulsion against arming slaves that had already been seen in the hostile reaction to the adoption of such a policy in 1775–1806 by John, 4th Earl of Dunmore, the last royal governor of Virginia.

Thus, the Americans were not to create a slave army to campaign in the West Indies, a key instance of strategic culture being moulded by domestic ideology. Aside from ideological opposition, there was not the institutional basis for such a policy of arming slaves. Slavery in North American was private, not public; it was an aspect of investment, not of governmental utility. There was also in America no halfway house equivalent to the military system run by the British East India Company.

A comparable force was certainly necessary if the Americans were to launch a large-scale policy of overseas conquest. The numbers of British troops sent to (and dying in) the West Indies—including thirty-three thousand sent in 1795, and forty-five thousand dying in 1793–1801, a figure that owed much to disease[51]—indicated the challenge if the USA was to mount any viable program of Caribbean conquest. The American filibusters were far less numerous, though they had some success in extending American power in the Gulf region in the 1800s and 1810s, and, in 1813, temporarily gained control of Texas (then part of the Spanish empire), before a larger loyalist force marched north from Mexico later that year and regained control. Filibusters can also be seen as playing a role in relations with Native Americans. It was far less possible, however, for filibusters to challenge the British in Canada successfully, and even less in Britain's extensive Caribbean colonies. Numbers of troops indeed were an issue for the USA in the War of 1812, not least because of the need to compensate for poor commanders and for the range of American operations.

## The Causes of the War of 1812

The cause of the war is a matter of historical debate. There is discussion of the respective roles of President Madison and of the War Hawks in Congress, headed by Henry Clay, Felix Grundy, and John Calhoun. Furthermore, it is difficult to disentangle and assess proximate causes from underlying attitudes. As far as the latter are concerned, a key element was that Jefferson and others over-estimated American power after his success in acquiring Louisiana from France in 1803: the Louisiana Purchase took American claims to territory up to the Pacific Ocean although, in practice, most of the territory was under Native American control. For 60 million *louis*, or $15 million, America gained over eight hundred thousand square miles with no clear borders, including all or much of the future states of Montana, North and South Dakota, Minnesota, Wyoming, Colorado, Nebraska, Iowa, Kansas, Missouri, Oklahoma, Arkansas, and Louisiana. The USA also claimed the Oregon Territory (which included the modern states of Oregon and Washington as well as part of Canada) as part of the Louisiana Purchase.

The gain of Louisiana, including the crucial port of New Orleans, ensured that the Spanish stranglehold on the Gulf of Mexico was broken, challenging the Spanish position to east and west, in West Florida and Texas, while, as a result of the purchase, America now had a far longer frontier with Canada. Jefferson indeed tried to gain Florida in 1806. The new gains to the west were explored in 1805–1807 by Meriwether Lewis and William Clark, who reached the Pacific coast at the Columbia River. Its largely overlooked counterpart, the Freeman-Custis Red River expedition of 1806 provided valuable knowledge, including a map of the river, that was to help subsequent American expansion,[52] but the results were less positive than for the Lewis and Clark expedition, not least due to a firm Spanish response, and this encouraged an end to government-sponsored exploration.

More generally, while Jefferson understood the potential of the West and was correct in his long-term appraisal that the USA would become a world power, he mistook America's marginal leverage in the bipolar dynamic between Britain and France for a situation in which all three were major powers, which was not to be the case until later in the nineteenth century. Madison, who had been Jefferson's secretary of state, followed this reasoning reflexively. This attitude ensured that American policymakers saw little reason to compromise in the disputes over neutral trade that played the key role in leading to war between Britain and the USA in 1812. Instead, they assumed that Britain would back down in the face of American anger and preparations for war, only to discover that they could not dictate the pace of events: Britain compromised, but inadequately, and too late for the Americans.

Manipulated by Napoleon,[53] possibly as part of his attempt to unite all naval powers against Britain, Madison foolishly thought he had won concessions from France that justified his focusing American anger and the defense of national honor on Britain. To leading

American politicians, Britain's maritime pretensions, which were more pressing than those of France, a weaker naval power, were a true despotism. In retrospect, John Threlkeld of Georgetown was to attribute the "wicked war" first "to the leaning of our government to that of France" and secondly to "the great desire of individuals to be general, colonel, captain, commodore, captain of frigates etc, privateers contractors etc."[54] In practice, French seizures of American shipping continued, leading in late 1812 to American requests that France settle commercial complaints, while Napoleon's tyranny was more antipathetic than British policy to American values. Moreover, other powers, such as Sweden, moved away from France and towards Britain.[55]

In an ahistorical moment, Richard Glover, a Canadian historian, compared the USA in 1812 to Mussolini's Italy which, in 1940, joined Hitler's Germany against Britain when the latter was weak and vulnerable as it had been in the face of Napoleonic power in 1812. The American press certainly carried extensive news of France's naval buildup, which underlined Britain's vulnerability.[56] Indeed, once the war had broken out in 1812, Robert, 2nd Viscount Melville, the recently appointed First Lord of the Admiralty, expressed his concern about naval overstretch. Writing to Commodore Sir Home Popham, who was seeking more ships and sailors for his squadron off the northern coast of Spain, Melville noted: "In addition to the American hostilities, which require to be met as they were likely to be of much longer duration than some people suppose, we have had since I wrote to you such demands for the Baltic and the Mediterranean as will completely drain us of all our disposable means, and still leave us deficient in many important points."[57]

It was also widely assumed that Napoleon would defeat Russia, not least as his invasion that year was supported by Austria and Prussia, each of which provided troops, as did lesser German powers such as Saxony and Bavaria.

A "visceral hatred of Great Britain" seems to have played a role for Jefferson and Madison.[58] Conversely, Spencer Perceval, the prime minister from 1809 until his assassination by a mad bankrupt on 11 May 1812, and Wellington's brother, Richard Marquess Wellesley, foreign secretary from 1810 to February 1812, have been criticized for a "visceral anti-Americanism" that harmed relations.[59] Indeed, this hostility can be linked to the shift from an attempt to woo the USA to, instead, a tendency to adopt a firm attitude. Robert Smith, the secretary of state, complained in May 1810 of British "indifference" to relations and "inflexible determination" in persisting in its policies.[60]

The American misjudgement of Napoleon included an assumption that war between France and Britain would be bound to continue[61] and thus place Britain under pressure in any conflict with the USA. In fact, on 17 April 1812, Napoleon offered Britain peace, essentially on the basis of the status quo. Suspecting an attempt to divide Britain from her allies, the British ministry, on 23 April, sought clarification on the future of Spain, as they were unwilling to accept its continued rule by Napoleon's brother Joseph. Napoleon did not reply,[62] and that ended the approach.

Neither side probably was sincere in suggesting talks, but the possibility, however distant, of a negotiated end to the war in Europe, or at least one between Britain and France, was one that would have put a bellicose USA in a very difficult position. As a result, the international situation in 1812 was very different to the situation in 1778. Then Britain had been weakened as far as the Americans were concerned because France had gone to war with Britain while avoiding the European alternative offered by intervention in the War of the Bavarian Succession (1778–1809), even though in this conflict France's ally, Austria, was at war with Prussia. In 1812, in contrast, the French turned east, albeit without ending their war with Britain; but this invasion of Russia was ultimately to lead to the downfall of Napoleon and end his war with Britain, and thus to weaken the USA.

Irrespective of French moves, Madison had departed from Jefferson's principles in foreign policy. Crucial to these were an attempt to maintain neutrality in great-power confrontation, which Jefferson presented as the way to avoid dangerous entanglements. This departure was to have a serious consequence for America. The domestic pressures on Madison, however, were serious and led Jeffersonians to fear for the survival of the republic. Unsuccessful as a tool of foreign policy, non-importation had also resulted in major economic strains, and this was increasing opposition to the government.[63] Indeed, having become much weaker, Federalist support was rising. Meanwhile, Britain was not yielding over trade or impressments. Madison thus appeared to have the choice of backing down in order to assuage domestic pressures, or of forcing Britain to back down. He underestimated the risks of the latter and failed to appreciate the prudence of the former.

In 1812, the British government itself did not want war with America.[64] For example, in 1811, Spain, then fighting as an ally of Britain against France, sought British help against American expansion into West Florida (the Florida Panhandle and over to the Mississippi, including coastal Alabama and Mississippi and part of Louisiana). The British government saw this expansion as unprovoked aggression against a close ally and instructed the envoy to protest, and to do the same if the Spanish colony of East Florida (modern Florida minus the Panhandle) was attacked. However, he was also ordered to avoid hostile and menacing language and informed that the government did not want to fight the USA.[65]

Madison, in his message to Congress on 1 June 1812 pressing for a declaration of war on Britain, emphasized maritime rights. He declared that Britain had been responsible for

> a series of acts hostile to the United States as an independent and neutral nation ... Thousands of American citizens, under the safeguard of public law and of their national flag, have been torn from their country and from everything dear to them ... Our commerce has been plundered in every sea, the great staples of our country have been cut off from their legitimate markets, and a destructive blow aimed at our agricultural and maritime interests.

Thus, as far as Madison was concerned, war was already in progress.[66]

This was a notion that was to dovetail with the idea that the new conflict was a second "War for Independence," a view that made the war seem necessary to some Americans[67] but that others rejected. A ninety-day embargo on exports had already been agreed by Congress in April. That June, Congress declared war, with the Senate, which adopted the War Bill on 17 June, taking far longer to persuade than the House of Representatives (adopted 4 June) where the War Hawks were powerful. Among the War Hawks, Henry Clay of Kentucky, the Speaker of the House, was especially important. In advancing his views, he also strengthened the role of the Speaker and used the Speakership to advance his cause.[68]

In part, the delay reflected the difficulties of justifying the war and the bitterness of divisions, which included opposition to the war in areas where there was majority support for it: the South and the West.[69] In the Senate, moreover, there was much support for avoiding full-scale war and, instead, limiting it to a naval conflict similar to the Quasi War with France, namely privateering and action against British shipping—in short a truly limited war that, in practice, was of the form of an armed demonstration. Initially, the Senate voted for such a limitation, but it subsequently changed tack and backed the House bill.[70] Had the Senate not changed its mind, as indeed seemed possible, then the House might have rejected its proposal, but that could simply have led to an impasse that would have forced attention back to diplomacy. On 18 June 1812, Madison signed the war bill into law.

That day, Augustus John Foster, who had been appointed British minister plenipotentiary the previous year, was informed that the USA would fight until Britain ended the impressment of sailors on American ships and also granted the USA the generous understanding of neutral rights offered to Russia in the Anglo-Russian Convention of 1801. This demand ignored the extent to which Russia was a much more powerful state whose support Britain had been seeking in 1801 after the two powers had come close to war.

The news of the declaration of war reached London on 30 July 1812. In fact, the British government had already lifted the Orders in Council on 23 June. This lifting was in order to try to maintain peace and to encourage trade with the USA, as well as in response both to French attempts to win over the USA and to economic problems within Britain. These had been focused with a major campaign in the provinces, especially in Liverpool, the key port for American trade, for the repeal of the Orders in Council. This campaign reflected the rise in provincial economic interests and lobbying that had been seen, for example, in the negotiation of the 1787 Anglo-French trade treaty.[71] The news, however, only arrived in North America after fighting had broken out. Lifting the Orders in Council in relation to the USA would have come sooner had it not been for the assassination of Spencer Perceval, the prime minister, and the resulting reconstruction of the government.

The British hope, once they knew that war had broken out, that the lifting of the orders would lead to its speedy end, was misplaced. This mistake can be seen as a product of the focus of British intel-

ligence collection on Europe and the war with Napoleon.[72] Admiral
Sir John Borlase Warren, the commander in chief of a combined North
American and West Indian station, was given instructions in August
to negotiate with the Americans.[73] In practice, the British move was
unacceptable to the USA as the British government insisted on the
right to reinstate the orders when they chose, while there had also
been no concession on impressments, which the American government insisted must be given up. On 17 September, Robert, Viscount
Castlereagh, the foreign secretary, told Jonathan Russell, the American envoy, that impressments could not be ended. Meanwhile, on 24–
25 June, Napoleon's forces had crossed the River Niemen without
resistance, launching his invasion of Russia. Over six hundred thousand French and allied troops were available for the invasion.

Congress had voted for war in part because of bellicose over-confidence, especially by the War Hawks, and in part thanks to patriotic
anger with British policies, but very much as a party measure by
the Republicans. Impressment of seamen from American ships was
seen as a particular outrage, as it represented an infringement of the
national sovereignty of American vessels and a denial of America's
ability to naturalize foreigners, but impressment was not only a natu-
ralization problem: short of sailors in an age when warships required
very large numbers to work the extensive sails and rigging, and to
man their numerous cannon, British naval officers also impressed
many native-born American seamen. This impressment was an extension of the forcible system used in Britain in order to raise sailors:
the press gang.[74] The maritime issues—Orders in Council and impressments—were crucial in the East, the region with most votes in
Congress. However, for the New England ship owners, they were
simply a cost of doing business that could be passed on to the Continental purchasers of American products. Impressment was emphasized by the bellicose Richard Rush, the comptroller of the treasury,
in his Fourth of July speech at the capitol that year. Rush linked this
issue to the quest to affirm national independence.

Yet, to add to the difficulties in assessing causation, other on-
going tensions were also important. These included American suspicions of relations between Native Americans and the British in
Canada, and the activities of British officials, officers, and traders on
the frontier that, in large part, justified these suspicions. Until Jay's
Treaty, the British had occupied bases such as Detroit, Mackinac, and

Niagara, while there was a degree of connivance with the attempt by the Iroquois leader Joseph Brant to create a Western Confederacy to keep the Americans out of Ohio. This attempt failed in 1794,[75] but tensions continued thereafter, as did American suspicions. On the British part, there were still hopes that influence, commercial and political, could be developed in the interior of North America.[76] There was also a sense of obligation to the Native Americans as past allies, not least because Britain had let them down in its treaties with the USA in 1783 and 1794. The idea of the "Noble Savage" retained a hold on the British imagination,[77] and indeed adapted to new themes. Thus, *Hermsprong: or Man As He Is Not* (1796), a novel by Robert Bage who ran a Staffordshire paper mill, offered a radical critique of the social system, using the perspective of an Native American who personified the virtuous "Noble Savage" in a more modern setting; but with the radicalism tempered by an appreciation of the constraints of society. As a result, the hero in the end returns to his true role as part of the establishment, and not as a rejection of it. Such images reflected a sympathy with the "idea" of Native Americans.

The British, in turn, were blamed in the USA for problems with the Native Americans and with the fur trade. Both administrators and army officers in Canada indeed were prime movers in instigating the Native Americans to oppose American expansion. Many administrators were former officers, such as John Graves Simcoe and Thomas Saumarez, each of whom had surrendered at Yorktown in 1781. However, the British were not responsible for the developing nativist movement that centered on Tecumseh and, even more, his brother, Tenskwatawa, "the Prophet," who had launched a religious revival in 1805.[78] This revival did not unite all Native Americans, and only a minority of the Shawnees followed Tecumseh and Tenskwatawa,[79] but tensions between Native Americans and the USA rose. More generally, many Native Americans had little interest in accommodating themselves to American interests and, instead, tended to see such a practice as weakness.[80]

Madison, in his message to Congress on 5 November 1811, urging it to prepare for war, made no reference to problems with Native Americans in his case for preparedness. Nevertheless, within the USA, the increasingly prominent (although only modestly represented in Congress) West, which then meant trans-Appalachia, especially Kentucky, Tennessee, and Ohio, was concerned about British aid to the Native Americans. This concern led to pressure for the seizure of Canada, which was seen as the base of, and the means for, this aid. Thus, expansionism arose in part from a defensive mentality. Prior to the War of 1812, the British government denied instigating Native American attacks on the Americans.[81] Insofar as such encouragement occurred, it was a case of policy being set by officials on the ground, especially military commanders, rather than by the foreign secretary and the diplomatic system. Indeed, the role of frontier disputes in relations with the USA provided the best example of the potential clash between formal diplomacy and other agencies of the British state.

From the American perspective, the reality on the ground, however, was a degree of cooperation between Britain and Native Americans that was a threat. As a consequence, defeating the Native Americans was, in part, to the Americans, a way of hitting Britain, whether or not the two powers were at war. In reality, Major General Isaac Brock, from September 1811 the commander of the troops in Upper Canada, and the acting administrator of the colony from the time he took command there, directed the Indian Department to exert its considerable influence over Native American frontier settlements in order to maintain the peace. Prevost sent an extract of Brock's letter to the British minister in Washington as well as to the Earl of Liverpool in order to show how British authorities on the spot were acting to restrain the Native Americans. In May 1812, at the Mohawk village on the Grand River, Brock told Native American leaders that the British could not help against American encroachment while they were at peace.

American expansion, however, was a source of pressure to the Native Americans. Ohio became a state in 1803, the year in which the Louisiana Purchase of lands from France led to an unprecedented westward extension of American sovereignty, and one that threw the status of the West and relations with Native Americans into greater prominence. The Greenville (1795) boundary rapidly became redundant as Native American lands in Ohio, Indiana, Illinois, and Michigan were purchased, particularly by the Treaties of Fort Wayne of 1809 which led to the acquisition of much of eastern and southern Indiana. In turn, this expansion led to an Native American reaction, which ensured that the fear of a renewed British-Native American alliance became a self-fulfilling prophecy.[82]

The Native American reaction helped cause fighting that was an immediate background to the War of 1812. Concerned about Shawnee opposition to the advance of American power, particularly opposition to land cessions by other tribes, William Henry Harrison (1773–1841), the governor of the Indiana Territory (and briefly president in 1841), advanced in 1811 to seize their base at Prophet's Town near the confluence of the Wabash and Tippecanoe Rivers. On 7 November, in what was subsequently known as the Battle of Tippecanoe, the Shawnees attacked first, but the early morning assault by about 450 natives under Tenskwatawa was fought off by about 910 Indiana militia. Tenskwatawa had misled the Native Americans by promising them impunity to American musket fire, a frequent theme in anti-Western movements that drew on religious inspiration. Harrison's robust defense exposed the claim and, their morale falling and ammunition running out, the outnumbered Native Americans withdrew, allowing Harrison to burn Prophet's Town and to claim a victory. Yet, it was soon apparent to Americans, Native Americans, and the British that the battle was not decisive. Indeed, Prophet's Town was repopulated and in June 1812 Harrison was to observe that the force there was as strong as that the previous summer.[83]

Tippecanoe indeed served to strengthen both the Native American determination to fight and Native American support for Britain, while also indicating the extent to which political issues were being militarized. In April 1812, Henry Clay, the bellicose Speaker of the House of Representatives, informed the House that "he had no doubts but that the late Indian War on the Wabash was executed by the British."[84] This was not the case, but it indicated the strength of a paranoid mood in the drive for war. Harrison himself had seen the treaties of Fort Wayne as simply the temporary prelude to fresh expansion but, ironically, the federal government was less than sympathetic, because Madison did not want a war with the Native Americans at the same time as he was pursuing the acquisition of West Florida from Spain, which he saw as more important. Jefferson, however, pressed for the conquest of Canada, informing John Adams in June 1812 that "the possession of that country secures our women and children for ever from the scalping knife, by removing those who excite them."[85]

During the War of 1812, the West was to feel it was fighting an offensive-defensive war against British containment, a continuation of the struggles of the 1790s. To Westerners, this was not a case, as the critical, largely antiwar Federalists quipped, of fighting on land to protect maritime rights (a charge designed to expose the flaws in government policy) because, to them, the war was about much more, although at the time a sense of vulnerability led some in Ohio and the Michigan Terriorty to oppose the outbreak of war.[86] More widely, American expansionism had contributed to the crisis in Anglo-American relations, although it is possible that historians have over-emphasized its role in bringing on the war, certainly insofar as Madison was concerned. This may indeed be an over-emphasis that reflects historians' need to integrate maritime causes with internal or domestic ones.

Aside from the specific issues in dispute or arousing disquiet, there was a more general sense, particularly among the Jeffersonians, that the Revolution was unfinished because Britain remained powerful; and that this power threatened American interests and public morality, as Britain was a corrosive but seductive model of un-American activity. This model moreover sapped American virility because it encouraged a trade that fostered a love of luxury, a love that corroded the necessary martial spirit.[87] Thus, Americans employed earlier British political discourse about the danger of luxury against Britain, rather as their predecessors had done at the time of the Revolution. The Revolution not only seemed incomplete. It also was incomplete as long as Britain could be seen as a menace.[88] A sense of superior American morality, but also of the challenges it faced, was captured in 1812 by Thomas Sully's painting *The Capture of Major Andre*. Sully, who, as a reminder of Anglo-American links, had trained in London in 1809–10, depicted the three young militiamen who captured André in September 1780 refusing a bribe, thus thwarting Benedict Arnold's plan to betray West Point. This refusal of the bribe, and the contrast with Arnold, was a symbol of the moral strength of ordinary American citizens, a strength that was the basis of the republic, but also of the need for vigilance against the British threat.

# 2

# THE AMERICANS ATTACK, 1812

The War of 1812 is difficult to discuss clearly because it was a particularly disparate struggle and, therefore, without any central narrative. There were separate campaigns on the Canadian frontier (which stretched from beyond Lake Michigan to Maine, a formidable distance by modern, let alone early nineteenth century, standards), as well as around Chesapeake Bay and its river system, and in the Gulf of Mexico. There was, moreover, warfare on the high seas, not only off the USA but also as far away as the Pacific.

The order in which these campaigns, or even only those on the Canadian frontier, are discussed appears to offer a prioritization that may be misleading. It also suggests a form to a war that in fact was curiously shapeless, as politicians and generals struggled to reduce the range of real and possible commitments to some order so as to be able to try to understand, respond to, and even direct, events. Indeed, these difficulties throw some light on the argument that the existence of strategy in this period is problematic. Indeed, the word "strategy" was not used in English until about 1800 when it was borrowed from the French. The earliest citation in the second edition of the *Oxford English Dictionary* is from 1810.[1] However, the concept as such was hardly new, and many eighteenth-century writers used the terms grand tactics or art of war to denote strategy. Moreover, discussion over whether, where, and in what force to attack involved strategic concepts. In the event, the Americans found the process of directing efforts and events across the range of their commitments particularly difficult, and largely beyond them. They were most successful, in 1814–15, when they were largely on the defensive and responding to the British attempts to shape the conflict. In their lack of success these British attempts, in turn, threw light on earlier American difficulties in mounting successful offensives.

In considering how best to present the conflict there is also the issue of participants. The war was far from being a straightforward struggle between American and British forces, and is not treated thus in the literature. Canadians played an important part in their own defense, a part indeed that was to be significant in the development of Canadian identity. Moreover, Native Americans played an independent and important role in the conflict. They were mostly allied, albeit often indirectly, with the British, although there were important exceptions both in the Northwest and in the South/Southeast. Inclusion of the Native Americans also serves to suggest a different geographical focus for discussion, for devoting appropriate attention to them leads to due consideration of both the western Great Lakes region and the Southeast. This is in place of the usual focus, which is on a more eastward view of the Canadian frontier, as well as on the Chesapeake. Discussion of the Native Americans, moreover, helps take the war into the Mississippi Valley, an area of strategic importance since the late seventeenth century; and also links the war to the longer-term development of American territorial power and the dislocation that caused for Native American society.

For the USA, this conflict is also a very instructive political episode. It was a highly divisive war, one in which many Americans refused to help. The Federalists, who were heavily represented in New England, but not only there, were opposed to war with Britain, which they correctly saw as likely to be expensive and harmful to trade. The Federalists also saw territorial expansion as intended to benefit the rival governing Democratic-Republicans. In addition, New England interests had only limited concern in the relations between Britain and the Native Americans that troubled the frontier regions. Commentators, indeed, had long detected regional rifts within the USA. Opposition in New England to the war looked ahead to limited New England support for the Seminole Wars in Florida and also for the Mexican-American War of 1846–48.

In 1812, the Federalists were outvoted by the Democratic-Repub-

licans, but the divisions on declaring war—79 to 49 in the House of
Representatives on 4 June, and 19 to 13 in the Senate on 17 June—
reflected the depth of disquiet. These votes showed that it was difficult to create both a nation-state and a nationalism that worked.
They also throw light on subsequent divisions in American history
over going to war, underlining the extent to which they were part of a
long tradition.

In 1812, the votes demonstrated division. As the Constitution
expressly conferred the power to declare war on Congress, and Congress alone could vote money to pay for the war and the military, the
potentially unifying position of the presidency was heavily qualified
thereby. Moreover, it was too early for the potential wartime powers
of the presidency to be fully explored. They only became clearer with
the Civil War fifty years later. Nevertheless, in 1812, division was
less bitter than at the time of the hard-fought presidential election in
1800, and this division did not lead to civil conflict. Indeed, it is
still appropriate to refer to American goals, albeit accepting that the
extent of dissension not only limited the availability of resources
available for the war effort, but also affected strategic options and
operational possibilities.


ATTACKING CANADA

The prime American strategic goal was the overcoming of Canada, an
issue that symbolized the extent to which the American Revolution
seemed unfinished abroad and, therefore, in some eyes unrealized at
home. It is unclear, however, whether, once conquered, the Madison
government wished to retain Canada, or to use it merely as a pawn in
negotiations with Britain over impressments and trade. In 1801–
1802, Jefferson had shown little interest in supporting Asa Danforth's
plan for a rebellion in Upper Canada, a plan that was dependent on an
American invasion. Jefferson had been more interested in expansion
at the expense of Spain.[2]

The complex nature of sectional interests was a factor in Ameri-
can politics in 1812. Far from being solely focused on Canada and
Native Americans, the British Orders in Council were blamed by the
Western and Southern War Hawks for agricultural problems in their
regions. Thus, alongside the issue of national honor, the need to force
Britain to change maritime policy was also seen there as a key sec-

tional interest. Maritime issues, in short, were not a diversion from Western and Southern concerns about Native Americans.[3]

The use of Canada as a negotiating pawn has been stressed in accounts that emphasize the defensive character of American policy; but, whether defensive or offensive, these goals required the seizure of Canada. So also, in the eyes of the many Westerners, did any settlement of the Native American issue. Henry Clay, a Kentucky landowner and lawyer, a leading Westerner, and a War Hawk, who was Speaker of the House of Representatives, was to write in December 1813: "When the war was commenced Canada was not the end but the means; the object of the war being the redress of injuries, and Canada being the instrument by which that redress was to be obtained." However, he also observed that, if Canada could be conquered and retained, it should be held.[4] That was very much a theme of the Westerners.

The defense of Canada was a very difficult task for Britain: Canada seemed both vulnerable to American attack and of limited importance to Britain. The American population of 7.25 million (the census of 1810) was far larger than that of British North America, which is estimated to have been between 400,000 and 500,000. Canadian militia[5] and Native American allies were supplemented by British regulars; but, in June 1812, there were only 9,777 of these in Canada, and no significant reinforcements arrived that year. A shortage of troops was a central aspect of the British position. Aside from a lack of regulars, there was scant artillery, and the Canadian militia were untried.

Canada was also vulnerable because the frontier across which the Americans could move forward was lengthy. There were, moreover, clear lines of American attack, not least the Lake Champlain corridor, which had been used successfully in 1760 when the British advanced on Montréal, and again in 1775 when the Americans did the same. The naval forces available to the British on the Great Lakes were limited, with only two warships on Lake Erie and three on Lake Ontario: these were the two key lakes.

The British suffered because they were unprepared for conflict in North America, had not sought war there, and did not take the military initiative. The lack of preparedness reflected the extent to which they were already heavily engaged against Napoleon's France. More generally, the British faced the problem of strategic depth. Whereas much of the American population was vulnerable, not to attack across the Canadian frontier but, instead, from the sea (the latter much more so than even thirty years later), the Canadian population was within ready campaigning distance of the frontier, which increased Canada's vulnerability.

Compounding the problem of defense, Canada, furthermore, despite its significance as a source of naval stores, was relatively unimportant to Britain compared to the war with Napoleon. He was as yet undefeated and, indeed, was at the height of his ambition and power in 1812. The war in Europe was going badly for Britain. Both Austria and Prussia were allied with Napoleon, and the British, while capable of defeating the French in battle in Spain, found it difficult to sustain offensive operations in the field there.

The struggle with France demanded the commitment of most of the British army, although it also provided valuable combat experience, while the army's organization and quality greatly improved in the 1800s.[6] The use of military intelligence was taken forward by Arthur Wellesley (later Duke of Wellington) in this campaigning in India and later Iberia and, by 1812, "multiple-scenario planning had become a staple of Wellington's decision-making process, and as well as being used to mitigate against intelligence failure, was used to shape enemy options."[7] The British were not to have this capability in North America.

In the absence of conscription, and in response to the need for much manpower for the navy, Britain faced many problems in raising troops, which resulted in considerable reliance upon Catholic manpower from Ireland. Although, from 1801, as a constituent part of the United Kingdom of Great Britain and Ireland, the latter was represented in the Westminster Parliament, it also had some of the attributes of an imperial possession. Nevertheless, the rebellion of 1798 had been crushed, and the British war effort against America was helped by the absence of another Irish rising.[8] There was no comparison with the discontent there in the early 1780s or even early 1800s, which was an aspect of the strategic situation in the broadest sense.

Prior to the War of 1812, France had already been defeated by the British at sea, and decisively so by Horatio, Lord Nelson in his dying triumph at the battle of Trafalgar in 1805. Subsequent French attempts to rebuild their navy had not been particularly successful, not least in terms of fighting effectiveness and due to a lack of trained sailors. This naval situation between Britain and France, which was completely different to that during the War of Independence, when the French navy was not defeated until 1782, is a reminder of the extent to which American history was dependent on relations between other powers. This is one of the themes of this book and accounts for the space devoted to this wider context.

In the case of the War of 1812, naval power meant that it was possible for Britain to put maritime pressure on America, not least by mounting a blockade, and also to send reinforcements, if any were available, to Nova Scotia and Lower Canada (Québec). On 14 August 1812, Sir John Borlase Warrer, the commander in chief of the combined North American and West Indies station, sailed from Portsmouth for Halifax with five ships of the line and three frigates. In contrast, because warships of any size could not pass the St. Lawrence rapids, the British were unable to send their ocean-going fleet there from the Atlantic to the Great Lakes. Furthermore, most of the British navy was still required for the blockade of France and French-occupied Europe.

Canada provided the Americans with a clear strategic goal. It was a conquest that would at once permit the pursuit of their imperial schemes and offer a bargaining counter for maritime concessions. Yet, the Americans were unable to devise an effective means to obtain this. The size of Canada helped make strategic planning for its invasion difficult, although the size of Upper Canada (Ontario) was irrelevant if the Americans had cut the St. Lawrence route above Montréal. The conquest of Lower Canada would have been difficult for reasons other than its size. Also making strategic planning difficult were the nature of contemporary communications, command and control, and the relationships between individual commanders. For these reasons, there was little prospect of the coordinated campaigning that would have been the best way to take advantage of the wide-ranging distribution of American military resources. The alternative, their massing in a single concentration of power, was not possible for political reasons, not least due to the major and autonomous role of state militias. Moreover, such a massing was not feasible in logistical terms, the last a very important qualification of military effectiveness in this period. In addition, a deficiency in American planning that, in part, reflected the lack of an effective planning structure and process, accompanied the organizational and political limitations that affected the war effort.

In contrast, the British benefited from methodical, planned, disciplined, and relatively orderly military and administrative structures, and also from the ability to purchase and reward military and civilian service. Sustained conflict with France had had an important impact in improving British military structures. The rise of the War Office under the secretary of war from 1783 had provided a larger and more effective bureaucracy for the conduct of overseas operations, especially so under the energetic Henry, 3rd Viscount Palmerston, secretary from 1809 to 1828, and later prime minister. The secretary of war, however, was an administrative budgetary officer, while, from 1794, policy was made and orders conveyed by the secretary of state for war. The process of administrative reform was taken further from 1806 with the appearance of the first of a number of reports by the newly established Commission of Military Enquiry.

The British war effort had also benefited greatly from a burgeoning economy and a robust oceanic trading system, the importance of which helped explain the significance of maritime disputes with the USA. The economy fed into strong public finances and, thanks largely to the introduction of income tax from 1799, direct taxation became far more significant, and tax revenues rose from £18.8 million in 1793 to £77.9 million in 1815.

The Americans could not match these strengths, while the absence of an effective American strategy made it difficult to make full use of the tactical and operational successes that were won, such as Oliver Hazard Perry's naval victory for the USA on Lake Erie on 10 September 1813 (see Chapter 3). William Henry Harrison took advantage of this triumph, but the victory did not lead to the rolling up of the British position in Upper Canada. Instead, such successes comprised parts in a whole that was absent. More particularly, multi-pronged American attacks were not coordinated, and did not exert simultaneous or sequential pressure on the British or, at least, did not succeed in doing so sufficiently to ensure a cascading dynamic of success. This was a particular problem with operations against Montréal, but was also an issue farther west in the Great Lakes region. Yet the Americans were not alone in these failings. A lack of cooperation between forces and operations on different fronts also detrimentally affected the British, especially in Upper Canada in late 1813.

A strategy of coordinated American attack on Canada would have been difficult to execute given the extent of operations. The war was extremely difficult to plan or manage because the territories involved were so large, although also because many of the fighting forces were not trained or equipped for the kind of warfare that resulted, and American leadership was unprepared for this struggle. Moreover, logistical and transport problems accentuated the problems of distance and communications. Many military goods and other supplies had to be transported, by both the Americans and the British, from the eastern seaboard. The distances were considerable and the circumstances difficult, as the British troops who marched to Lower Canada from the Maritime Provinces (Nova Scotia and New Brunswick), such as the 104th Foot in February–April 1813 abundantly realized. It was not possible to obtain sufficient supplies in the relatively unpopulated frontier areas, which were richer in trees than food, and it was not possible for the Americans to transfer the burden to the Canadians by invading, for the border areas of Canada also had insufficient supplies. Nor was it possible for the American forces to transport the food and matériel they required: aside from transport and logistical problems, the necessary administrative structure was lacking. These deficiencies greatly affected American operations.

The British conquest of Canada in 1759–60, the sole successful conquest of that country, then New France, was carried out by regulars and had required a formidable logistical underpinning.[9] Furthermore, it followed several years of unsuccessful British campaigning in North America (1754–58) which, itself, indicated the difficulties of the task, as well as providing a less critical comparative context for American efforts in 1812–13. This was a point made in September 1813 by an American supporter of the war, Richard Rush, the comptroller of the Treasury. He drew attention to the time the British had taken to conquer Canada,[10] not that New France was more than a fraction of modern Canada.

The romantic concept of American warriordom as self-sufficient, rugged individuals at one with the terrain is a highly misleading image of the forces deployed against Canada in the War of 1812 and, more generally, underrates the long-term theme of professionalism in the American way of war. Yet the necessary professionalism was lacking in 1812, and this was to prove a conspicuous problem in the case of many of those who were appointed generals.[11] Aside from problems with the regulars, federal law limited the militia to three months of service out of every year. They were differentiated from volunteers, a new class of citizen-soldiers who could be raised to fight for nine to twelve months, but the latter also lacked the training of regulars.

Moreover, institutionally, America was not a war state. The absence of a commanding general, let alone a general staff, threw command functions on land onto the secretary of war, who had a myriad of responsibilities and little power. This was compounded in 1812 by the deficiencies of William Eustis, the secretary of war, who was not up to the role of providing or supporting leadership. He was not a shadow of Berthier and Clarke, French ministers of war in 1799–1807 and 1807–14 respectively, each of whom helped organize Napoleon's war-making, although Berthier insisted that he just implemented Napoleon's instructions, efficiently turning his broad directives into detailed ones.

Rather than preparing adequately before the war, Congress in 1812 sought to remedy the institutional crisis by establishing quartermaster, ordnance, hospital, pay, adjutant and inspector general, and commissary departments. However, these departments proved poorly prepared for their tasks, and this contributed to serious logistical failures, especially once forces advanced into Canada. The Americans, moreover, suffered from a lack of specie and from limited confidence in the financial system, which was far weaker than that of Britain.[12] These failures help to explain the lack of operational movement that characterized much of American campaigning, and its start-stop or episodic character. Continuous pressure on the British could not be provided. The deficiencies exacerbated, and were exacerbated by, the poor state of internal transport (both in terms of routes and of other aspects of infrastructure) to the area of hostilities and within it. Land transport was slow, cumbersome, and expensive. Poor weather added to the problems.

This situation was abundantly seen with the drawbacks that affected William Hull's advance in 1812, problems that more generally showed the difficulty of transforming strategic planning into operational success. Hull, who had served extensively during the War of Independence, had been made governor of the Michigan Territory by Jefferson in 1805. In March 1812, still governor, he proposed a bold plan as relations deteriorated with Britain. Hull wanted a large force to be sent to Detroit with a defensive/offensive objective: to protect Michigan and Ohio, and to drive the British from Lake Erie and Upper Canada. Hull was appointed brigadier general and given command of the Northwestern Army, an army that was in fact not yet in being. Leaving Washington on 9 April and reaching Dayton on 25 May, Hull organized a force of twelve hundred Ohio militia that was to be strengthened by eight hundred regulars of the 4th U.S. Infantry. Hull, however, was hindered not only by his own unsuitability for the command, but also by serious disagreements between militia and regulars.

A key issue was transport. An Ohio volunteer noted of the march north of Hull's forces through Ohio in June 1812, "A continued rain for a number of days had tended to render the roads we had to travel . . . uncommonly bad and almost impassable for our wagons."[13] Again discussing the Northwest front, Harrison wrote the following January of "a most unfortunate rain, which has broken up the roads, so as to render them impassable for the artillery, although it is fixed on sleds."[14] The transport of cannon and supplies was seen as crucial by Madison, who argued in September 1812 that there was no point in attacking Detroit and invading nearby Canada unless they were available, and that troops without such support were of scant value.[15] Indeed, uncertainly about the movement of supplies made planning difficult, at least insofar as time factors were concerned. James Monroe, the secretary of state and later Madison's successor as president, commented that month: "6 24 pounders, 10 18s, 10 12s, 6 6 pounders, and 14 8-inch howitzers are ordered to Fort Pitt. They are necessary to batter and take Detroit and [Fort] Malden [Amherstburg], and, although they may not be got there this year, they will be ready for the spring."[16]

The serious structural problems that face any military that rapidly expands under the pressure of war, problems which were to be seen by the Americans (both sides) in the Civil War and in the two world wars, and by the British in the world wars, were compounded for the Americans in the War of 1812 by administrative weaknesses. These included a failure to provide a clear ranking of officers, not least to define relations between regular and militia commanders, a repeated problem during the war and one that seriously affected operations. Thus, in the autumn of 1812, Madison's wish that Monroe replace Hull as commander in the Northwest in order to repair the serious damage caused by the latter's surrender of Detroit[17] was thwarted because Charles Scott, the governor of Kentucky, gave Harrison control over Kentucky forces serving in the Northwest. Harrison was also made a major general of the Kentucky militia, which gave him precedence over James Winchester, a brigadier general in the regular army who was unpopular with the militia. Tension between the two men affected that winter's eventually unsuccessful campaign.

These institutional weaknesses were then played out in a situation made bitter by a shortage of money and matériel, especially the first, and with issues provided by problems such as the absence of any comprehensive set of general regulations or any uniform system of tactics. There was a lack of new weaponry while, in October 1812, Henry Dearborn, the newly appointed major general in charge of the northern border, complained about a lack of musket cartridges.[18] Supply shortages hit morale and health and encouraged desertion,[19] which had also been a problem in the War of Independence. Moreover, the militia tradition ensured not only that the regular army was too weak but also, as a result, left the war effort dependent on militia forces that were unsuited to the task of sustained offensive operations,[20] not least because many units refused to cross the border. In 1814, the militia were also to prove poor in defense, both in the Chesapeake and in Maine. Madison complained in September 1812:

> Proofs multiply daily, of the difficulty of obtaining regulars, and of the fluctuating resource in the militia. High bounties and short enlistments, however objectionable, will alone fill the ranks; and these too in a moderate number. This plan would have given us a greater force in July, when the enemy were unprepared, than we shall have in November when it is possible reinforcements may have reached Canada from England.[21]

Even if morale was high, there were other problems, aside from issues of supply. Harrison reported from Cincinnati in southern Ohio in August 1812: "I have an army competent in numbers and in spirit equal to any that Greece or Rome have boasted of but destitute of artillery, of many necessary equipments and absolutely ignorant of every military evolution, nor have I but a single individual capable of assisting me in training them."[22]

Functional problems alone were not responsible for the American failure of coordination. There were also serious political divisions over strategy. There was much support for a focus on the Lake Champlain corridor in order to advance north, first to divide Montréal from Québec and capture Montréal, and then to besiege Québec.[23] Dearborn agreed that the main thrust should be north from the Champlain corridor, but also pressed for ancillary assaults from Detroit and the Niagara frontier. Westerners, however, were opposed to an emphasis on the distant (to them) Champlain corridor and instead wanted to prevent British help to the Native Americans, in particular by advancing on Fort Amherstburg from Detroit. Dearborn himself was a veteran of the Revolutionary War, but had been captured then in operations at Québec, which the Americans had unsuccessfully besieged in 1775–76. He had served from 1801 to 1809 as Jefferson's secretary of war, and his new position was another sign of continuity from the Jefferson presidency.

Optimism was no substitute for planning, but it was widely assumed that the British could be easily and rapidly beaten. Henry Clay declared in 1812 that the Kentucky militia alone could conquer Montréal and Upper Canada. He also suggested to Monroe: "If you carry your recollection back to the age of the Crusades . . . you will have a picture of the enthusiasm existing in this country for the expedition to Canada." This was ridiculous. More pragmatically, Clay accepted that French claims about the right to blockade Britain also threatened American trade, a reasonable criticism of American policy; but he noted that "the one [Britain] we can strike, the other [France] we cannot reach." The anglophobic Jefferson, who claimed that the war would be a "mere matter of marching," hoped to drive the British from North America: Québec was to be taken in 1812, and Halifax, Nova Scotia, Britain's naval base in North America, in 1813.[24] Such vain remarks make for painful reading in light of the numbers who died.

In practice, despite the length of the Canadian border, there were few corridors in which the advance of a force of any size was viable. As a consequence, it was possible for a smaller defensive force, if properly deployed, to block advancing armies, which thwarted the Americans in 1812–13 and, in turn, the British in 1814–15. Water transport was important to both sides, and control of the Great Lakes therefore had a major impact on mobility and on operational possibilities. However, such transport was of limited use for the north-south movement of forces away from the lakes, which instead principally offered east-west routes. An important exception was provided by the Hudson/Mohawk route. It was readily possible to carry goods up the Hudson River from New York City, a key logistical and communications center, to Albany. It was then necessary to move sixteen miles overland to Schenectady. There, the Mohawk River became navigable and, thanks to works by the Western Inland Lock Navigation Company, there was a continuous water route to Oswego on Lake Ontario, which proved a key point in the American supply infrastructure. This route proved particularly important to the movement of naval supplies, which allowed the Americans to contest control of the lake, and was also significant to the more general issue of American power projection and capability on the frontier.[25]

## THE NATURE OF CONFLICT

Before beginning a narrative, it is appropriate to offer an introduction to the nature of combat in the Western world. The various forces taking part, excluding the Native Americans, had more in common in terms of armaments and tactics than is sometimes appreciated, although the advantage brought by the experience of British regulars was significant, not least for their fire discipline.[26] Partly as a consequence of this similarity, battles, and the smaller-scale clashes that were far more common (but that cannot always be readily differentiated from battles), were usually won in Europe and North America in 1775–1815 by experienced and motivated troops whose dispositions had been well arranged. If forces were evenly matched, engagements were either inconclusive encounters or were determined by other factors, such as terrain and the availability and, more significantly, employment of reserves. In comparison, innovative ideas about deployment and tactics were not necessarily superior, while numbers alone were only of value if they were handled ably.

Infantry were mostly armed with a flintlock musket equipped with a bayonet. This weapon provided both the offensive and the defensive capacity of the infantry, and its multi-purpose character ensured tactical flexibility. Rifles were less common.[27] In the flint-lock musket, powder was ignited by a spark produced through the action of a flint on steel. The rate of fire was helped by the use of pre-packaged paper cartridges, which provided the correct amount of powder. There were, however, serious problems with the musket. Its fire could readily be disrupted by poor weather, especially by rain and, to a lesser extent, wind. Damp powder caused misfires.

Even in perfect conditions, effective range for an individually aimed musket shot was limited, while it was unusual to exceed three shots a minute. Accuracy was compromised by the nature of the barrel, which was unrifled and, in order to avoid fouling by powder and recoil, generally a loose fit for the shot, and therefore of limited accuracy. The shot, as a result of the significant windage (gap between barrel and shot), "bounded" down the bore, and might then leave the barrel in any direction, a process known as balloting. Moreover, the rough-cast shot was often elliptical and thus unlikely to travel as designed. In addition, the ramrods used to drive down the shot often bent and jammed in the musket, broke or went rusty; and frequent use of the ramrod distorted the barrel into an oval shape. The lock speed of muskets was slow, and they also had no sights. Worn flints and blocked touch-holes caused misfiring. Reloading became more difficult as the bore fouled with powder.

It was not surprising, given the nature of the weaponry, that infantry tactics on both sides emphasized the volume of firepower rather than aimed fire. The same was true at sea. It was difficult in any case to aim in the noise and smoke of a battlefield, and the heavy weight of muskets led to musket droop: firing short. Another reason for poor aim was the bruising produced by the recoil if the firing was heavy. Volume firepower was achieved by arranging the infantry in closely packed, shoulder-to-shoulder linear formations and training them to fire as fast as possible, a measure that further inhibited individual aiming. Soldiers fired by volley in a process designed to maximize the continuity of fire, rather than employing individually aimed shot. Training through drill was also the best way to use soldiers whose lack of experience resulted from the continual infusions of new recruits. The speed of fire was enhanced by the use of paper cartridges, with the ball, powder, and wadding in a single package, which made reloading easier, and which also allowed each soldier to carry more ammunition. As a weapon capable of killing and used in volleys, the British "Brown Bess" flintlock certainly achieved its purposes at 100 or 150 yards.

Despite the bayonets, most casualties were caused by shot. Indeed, the exchange of fire at close quarters between lines of closely packed troops could lead to high casualty rates. Low muzzle velocity, moreover, led to dreadful wounds, because the more slowly a projectile travels, the more damage it does as it bounces off bones and internal organs. As a result, the sight of the dead and mangled, and the cries of the wounded, in the aftermath of battles were horrific.

Due to the close-packed and static or slow-moving formations that were adopted to maintain discipline and firepower, unbroken infantry were vulnerable to artillery. Cannon were employed on the battlefield both to silence opposing guns and, more effectively, to weaken infantry. Grape and canister shot were particularly deadly: they consisted of a bag or tin with small balls inside, which scattered as a result of the charge, causing considerable numbers of casualties at short range. John Norton described how at the battle of Queenston in 1812 the American grapeshot "rattled around."[28]

Alongside an emphasis on battles and formations, it is appropriate to note the extent to which much conflict was a case of what has been termed "small warfare." Aside from being a smaller-scale variant of larger unit conflict, this warfare had different characteristics and served a number of functions, not least raiding. At this level there was an emphasis on march security, surprise, and cover. Many actions took place around small positions that one side had occupied for their defensive value, and most were decided within minutes of the first volley. The rushing of positions was also significant, as in the successful attack across the frozen St. Lawrence River on Ogdensburg on 22 February 1813 by eight hundred Canadians and Native Americans under Lieutenant Colonel George MacDonnell. Although, in this case, spies ensured that the outnumbered Americans knew of the forthcoming attack, small warfare placed a premium on surprise attacks launched without the delays or concentration of force required if artillery was to be deployed.

An emphasis on the attack does not necessarily lessen the value of firepower, especially because the latter could be used to prepare for the assault as well as to counter it. However, this emphasis suggests that any account that approaches tactical success in terms of the technological (weaponry) and organizational (tactics, drill, discipline) factors that maximized firepower is a limited one. The real point of drill and discipline was to prepare a unit to remain intact in the face of death, regardless of casualties. The issues of firepower versus shock, or defense versus attack, were not as important as a unit remaining able to act, and tractable to its commander, while receiving casualties, which could be very heavy, particularly as a result of close-quarter volley or cannon fire.

Small warfare, far from being an inconsequential echo of decisive battles, could serve not only as a description of particular kinds of actions, but also to characterize military operations as a whole.[29] This was not only true of North America, and thus throws light on the debate as to whether there was a distinctive American way of war, not least, as has been suggested, an effectiveness in small warfare and a practice of achieving victory by devastating Native American society.[30] This argument for a distinctive way of war, which draws on the idea of particular military cultures, and also matches the more general theme of American exceptionalism,[31] has been countered, for example by Guy Chet, with the argument that American warmaking had many similarities with more formal European techniques.[32] In practice, it may be most pertinent to join the two and to say that there was a similar continuum in European and American warmaking. As a result, there was no clear difference in doctrine and experience between them, and no automatic superiority for either. This helps explain the lack of any clear capability gap between the two sides during the War of 1812, certainly at the overall level, although the situation was different in individual clashes.

At one level, small warfare overlapped with the tactics and goals of the Native Americans and, at another, with the European interest in light infantry.[33] The latter was a cause associated in particular in Britain with Sir John Moore who, in 1803, was appointed commander of a new brigade at Shorncliffe Camp in Kent, which was designed to serve as the basis of a permanent light infantry force. Particular emphasis was placed upon marksmanship. Moore's force was to become the Light Brigade and, subsequently, the Light Division. The cause of light infantry was supported by Frederick, Duke of York, George III's second son, who was commander in chief of the army from 1795 to

1809 and 1811 to 1827. Derided in nursery rhymes as the "Grand Old Duke of York," who was an unsuccessful commander in the field in Holland in 1799, he was, in fact, a committed reformer.

On the other hand, after York was forced to resign when a former mistress, Mary Anne Clarke, falsely accused him of selling promotions, the commander in chief from 1809 to 1811 was General Sir David Dundas. He placed the organized firepower of the close-order line at the center of military practice, and was much less concerned with light infantry. Yet, heavily encumbered regular units, maneuvering and fighting in their accustomed formations, were vulnerable in the face of entrenched positions and were unsuited to the heavily wooded and hilly terrain of the Canadian frontier. Instead, this was terrain suited for the defense, as both the British and the Americans showed during the war. Narrow valley routes were flanked by dense woodland, while deep rivers often had few crossing points. This posed serious problems for commanders. It was not easy to execute flanking maneuvers in this terrain.

Cavalry played scant role in the War of 1812, although it offered more in the South. The Southern Pine, straight and thin with no branches and growth till the top, allowed for easy maneuvering on horseback, and there were no fences. Forage for the horses, however, was a major issue: it was bulky, difficult to transport, and precious. Furthermore, the transportation of horses by sea posed serious difficulties for the British, not least those of providing sufficient food and preventing horses from breaking their bones in unstabilized ships, while acquiring sufficient suitable mounts in North America was not easy.

Initially, in 1812, the Americans planned a wide-ranging attack that was intended to conquer much of Canada. Simultaneous offensives were to achieve particular goals and to put cumulative pressure on the British. The foci of attack were to be Fort Amherstburg in the west and Montréal in the east, but there were also to be advances on Kingston and the Niagara peninsula in the center. These multiple attacks, and the widespread deployment of troops they entailed, also provided the Americans with the opportunity to defend key sectors against possible British advances. Madison explained to Jefferson that a concentration on Montréal "could not be attempted without sacrificing the Western and N.W. Frontier,"[34] an argument that reflected not only political practicalities but also a sense of vulnerability to Anglo-Native American attacks in the Northwest.

In opposition, the British were short of troops. Aside from the regulars in Canada, there was a larger force of local troops, but their effectiveness was unclear to British commanders. The British were also affected by divisions among their leaders related to strategy. Lieutenant General Sir George Prevost, who was governor in chief of British North America, and also captain general, vice admiral, and commander of all His Majesty's Forces in North America, was not keen on war with the USA. Moreover, although Prevost had considerable combat experience in the West Indies, he lacked the necessary drive and fighting zeal in his new command, although he also had the difficult task of avoiding defeat when attacked by larger forces and without the prospect of reinforcements.[35] From the outset of the war, Prevost was repeatedly and emphatically instructed to follow a defensive policy. He was not prepared to abandon Upper Canada, where he sent arms and ammunition and agreed to the recruitment of the Glengarry Fencibles. Prevost also ordered the construction of another schooner on Lake Erie and sent a naval captain to consult with Major General Isaac Brock, the local commander, about strengthening naval forces on Lake Ontario. However, Prevost was more committed to the defense of Lower Canada.

## The Detroit Front

Brock, the commander of the troops in Upper Canada, who was also the acting administrator of the colony in the absence of its lieutenant governor, Francis Gore, had no intention of yielding Upper Canada. Instead, he followed an active policy of strengthening the militia and also seeking support from the Native Americans. Indeed, he saw the support of the latter as crucial to any successful offensive strategy and also as being a byproduct of such a strategy. To strengthen Native American support, Brock ordered an attack on Fort Mackinac in modern Michigan as soon as the war broke out. This was seen as likely to impress the Native Americans in the Upper Lakes. The fort was surprised and captured on 17 July.

In the event, in 1812 campaigning focused on the western end of the frontier zone. The British were able to gain the initiative there after an American offensive was defeated. Brigadier General William Hull, governor of the Michigan Territory and commander of the Northwestern Army, invaded Canada on 12 July at the western end of

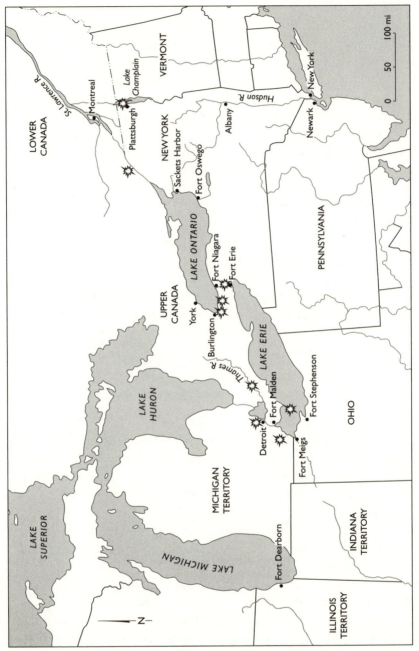

**Northern Theater**

Lake Erie with twenty-five hundred men, a significant number of non-Native Americans for this region. Hull occupied Sandwich (now Windsor) and from there threatened the British position at Fort Amherstburg on Lake Erie, which had a garrison of about three hundred. The garrison was affected by militia desertion and a lack of solid civilian support, but the hesitant Hull did not press his advantage. There were four skirmishes nearby between 16 and 25 July, but they settled nothing.

The fighting effectiveness of Hull's army was limited. His largely volunteer troops were untrained. Moreover, in what proved a serious operational drawback, the Americans were dependent on a long and precarious supply line that was vulnerable to Native American attack. The capture of Hull's military papers on the schooner *Cuyahoga* on 2 July was also unhelpful. Brock learned a great deal about Hull's forces, particularly their weaknesses and vulnerabilities. In effect, he gained inside intelligence about the enemy and put this knowledge to use in his attack on Detroit.

Colonel Henry Procter was sent by Brock to take charge of the garrison at Fort Amherstburg, which he ably rallied. Procter proved a bold commander who made a major effort to win and use Native American support. Helped by Tecumseh, he won over the Wyandots, who had been neutral, and, with their help, cut Hull's supply line in clashes at Brownstown and Maguaga on 5 and 8 August respectively. These thwarted American attempts to reach Frenchtown and secure supplies there.

Hull's morale had also been affected by news of the fall of the American position at Fort Mackinac. Supply problems and a collapse of nerve led Hull to abandon his plan to attack Fort Amherstburg and, instead, to retreat to Detroit. Shadrach Byfield of the 41st Foot commented, "The Americans had erected works at Sandwich, but hearing that we were advancing, they burnt and destroyed them, and returned over to Detroit."[36] Hull also ordered the evacuation of the garrison of Fort Dearborn, a vulnerable position near the mouth of the Chicago River. The retreating column, however, was ambushed and destroyed by Potawatomis on 15 August. Thus, fear of the impact of Native American hostility had wrecked the American position west of the Great Lakes, ending the prospect of using the fort as a base.

Although he had had extensive military experience in the American Revolution, Hull (1753–1825) was neither young nor well and, more seriously, he was unable to bring coherence to his command and inspire it. Having retreated to Detroit, Hull faced complaints and the threat of mutiny. He then surrendered Detroit, on 16 August, to a smaller British force of about three hundred regulars, four hundred militia, and six hundred Native Americans. This force was led by Brock, who had arrived at Amherstburg on 14 August and taken over the command from Procter. Tricked into believing that he was faced by an overwhelming horde of Native American warriors, Hull feared massacre at their hands if Detroit was stormed. Unable and unwilling to rally support, Hull surrendered even though supplies were plentiful. Byfield recorded that, when Brock was asked for a cessation of hostilities for three days, "our general replied that if they did not yield in three hours, he would blow up every one of them."[37]

Failure was not treated sympathetically. Jefferson, who had in fact not behaved appropriately as governor of Virginia when the British attacked the Chesapeake in 1781, thought that Hull should be shot.[38] He was court-martialed in 1814 and sentenced to death for neglect of duty and cowardice, although the recommendation of mercy was accepted. In contrast, Brock was made a Knight of the Bath on 10 October 1812, shortly before he died, while the British troops were rewarded with prize money.

Brock appointed Procter, who had gained plaudits for successfully isolating Detroit, as administrator of the Michigan Territory. This was a step that reflected the reality that authority in the territory had been given up by Hull and it had to be assumed by someone in order to ensure that the laws and property rights of the permanent residents would be secure. Yet territorial ambitions were also in play and Henry, 3rd Earl Bathurst, the secretary for war and the colonies, was urged to support a new frontier along the rivers Miami and Wabash, that would secure the Native Americans and prevent the USA from blocking British influence in the interior as far as the Pacific.[39]

The Americans, indeed, feared that the British might exploit their success to capture, first, Fort Wayne, and then Fort Harrison on the Wabash River, and Vincennes, which would be a major advance south in the Indiana Territory. Vulnerable as a result of its small and weak garrison—seventy effective troops and four small cannon—Fort Wayne was in fact besieged by about five hundred Native Americans from late August 1812, with attempts to set it on fire using flaming arrows. The siege, however, was unsuccessful. Moreover, the Native

Americans did not only fail there. On 4 September, Captain Zachary Taylor (who was to be elected president in 1848), successfully defended Fort Harrison against attack by Tecumseh. Vincennes was not attacked.

Farther north, the British had, on 17 July 1812, already surprised and captured Fort Mackinac on Mackinac Island, near where Lakes Michigan and Huron meet. Like their capture of Detroit, this both impressed the Native Americans and helped the British to sustain their physical links with them from Canada. The Native Americans, in turn, were particularly important to the defense of Canada on this flank. They both diverted American attention from the Lake Champlain corridor and gave the British important strategic possibilities,[40] although the idea of Britain recruiting support from the distant Sioux[41] was fanciful.

The victory at Detroit moreover brought the British a welcome supply of weapons, as well as stiffening the morale of Upper Canada. The Americans were to relieve Fort Wayne from Native American pressure on 12 September 1812, to regain Detroit in September 1813, and to replace the troops they had lost, but they had been pushed onto the defensive on this front by Brock's success, and this gave the British in Canada a welcome strategic advantage.

However, the prospect of more lasting British strategic success in the Northwest was squandered in late 1812 by a lack of cooperation with the Native Americans. There is a legend that after the fall of Detroit, Brock gave Tecumseh his sash (which Tecumseh handed on to a senior chief) and a brace of pistols, whereupon Tecumseh handed an elaborate belt to Brock. No contemporary eyewitness recounts this exchange and its origins have been traced to early nineteenth century secondary accounts. More prosaically, the impetus was lost after the capture of Detroit. Brock left for the Niagara front on 19 August. Moreover, Prevost's pursuit of a ceasefire in order to see the consequences for American opinion of the repeal of the Orders in Council, led to a failure to support Native American operations in Indiana. This failure angered Tecumseh. A peaceful settlement would entail the surrender of Native American interests, which indeed occurred in the eventual settlement. Those terms, however, reflected the serious British-Native American defeat at the close of 1813 (see Chapter 3), and, in 1812, the situation was totally different.

Prevost also suggested that Brock move troops from the Detroit front to the Niagara to face the growing threat of attack from the Americans. Looked at more critically, Brock's victory was one that was ripe for exploitation. It was Prevost's failure to grasp this, indeed the absence, in his case of what is sometimes seen, with particular reference to India, as an ambitious, expansionist, proconsular stance on the part of British imperial governors,[42] that played the key role in ensuring that there was no real exploitation. This stance was more generally lacking of the governors from Guy, 1st Lord Dorchester, lieutenant governor and then governor of Québec from 1766 to 1791 and of Lower and Upper Canada from 1791 to 1796, to Prevost. Unlike the Chesapeake in 1813–14, this was a region where the British could attack effectively, in large part thanks to Native American support. However, due to Prevost, Procter did not send troops to help the Native Americans besieging Fort Wayne until 14 September.

This dispatch of troops was too late to prevent Harrison's relief of the fort on the 12th, and they fell back in face of the larger American force.[43] This delay is one of the major might-have-beens of the war. The fall of Fort Wayne would have ensured that any American counterattack had more ground to cover and would also have diverted American strength from the Niagara front.

Five days earlier, as part of a changing international context that was to transform American chances and as a reminder of a very different scale of conflict, 233,000 men and 1,227 cannon clashed in a battle of attrition at Borodino as the Russians unsuccessfully sought to stop Napoleon's advance on Moscow. Napoleon lost a quarter of his force, while Russian casualties were even heavier. The Russians resisted successive attacks and, when finally driven back, did so without breaking.[44] On 14 September Napoleon entered an undefended Moscow, only to find the city set ablaze that night, probably by the Russians. He had no terms to propose that Alexander I would consider, indeed crucially faced an opponent who would not negotiate, and thus could not translate his seizure of Moscow into negotiations.

## THE NIAGARA FRONT

Meanwhile, failure at Detroit led the Americans to act elsewhere, with Madison pressing Dearborn for action on the Niagara front and in Lower Canada, although he was sceptical that this could reverse the recent blow at Detroit: "I perceive no foundation for sanguine hopes, of a success in either quarter that will heal the wound which Hull has given to the campaign. It becomes the more necessary, to avail ourselves of the Western spirit in order to recover if possible what he has lost, and even to accomplish what he might have gained."[45]

This emphasis on "spirit" was a response to Hull's failure and was typical of a new government proclaiming the value of its virtue, but the emphasis led to an underplaying of the need for professionalism and for improvement by that means.

In October 1812, the Americans struck closer to the center of British power in Upper Canada by advancing across the Niagara River. This was also a more convenient area for American operations, not least for logistical reasons, although also because the role of Native Americans, who tended to favor the British, was less important than farther west. As William Eustis, the secretary of war, noted in September 1812 from Pittsburgh: "[T]he march to Detroit by the way of Cleveland is near 300 miles—that to Niagara not much more than 200, the former through a wilderness, the latter principally through a settled country . . . provision to and at Niagara more plentiful and less expensive by 50 per cent."[46]

As so often with the American war effort, the Americans, however, suffered as a consequence of poor command structures, particularly the tension between regular and militia officers. The senior regular officer on the Niagara front, Brigadier General Alexander Smyth, was placed under Major General Stephen Van Rensselaer, a well-connected militia commander, which led Smyth to refuse to cooperate, even though he was instructed to do so. Van Rensselaer was in command of about 1,650 regulars and 4,300 militia, while his opponent, Brock, had about 1,600 regulars and militia, as well as about 600 Iroquois. More mundanely, as an instance of poor preparation, the oars were missing from the boats intended to take the Americans across the Niagara River, and this led to the delay of the attack from 10 to 13 October.

The American advance force finally crossed under darkness in the early hours of 13 October 1812. Some boats, however, were driven downstream by the strong current (a problem that was to affect attacks by both sides), and the troops who landed at Queenston came under British fire. Nevertheless, they were able to find a path that enabled them to surprise the British position. The Americans then deployed on Queenston Heights, while the British under Brock regrouped. They attacked the Americans only for Brock to be killed. This was a reminder of the problems caused by leading from the front and of the risks to which officers exposed themselves.

The Americans initially held their position at Queenston, but they received inadequate support, in part because of the unwillingness of the militia to cross the river into Canada. This refusal was based on the constitutional specification that federalized militia could be used only to repel invasions, suppress institutions, and enforce the laws—and not to invade foreign countries. This stricture continued to hamper American offensive operations throughout the war. In this battle, the British used spherical case shot, subsequently called shrapnel, which had been invented by Henry Shrapnel in 1784. Employing it, two British 6-pounder guns were able to silence American cannon across the Niagara River, as well as sink three or more American boats. This capability helped thwart American preparations to cross. Moreover, Smyth was unwilling to employ his regulars and refused to heed Van Rensselaer's order to take part in the attack. Moreover, Native American warriors led by John Norton, William Kerr, and John Brant played a crucial role. Their presence on the heights prevented the Americans from advancing inland or even consolidating their position there. Thus, Brock's replacement, Major General Roger Sheaffe, was given time to bring up reinforcements and organize them on the heights to fight a successful action.

The battle slipped away from the Americans. More British reinforcements from Fort George several miles to the north arrived in the early afternoon, and they attacked with the aid of Iroquois allies. By the evening of 13 October the outnumbered Americans had been driven back, some jumping into the river, or had surrendered to Sheaffe.[47] In most of the battles of this war, the numbers of those engaged, killed, wounded, and captured are always uncertain. The Americans did not produce a return of their casualties but, on 15 October, Major Thomas Evans from the British side reported 925 prisoners taken and estimated American killed and wounded at about five hundred.[48]

The battle was a major boost for Canadian morale, although Brock's death was a serious loss. He was a skillful and inspiring, as well as vigorous, leader, and was praised to Wellington by Henry, 3rd Earl Bathurst, the secretary of state for war and the colonies.[49] Moreover, Brock could see Upper Canada as a single unit for military purposes, and was ready and able to move troops between fronts within it. Brock was to be a hero in Canadian history.

In contrast, Major General Francis de Rottenburg, who was moved in June 1813 from command in Montréal to command in Upper Canada, based in Kingston, lacked that strategic vision, and this had fatal consequences for the British in late 1813 (see Chapter 3). The situation in Canada, indeed, anticipated that following the death of Major General Robert Ross during the advance on Baltimore in September 1814 (see Chapter 5), although, in the event, the deleterious effect of Ross's replacement by Colonel Arthur Brooke proved tactical and operational rather than strategic, as Ross had simply been charged with command of an expedition.

The Americans achieved little in the remainder of the 1812 campaign. Van Rensselaer resigned on 16 October, to be replaced by Smyth, who attempted to do better and to capture Fort Erie, a key position on the Niagara front. It covered the junction of the Niagara River with Lake Erie. Smyth, a lawyer who was a Republican politician in Virginia, became a colonel in 1808 and an author of a drill manual for the American infantry, which in fact was only a translation of the French regulations of 1791. In July 1812, Smyth was made inspector general for the army, as well as a brigadier general. In this role Smyth was largely inactive, but he pressed for a field command, for which he had no experience. Although he had acted a poor part at the battle of Queenston, Smyth was on the spot and he clearly enjoyed Eustis' confidence. This career was all too typical of the politics of American generalship.

In command, however, Smyth did little to fulfill his promises of attack and victory. He benefited from reinforcements, especially two thousand Pennsylvania militia. However, on 28 November and 1 December, having ordered troops into the boats, Smyth countermanded the planned crossings of the Niagara River. He was concerned about a lack of militia support, particularly on 1 December. Smyth was also worried about what he could achieve with the relatively low numbers who embarked against prepared British troops. The American forces were affected by disease and a lack of supplies. They had also been disrupted by British bombardment and, more seriously, were affected by the extent to which the British were clearly prepared for an attack. This preparedness was serious as it suggested that, wherever the Americans attacked, the British would be able to respond rapidly. As a result, the second projected American crossing had a target down-river of Fort Erie. Concerned about British preparations, however, Smyth did not wish to cross with fewer than three thousand troops, and that number was unavailable on 1 December.

Whatever the reasons, Smyth's leadership was poor. This led to mutinous behavior among his angry troops, with the militia firing off their ammunition and, on 12 December, to a duel with Brigadier General Peter Porter, who had accused him of cowardice. Neither was hurt in the exchange of shots. Smyth went home on leave and was not employed in the army again.

The campaign had been a disaster, which was particularly serious because the Americans were far better able to deploy their forces on this front than farther west where logistics posed greater problems. Furthermore, success here would have put considerable pressure on the British position in Upper Canada. The lines of communication to Detroit and Fort Amherstburg would have been cut, and the Americans would have been able to threaten York (now Toronto).

## The Lake Champlain Front

Politics also played a role in American difficulties. Unsuccessful in preventing the conflict, the Federalists did not offer a political challenge to the war effort at the national level, but the fissiparous tendencies integral to state authority were fully revealed in the politics of the war. Indeed, during what they termed "Mr. Madison's War," New Englanders, especially in Connecticut, Massachusetts, and Rhode Island, were opposed to the conflict, unhelpful to the war effort, and keen to retain links with Britain.[50] This situation was very different to that during the War of Independence. Adams had warned Jefferson in June 1812 that the federal failure to spend on maritime defense had endangered support in New England while, at the outset of the war, Rush had "feared that the powerful and intelligent state of Massachusetts will not yield her zealous cooperation to the nation."[51] In those three states, and particularly in Rhode Island, there was opposition to the use of the militia in the war. The Rhode Island legislature voted not to send the militia to act alongside the army, although about five hundred state citizens did serve with the latter.

In turn, the British sought to exacerbate American divisions with their blockade because, initially, "licensed" neutral commerce was permitted with New England. This permission was seen as a way to encourage opposition to the war. Indeed, economic links between the two sides remained important, and Canadian deficiencies in food and other supplies were rectified by American smuggling by sea and land, a source that was very important in feeding the British troops.

The attitude in New England made it harder to raise the man-power and logistical support for striking at the St. Lawrence artery of British power in North America. Monroe complained in September 1812: "From the northern army we have nothing which inspires a confident hope of any brilliant success. The disaffection in that quar-ter has paralyzed every effort of the government."[52] Failure could thus be blamed on the Federalists. However, as in other crises in Anglo-American relations, a lack of the relevant naval capacity was also a key issue in affecting American capability, as it made it necessary for the Americans to have overland supply routes and also to strike over-land at Canada.

As another instance of American hesitation, Henry Dearborn—"Granny" to his justifiably critical subordinates—had responded positively on 8 August to the offer of an armistice made by Sir George Prevost, the governor general of Canada. This offer reflected the sense that the British lifting of the Orders in Council made peace a prospect, and Prevost hoped that this would be the case. Madison, however, rejected the idea as soon as he was informed of it on 8 Sep-tember. In terms of the politics of the moment, and the grudging nature of the British offer, it was understandable that Madison did so. As yet, the American attacks had not been launched on the Niagara and Champlain fronts, and there was no reason to predict failure against a Britain embroiled with an undefeated Napoleon. Moreover, the *Constitution*'s capture of the British frigate *Guerrière* on 19 Au-gust after a dramatic battle boosted American morale. In light of the strategic situation in 1814, and indeed the terms that were to be ac-cepted that year, this might seem a serious mistake; but, against that, the defensive successes of 1814–15 proved important in fostering a sense of national fortitude and destiny; while the course of the war also helped the governing party far more than it did the Federalists.

In November 1812, Madison won re-election as president, but his opponent, DeWitt Clinton, the mayor of New York, won 89 electoral votes (to Madison's 128) and carried every coastal state from New Hampshire to Maryland. Clinton was a Republican who had become disillusioned with Jefferson, not least on the grounds that the Virginia politicians who dominated the party were keener on agriculture than trade, and that the 1807 embargo had harmed mercantile interests. His candidacy also reflected a more general hostility to Virginia's dominance of both party and government. Clinton was critical of the war's goals and of Madison's leadership, and drew on both opposition to the war and growing pressure for the more successful conduct of hostilities, the two linked by the idea of a rapid close to the conflict.[53] In the event, Pennsylvania's support proved decisive to Madison's electoral victory. Far from being extraneous to the narrative of the war, this political dimension needs underlining at every stage as it was crucial to the command context and also affected strategic options.

In November 1812, the seriously belated American attack from New England toward Montréal collapsed due to inadequate logistics and poor command. At a very different scale, and facing much greater difficulties, these factors also hit Napoleon's invasion of Russia. Abandoning Moscow on 19 October, the French lost heavily as a result of starvation, exposure, and Russian attacks. The army that left Russia suffered more than three hundred thousand casualties. The winter had already claimed the life of Joel Barlow, American minister to France, who had arrived in Vilnius on 18 November and witnessed the destruction caused by Napoleon's campaign. Initially confident that Napoleon would be triumphant and that a Franco-Russian treaty would be concluded, Barlow found that the French foreign Minister, Huges Maret, prince of Bassano, ignored him.[54] In his last poem, "Advice to a Raven in Russia," Barlow hoped that "this king of woes" would be hurled "from his blood-built throne."

Dearborn, the commander of the American advance on Montréal, claimed that the transfer of troops to the Niagara front had lessened his options, and yet that any successful move towards Montréal would depend on prior victory on the Niagara front.[55] He lacked enthusiasm for the new offensive, scarcely pressed it after troops crossed the frontier on 19 November, and withdrew his force to winter quarters on 23 November as soon as it met resistance. Montréal was the most vulnerable point in the British defense system for Canada as a whole, as British supply routes to Upper Canada ran through it. In 1822 Winfield Scott was to argue that the Americans should have focused on an attack there as part of an invasion of Lower Canada.[56]

Montréal, however, was also a serious challenge to the Americans. It was easier for the British to reinforce Montréal than positions farther west, such as those on the Niagara front. Moreover, the terrain to the south of Montréal was difficult for American advances (as it had been for the colonists advancing north in 1709, and the British advancing north in 1758 and 1760, and south in 1776 and 1777), while local logistical capability for supporting an advance was weak. Command and control were difficult not only due to the nature of communications, but also because the Americans lacked any tried system that was responsive to their circumstances.

In 1813 a similar attempt was abandoned when Wilkinson realized that there was going to be no overwhelming concentration of American strength near Montréal. Although command issues were important in both campaigns, American strategic options were directly related to the domestic political situation. In particular, thanks to a lack of support, there were logistical and other problems with using New England as a base for operations, and these drawbacks also affected the prospect of an advance along the Champlain corridor. This problem encouraged the tendency to think of invading Canada, at least in part, farther west than was possibly militarily most wise. The reasons why this was unwise were twofold. Not only were supply routes longer farther west, which led to delays and made it harder to sustain forces, but also American success there would not have overcome the key British positions in Lower Canada: Québec and Montréal. Indeed, had they only held Lower Canada, the British, having less of Canada to protect, would have been able to concentrate their meager forces there. This situation would have been even more the case had they only held Nova Scotia and Newfoundland—although, in that case, the Americans would probably have seen themselves as already successful.

The contrast between the invasions of Canada in 1775 and 1812 was a painful one for the Americans, although the Americans in 1775 had benefited from a greater lack of British preparedness. In 1775, as in 1812, there was a large degree of wishful thinking on the part of the Americans, although in 1775 this focused on the likely response of the French population of Québec. The Americans hoped that they would help their invading forces, but this was not to be the case. More generally, basing campaigning on popular support posed a major challenge to the Americans, both operationally and strategically, in Canada and in the USA. The challenge in the USA had not been conceptually overcome by 1812, while American failure at the frontier disguised the wider problem there of being unprepared for conquest and occupation in Canada.

The earlier invasion suggested that the Americans would be able to achieve much in 1812. Logistics had also been a major problem in 1775, but the Americans then were able to capture British fortresses at Ticonderoga (10 May), Crown Point (12 May), St. Johns (2 November), and Montréal (12 November); although they were a smaller force than their successors in 1812–14, and also had fewer opponents. Also in 1775, a separate force of 1,050 men under Benedict Arnold invaded Canada in a way that contrasted greatly with the more hesitant approach in 1812. Advancing in September 1775 from Newburyport in Massachusetts, they crossed Maine. Landing at Gardinerstown on the Kennebec, Arnold was handicapped by geographical ignorance, rain, a shortage of food and maps, strong currents on the rivers, and rough trails across the intervening carrying places. Nevertheless, in a megalomaniac fashion, having underestimated both distance and obstacles, he pressed on. Some men died and several hundred turned back, so that only about six hundred arrived opposite Québec on 9 November. Joined by troops who had advanced from Montréal, the Americans then besieged Québec, before being defeated when they attempted to storm it on 31 December 1775. This failure was followed by a resumption of the unsuccessful siege of Québec, before the Americans were driven out when the breaking of the ice permitted the arrival of a British relieving force in May 1776. The contrast with the far more limited pressure brought to bear on the British in 1812 was clear. Indeed, in January 1813, Major William Drummond, the commander of the British garrison at St. Johns (which had fallen in November 1775), noted that, although he had "been sometime past expecting to be attacked" he was "not yet swallowed up by the Yankees."[57]

The inspired improvisation that both sides had displayed in the winter of 1775–76 was lacking in 1812. However, had the Americans then advanced farther, they might well have found themselves exposed as their predecessors had been in 1775–76: short of provisions, matériel, and money, lacking support from the local population, unable to capture fortified positions, and worried about what the breaking ice on the St. Lawrence might bring. Québec's fortifications had been strengthened after the siege of 1775–76, and a citadel had been completed in 1783. In light of these defenses and of American deficiencies in 1812, it was just as well that the Americans did not press on. Indeed, the pathetic campaign of November 1812 probably saved them from a disaster. Similarly, George Washington had benefited from the extent to which failure in 1776 led to the closing of the Canadian option for American operations.

Dearborn himself sought permission to resign at the end of the 1812 campaign, only for Madison to turn him down. The resignation of William Eustis, secretary of war since April 1809, was, however, accepted. Offered on 3 December, it took effect from the end of the year, and James Monroe, the secretary of state, was given temporary care of the department, being succeeded on 5 February 1813 by John Armstrong.

CONCLUSIONS

Jefferson meanwhile remained a brooding presence, troubling because of his prestige and a problem for American policy due to his misplaced optimism. In November 1812 he outlined to Madison a path of partial victory that he thought viable despite the failures in the Northwest and on the Niagara front: "If we could but get Canada to Trois Rivieres [on the St. Lawrence between Québec and Montréal] in our hands we should have a set-off against spoliations to be treated of, and in the mean time separate the Indians from them and set the friendly Indians to attack the hostile part with our aid."[58]

Thus, gains in Canada were to be negotiated against British exactions on American trade. However, Jefferson's confidence in Dearborn had been proved misplaced and, at the close of 1812, the Americans faced the realization that the war would be more difficult than they had anticipated. They lacked the forces, land and naval, and institutions necessary for the task; and, within these limitations, had also performed badly. The requisite urgency was absent, and the attacks on Canada had not been properly coordinated. Yet, when American supporters of the war reviewed the events of 1812, they were more positive than this suggests largely because they believed that the war had gone so well at sea. The frigate victories (see Chapter 4) lifted American moral. To many Americans, the defeat and sinking of the *Guerrière* by the *Constitution* under the command of Isaac Hull was more important than the loss of far-off Detroit (commanded by William Hull, Isaac's nephew). The Americans entered 1813 with great hopes for the navy.

Nevertheless, a comparison with 1775, the first year of the War of Independence, was scarcely encouraging, but was one that seemed most valid to Americans. The British in 1775 had not been prepared for a widespread conflict in North America, although then, unlike in 1812, they did not have the commitment of a major war with France to distract their efforts. In 1775 the British forces in the thirteen colonies were already concentrated in Boston when conflict began. As a result of American operations, these forces were to be essentially confined there that year. The casualties inflicted on the British in the battle of Bunker Hill, and the strength and resolution of the (only in the end unsuccessful) American resistance there, had given the Americans an important psychological advantage in the war. In part this was misleading, as subsequent American defeats at Long Island (1776) and Brandywine (1777) were to show. Nevertheless, this advantage was important. The Americans at the close of 1775 had also been more successful in their invasion of Canada than they were to be in 1812.

If this was not an encouraging historical comparison for the Americans at the close of 1812, the international situation was also increasingly troubling for them that year. It was true that in Britain the large-scale Luddite riots against new industrial technology, and against the labor discipline and unemployment it caused, led to the deployment of over twelve thousand troops to deal with popular unrest in the Midlands and North of England.[59] However, the main British field army under Arthur, Earl (later Marquess and then Duke) of Wellington had defeated the French in Spain at Salamanca on 22 July, a major victory that underlined British fighting quality and led to fourteen thousand French casualties.[60] This triumph encouraged British confidence in their army.

There was also growing uncertainty in America over the fate of Napoleon's invasion of Russia. Even the distant Balkans were of importance. Russia's position was strengthened in May 1812 by the Peace of Bucharest with Turkey, which brought to an end the war between the two powers that had started in 1806. In this conflict, the Russian supply system broke down due to transport problems, but expedients were sufficient to permit a long-range Russian advance south of the Danube into Bulgaria, which was part of the Turkish empire.[61] Although Russia did not acquire Moldavia and Wallachia (both now in Romania), or an alliance with Turkey in the peace, as had been hoped, Russia gained both Bessarabia (now Moldova) and an end to the war.

This settlement made it easier for Russia to focus on France, both defensively in 1812 and on the offensive the following year. Thus, France was less able to act as a counterweight to Britain and, indirectly, to help the USA. Back in North America, the American army appeared too small to conquer Canada, and there were also serious problems with the militia.[62] 1813 was to reveal that more of the same was not to transform the situation.

# 3

# THE ATTACK RENEWED, 1813

In 1813, unlike in 1812, there was no uncertainty that there would be war and, as a result, the Americans were able to attack from the outset of the year. It was hoped that this would ensure success and thus rally popular support.[1] This was regarded as important, for Madison's success in the elections the previous year did not lead to any sense that such approval was no longer crucial. Moreover, an important aspect of support that was urgently sought was financial backing for the war effort.

In contrast, there could be no such focus on the part of Britain. Indeed, in February 1813, Britain's leading general, Arthur, Marquess of Wellington, informed Henry, 3rd Earl Bathurst, secretary for war and the colonies, that he wanted the British war effort to focus on Iberia (Portugal and Spain), where Wellington had been heavily engaged for several years as commander of Britain's leading expeditionary force. Wellington's major victory at Salamanca the previous July had been followed by the occupation of the Spanish capital, Madrid, on 12 August; but Wellington was forced to retreat in the autumn of 1812 in the face of larger French forces after his attempts to storm the fortress of Burgos had failed, not least because he had insufficient artillery. This failure, which arose from Wellington's risky strategy and tactics, and in which the British lost two thousand men to no purpose (prefiguring the defeat of Wellington's brother-in-law at New Orleans in January 1815), led to criticism of his generalship and disputes with his subordinates—the last a frequent feature of general-ship in this period, as the War of 1812 was abundantly to show. Along-side Napoleon's disaster in Russia and the inability of the Americans to invade Canada successfully, Wellington's defeat at Burgos was the third of the failed advances in 1812. The French, moreover, had re-covered the strategic initiative by abandoning Andalusia (southern Spain) and thus concentrating an overwhelming field force against Wellington. The British suffered many casualties in the retreat from Burgos, in part because of a breakdown of the supply system. Welling-ton spent the winter building up his army's strength, and did not invade Spain again until May 1813.

This failure in the prime sphere of operations was not the best background for the British war effort in North America, which was only a secondary goal. It was scarcely surprising that Wellington, who was always deeply suspicious and critical of British efforts being di-verted from the peninsula, sought to persuade Bathurst that only so many resources should be devoted to North America. In response to the decision to send a regiment from Spain to Canada, Wellington wrote to Bathurst from Frenada in February 1813:

> I am very glad to find that you are going to reinforce Sir George Prevost, and I only hope that the troops will go in time; and that Sir George will not be induced by any hopes of trifling advantages to depart from a strong defensive system. He may depend upon it that he will not be strong enough either in men or means, to establish himself in any conquest he might make. The attempt would only weaken him, and his losses augment the spirits and hopes of the enemy, even if not at-tended by worse consequences; whereas by the other system, he will throw the difficulties and risk upon them [the Ameri-cans], and they will most probably be foiled. If they should be so, and they should receive a check at sea, their arrogance will be lowered a little, which will give me more satisfaction than any thing that has occurred for a length of time, and they will be obliged to ask for peace.[2]

Wellington had always been doubtful that the Americans could be attacked in a way that would compel them to capitulate. He clearly hoped that the Americans would be caught in a disadvan-tageous stalemate with an adequate but economical British defensive posture on land and an aggressive blockade at sea, where the British had more military assets, which would leave the Americans with few realistic options other than to seek peace. Wellington, indeed, had always realized that the war with the USA was of necessity a secondary matter that had to be conducted for very limited ends with very limited means. Wellington's remarks about the danger of increasing "the spirits and hopes of the enemy" and instead about lowering "their arrogance" so that the Americans would seek peace indicated his well-grounded conviction of the importance of ensuring the perception of success in a limited war. He pressed the value of the British remaining on the defensive in order to thwart an appearance of American success. This perception indeed was to be an important after-echo of the conflict (see Chapter 8).

Wellington's stress on the need to focus on the conflict with France in Spain is a reminder of the wider international context within which the operations of the War of 1812 have to be considered. A more pointed reminder was seen in April 1813 when Sergeant James Commins and his colleagues of the 8th Foot heard an inaccurate report that French troops had joined their American opponents and would soon face the regiment in battle.[3] Yet, although the continued war in Europe and, more specifically, the operations in Iberia were the focus of Britain's troop commitments, it still proved possible, by the summer of 1813, to increase the number of regular troops in North America to over twenty thousand; while British naval forces in the Great Lakes and off North America also rose. This buildup reflected the end of French resistance in the West Indies, with the British conquest of the island of Guadeloupe in February 1810 and the ability of Britain therefore to move troops and warships from the Caribbean to North America. Ironically, this was an echo of the French success in doing the same as a prelude to the Yorktown campaign in 1781.[4]

Moreover, Britain's alliance with Spain from 1808 ended the earlier mirage of British gains in Latin America while Spain had been allied to France, and thus closed the distraction of possible operations there. As a result of the troops sent to North America, Wellington lost three or four and possibly more battalions of good infantry in 1812 as well as two battalions of marines; but these numbers were far less than those sent as reinforcements to his army which, indeed, remained the focus of British attention.[5] Moreover, the figure for regulars in North America did not mean that that force could be deployed in offensive operations because it included troops in defensive positions distant from the sphere of operations, notably in Nova Scotia.

The lack of American long-range amphibious capability ensured that the British also did not have to retain many troops in the West Indies to repel possible attack, which contrasted with the situation in 1778–83 during the War of Independence. Then, an undefeated France (at least prior to the victory of the British fleet in the battle of the Saints on 12 April 1782) threatened British colonies, capturing, for example, the islands of Dominica (1778), Grenada (1779), Tobago (1781), Nevis (1782), St. Kitts (1782), Montserrat (1782), and the Turks Islands (1783). This contrast is another illustration of a central theme of this book, the importance of the international context. It was relevant both because of what happened and due to what did not happen.

## THE WESTERN FRONT

The ability of Britain to send reinforcements to North America in 1813 directs attention to the significance of early moves by the Americans before these reinforcements arrived. The Americans were to take the initiative on Lake Ontario and the Niagara front in the spring, but, at the outset of the year, the key American advance was an attempt to reverse the collapse of their position to the west of Lake Erie the previous autumn.

Although feeling that Canada should be attacked farther east,[6] and seriously constrained by logistical problems, which were exacerbated by the distance from American bases, William Hull's experienced replacement, William Henry Harrison, had brought a necessarily more robust note to American operations in the west in late 1812. He relieved Fort Wayne from attack by the Wabash tribes and, in turn, stormed Native American villages. These were the targets that could most readily be attacked and were also seen as crucial to Native American society and thus to its ability to sustain conflict. Harrison had benefited from the concern caused by Hull's defeat which had led to the dispatch to this front of troops that might otherwise have acted on the Niagara front. A sense of existential struggle was presented by American commentators, for example in September 1812 by Henry Clay, who at this stage was never one to counsel restraint:

"Savages . . . must be made to feel the utmost vigor of government. . . . The progression of the Whites westward—the death
of the old warriors—the springing up of a new race of young
ones—the natural propensity of savage man to war, are sufficient to account for Native American hostilities, without re-
curring to the most fruitful source of them, British insti-
gation."[7]

Four months later in a speech on the bill to expand the army, Clay
blamed Britain for Native American policy, declaring: "Is it not in
Canada that the tomahawk of the savage has been moulded into its
death-like form?" Such claims captured the sense that Canada and
the Native Americans were a seamless problem, and that security
from Native Americans could not be obtained unless Canada was
dealt with. Looking back, Clay asserted that, but for Detroit, the Indian War in 1812 had gone well: "The Indian towns have been swept
from the mouth to source of the Wabash, and a hostile country has
been penetrated far beyond the most daring incursions of any campaign during the former Indian war."[8]

There were serious operational problems facing the Americans,
however, not least a lack of cooperation between Harrison and James
Winchester, who was a brigadier general in the regular army. Harrison had ordered a concentration point at the Maumee (Miami) River
rapids, but on 13 January 1813, Winchester was informed by the exposed settlement at Frenchtown (today Monroe, Michigan) on the
River Raisin that it feared immediate attack. In response, he moved
forward, and on 18 January reached Frenchtown, from which he drove
a small British force.

This was a threat to the British in Detroit and Fort Amherstburg.
In response, Brigadier General Henry Procter organized a riposte. The
regulars, militia, and Native Americans under Roundhead, the Wyan-
dot chief, that he was able to deploy reflected the range of forces upon
which the British could call. On 22 January, Procter attacked Winchester, who had failed to organize his troops to face assault and had
also neglected security. In the event, the Americans were taken by
surprise by a rapidly advancing British-Native American force supported by artillery and, as a result, their dispersed troops formed up in
disorder. Winchester was captured as he sought to join them, and then
surrendered his whole force even though the left-wing of it was fight-

ing on with some success. Indeed Byfield, who was badly wounded, recorded: "Under cover of a wood we approached near to them unperceived. We formed the line and had a view of them as they surrounded their fires. . . . Before daylight we had charged them several times, thinking that we were close upon their lines; but our men were so cut up that after every attempt we were obliged to retreat to the cover of a rising piece of ground with considerable loss."[9]

Of 934 Americans engaged all bar 33 were killed or captured. This type of rapid-attack victory was relatively common in North America where only small numbers of troops were available to be deployed on the battlefield. Commanders therefore showed their mettle in knowing how to shape such engagements, both being able to mount such attacks and also knowing how to respond.

Procter subsequently withdrew to Brownstown, leaving the wounded prisoners under Native American control at Frenchtown. About thirty were killed on 23 January; an episode that then became a major part of American war propaganda, matching similar use of atrocities during the War of Independence, for example the scalping of Jane McCrea in 1777.

The American defeat blunted their winter campaign to retake Detroit. It indicated the problems posed by dispersed forces, as the American position would have been stronger had Winchester waited for Harrison. The consequences of inadequate defensive preparations were also underlined, as they had been earlier and more spectacularly with the more serious Anglo-Hessian failure in the face of George Washington's surprise attack across the Delaware River at Trenton in December 1776. Winchester's flaws in the battle on the River Raisin again indicated that inadequate commanders and poor command decisions could have a fatal impact.

More generally, the Americans lacked sufficient troops properly prepared for frontier warfare. This was true of both regulars and militia. Most American troops, whether regulars or militia, were armed with muskets. These could bear bayonets, which gave them an advantage over the slower-firing rifles in the wooded terrain in which most of the war was waged. Most rifles did not have bayonets, although British Baker rifles were equipped with a sword bayonet. Rifles had greater range and accuracy than muskets but, in judging weapons, much depended on the nature of the terrain, the quality of the troops involved, and the quality and morale of their opposition.

The degree of accuracy needed in wooded terrain also depended on length of line-of-sight between trees. In thickly wooded terrain, where fighting was conducted at close quarters, a slow-loading rifle with a range of two hundred to three hundred yards was outclassed by a quick-loading musket whose bayonet also turned it into a pike. At close quarters, the superior accuracy of rifles could be superfluous, whereas the rate of fire could mean the difference between life and death, giving musketeers an advantage.

Advancing to relieve Fort Pitt in 1763 during Pontiac's War, Lieutenant Colonel Henry Bouquet found the bayonet superior to firepower in defeating Native Americans at Bushy Run, but that was because the Native Americans abandoned their distant fighting tactics, so that the British troops could use their bayonets. General Anthony Wayne, who successfully fought the Cherokees toward the end of the War of American Independence and defeated the Ohio Native Americans at Fallen Timbers in 1794, felt likewise. Wayne claimed: "The rifle and the tomahawk are unavailing when confronted by the bayonet in close quarters." Harrison learned much about how to campaign in the Old Northwest and defeat hostile tribes while serving Wayne as an aide in the 1790s.[10]

Seeking to maximize their opportunity to deliver aimed fire and to minimize the target they offered, the Native Americans fought in open, not close, order; but the Americans lacked the confidence and training to do so, although, when their troops held their order, they tended to do well. The American militia, however, usually lacked relevant experience. Moreover, their lack of enthusiasm for discipline made it difficult to compensate with training for an absence of experience, which had serious consequences in conflict. For example, a detachment of Kentucky militia panicked and ran during the effort to relieve Fort Meigs on 5 May 1813. In 1812, Colonel James Smith had published his *Treatise on the Mode and Manner of Indian War*, which laid down "Their Tactics, Discipline and Encampments, the various methods they practise, in order to obtain the advantage, by ambush, surprise, surrounding, etc. Ways and Means proposed to prevent the Native Americans from obtaining the advantage. A chart, or plan of marching, and encamping, laid down, whereby we may undoubtedly surround them, if we have men sufficient."[11] Reality, however, was less controllable.

In December 1776, Washington's success in his surprise attack on the Hessians at Trenton turned the tide in a war, puncturing the run of British success that had followed victory at the battle of Long Island earlier that year, whereas, in 1813, the River Raisin battle simply broke the run of American success for a campaign in one theater. Nevertheless, the battle was significant for the flow of campaigning in the West. The impression of American failure created by the campaign the previous year was underlined, which was valuable for British relations with the Native Americans and also in counteracting the idea that they might abandon the region in order to concentrate resources farther east.

Furthermore, the British gained a vital period of time before Harrison attacked anew in late September 1813. Counterfactuals ("what-ifs") are always problematic, but had Procter failed at Raisin River, or Winchester simply not detached and exposed his force, then Harrison might well have recaptured Detroit and invaded Upper Canada earlier. Hypothetical factors again come into play, as it is unclear what such an invasion would have entailed in terms of logistical capability and problems, not least given the situation on Lake Erie which was not yet dominated by the Americans. In particular, in the absence of a defeat on the lake, comparable with what was to follow at the hands of the Americans on 10 September 1813, Procter might still have held Fort Amherstburg and Harrison's campaign, if staged earlier, might therefore have come to a close in besieging the fortress, whether or not it was captured. Furthermore, in the absence of an American victory on land like the Battle of the Thames on 5 October 1813, Procter's force would have remained in being as a threat to any American advance, not least to its lines of communication; rather as Morrison challenged Wilkinson's advance toward Montréal in November 1814 by shadowing his advance (see Chapter 5). This suggestion is possibly pushing the might-have-beens too far. If they establish that a Harrison advance in early 1813 might not have led to the collapse of Upper Canada, that does not mean that it might not have been decisive on this front. Moreover, the consequences that could have flowed for the war farther east, for American morale and for eventual peace negotiations, were considerable. For the British, 1813 would have been even more a year spent on the defensive, and there would have been more losses to compensate for in advances in 1814. Given

the British determination not to accept territorial losses, this, however, might have encouraged a greater British military effort in North
America in 1814.

In any event, moving back from hypotheticals, and in response to
the setback at Raisin River, Harrison, who had been instructed to stay
on the defensive by John Armstrong, secretary of war from 5 February
1813, sought to consolidate the American position in the Ohio country by building Fort Meigs overlooking the rapids of the Maumee
River. Covering nearly ten acres and named after the governor of
Ohio, this was the biggest wooden fort built in North America, and
the effort involved testified to American anxieties. The availability of
resources was also indicated by the five artillery batteries located
around the perimeter of the fort. Fort Meigs was designed to resist
British attack as well as attack by Native Americans. Harrison was
borrowing a lesson from his old commander, Wayne, who set the
pattern of building forts to consolidate American gains during his
1793–94 campaigns; and Wayne learned that from the Romans who
habitually fortified their camps at the end of a day's march. Moreover,
the French fort-building campaign of 1748–54 in North America, especially in the Ohio Valley, provided a pattern of encroachment and
claim "by fort," while a wilderness warfare centered on forts and
routes of communications was also developed by the British.

Armstrong's emphasis, however, was farther east. Thus, both the
British and the Americans did not focus their attention on the western sphere of operations. This choice matched the situation in previous conflicts involving the British in North America. In the conquest
of Canada in 1758–60, the stress had been on the Champlain corridor
in 1758 and the St. Lawrence in 1759, and not farther west, although,
in 1755 and, successfully, in 1758, there had been important British
offensives into the Pittsburgh area and, in 1759, the conquest of the
French positions in the Niagara area. In the War of Independence most
of the key campaigning had been near the coast, although the American invasion of Canada in 1775 had been mounted along the Champlain corridor as, in the opposite direction, had been the British invasion under Burgoyne in 1777, while the Americans had fought Native
Americans in the interior.

In the War of 1812, there was also, as a major sphere for American
operations, the Niagara front, an advance from which appeared to
threaten the British position in Upper Canada; but the Detroit front

seemed less consequential for Upper, let alone Lower, Canada. This impression made sense in terms of logistics and the strategic articulation of military power along the entire frontier, but also entailed a failure to place due weight on the potential and problems posed by the Native American dimension. Nevertheless, cutting British supply routes farther east by advancing from Lake Champlain or the Niagara front would have made it difficult for the British to supply their Native American allies, while Brock, in August 1812, had warned about the susceptibility of Canadian opinion to military success.[12]

Seeking to advance south from Lake Erie, and to disrupt American preparations, an Anglo-Native American force under Procter sailed from Fort Amherstburg for Miami Bay on 23 April 1813 and pressed on to besiege Fort Meigs on 1 May. In an important addition of support, Tecumseh had rejoined Procter after seven months' absence. Procter had two thousand regulars and militia, while Tecumseh led over one thousand Native Americans. The British erected batteries and the two sides bombarded each other. On 5 May, a relief force of twelve hundred Kentucky militia under Green Clay and William Dudley approaching Fort Meigs suffered heavy casualties, in part due to a Native American ambush, but still compelled the British to lift the siege. British batteries were spiked by the Americans in the fighting of that day, and Byfield recorded, "We charged them close under the fort, but were obliged to retreat because of their great guns."[13] The strength of the American resistance discouraged the Canadian militia and Native Americans supporting Procter. Some militia and Native Americans left the siege, which led Procter to decide to abandon it. Now faced by larger American forces, he could not risk his army dissolving and was concerned about his lines of supply. Procter's force was short of food and affected by dysentery and flu.[14] As so often, the ability of a fort to resist attack, however briefly, dismayed the attackers, who had relied on its rapid fall. Moreover, this setback discouraged the Native American leaders who criticized the failure of the British to deploy larger forces in the region. Indeed, pressure on the Niagara front, where Fort George fell to the Americans on 27 May prevented the dispatch of British reinforcements that had been promised for operations farther west.

Forts were important to the advance of American power, and also in limiting the prospects for any rapid British advance. In 1811, Harrison had built Fort Harrison (Terre Haute), when he advanced against

Prophet's Town; and, in 1813, he built Fort Stephenson (Fremont, Ohio) as well as Fort Meigs to stabilize the situation after Winchester's defeat. Such forts were valuable because Native Americans were unwilling to mount frontal assaults on forts, and there were generally too few British regulars for the task; while the British and, especially, the Native Americans also lacked the heavy guns necessary to overcome fortifications. In September 1812, the Native Americans tried to make two cannon out of hollow logs when they unsuccessfully attacked Fort Wayne. Neither these, nor the fire arrows (which the Americans countered with using buckets of water to keep the defenses wet), led the defenders to surrender that fort, and the Native Americans did not mount a frontal attack.

A second attempt was made on Fort Meigs in July 1813. Procter, who had been promoted to major general the previous month, returned to the attack, and with more Native American support. In part, indeed, this attempt was launched in order to satisfy Native American demands for action. Procter, however, was under pressure not only because troops and supplies were retained for the Niagara front, but also due to American naval preparations on Lake Erie. These threatened Procter's line of supplies along the lake and, in particular, the viability of Fort Amherstburg.

Procter's force reached Fort Meigs on 20 July, but the American garrison under Green Clay was well prepared. Procter encircled the fort, but was unwilling to assault its defenses. Instead, he feigned a battle with an imaginary American relief force, hoping to lure the Americans from their defenses. Correctly fearing ambush, Clay did not rise to the bait, and this led Procter to turn, instead, to an apparently more vulnerable target.[15]

Nearby Fort Stephenson on the Sandusky River, however, successfully resisted attack. On 1 August, the sole American cannon in the fort, a 6-pounder firing grapeshot, inflicted heavy casualties on the advancing British regulars, discouraging the Native Americans from acting. Although heavily outnumbered, with only 160 troops, compared to Procter's 400 regulars and 400 Native Americans, the American commander, George Croghan, had out-thought his opponents, not least in locating his cannon where it was most likely to counter the attack. Grapeshot—bags with small balls inside which scattered as a result of the charge—caused considerable numbers of casualties at short range. Croghan had only eight casualties, whereas the British had eighty-nine, a high ratio of their force. Byfield recorded, "We advanced in file and formed near the ditch and found it much deeper than we expected and the fence much higher." Unable to storm the position, the trapped troops took many casualties in the ditch.[16]

This success, so rare for the Americans at this stage, made Croghan a hero. Kentucky-born Croghan had been an aide to Harrison in the Tippecanoe campaign, and the latter's patronage had got him a commission as a captain in the regular army when the War of 1812 led to military expansion. Born in 1791, Croghan exemplified not only the prospects for wartime expansion, but also the value of bold and determined young commanders, and he was a major before he became twenty-two.[17]

After his failure at Fort Stephenson, Procter retreated to Fort Amhertsburg on the northern side of Lake Erie. That his nighttime withdrawal was followed by a safe retreat was the silver lining for the cloud as far as the British were concerned. Keeping the force in being meant that there was a danger that it would return. Procter's safe retreat was not the fault of Croghan but of Harrison, who was only ten miles away at Fort Seneca, farther up the Sandusky River. He was criticized for failing to come to the relief of Fort Stephenson. Indeed, Harrison had ordered Croghan to evacuate and burn the fort if Procter had cannon.

Yet again, this campaign demonstrated the narrowness of the margin of success. The campaign underlined the tensions in command arrangements that were to be seen repeatedly, and on both sides, during the war. The Americans alone were not at fault. Indeed the self-righteous Prevost's failure to support Procter was a serious issue. He consistently failed to provide Procter with sufficient troops, even though Brock had thought it necessary to deploy more troops, including sixteen hundred at Fort Amherstburg. Earlier in 1813, Prevost had prevented an exploitation of the victory at Raisin River by arguing, as a reason for not sending troops, that winter operations were dangerous. This neglect continued during 1813.

As a consequence of the failure to provide troops to exploit the victory on the Raisin River, Fort Meigs could not be attacked by the British until after its defenses were finished in April 1813. Aside from handicapping Procter, this lack of support greatly affected Native American opinion. The consequences of the unwillingness to send troops were also exacerbated by the build-up of American strength.

It is all too easy to explain command tensions in terms of personality differences, however important these may be. There were also
major institutional rifts, with commanders answering back to their
respective constituencies, whether, for example, regular or militia
forces, or federal or state authorities. Furthermore, there were significant differences over strategy and operations, reflecting contrasting
perspectives on what was appropriate and feasible, and concerning
the relationship between particular fronts. Thus, Prevost felt that it
was most sensible to rest on the defensive in the face of superior
American resources, and this left him opposed to requests from
Brock, and then Procter, for troops for the Detroit front. Indeed, Prevost had been instructed, in the name of the Prince Regent, the future
George IV, that he was not to advance "except it be for the purpose of
preventing or repelling hostilities or unavoidable emergencies."[18]
Prevost may have conformed too much but, until 1814 brought a
transformation in the military situation, he knew his resources for
defense or attack were limited. Effective campaigning south of Lake
Erie would have to be carried out by regular troops because Upper
Canada militia could not be spared from their homes for long campaigns while the numbers as well as enthusiasm of the Native Americans constantly varied. Regular British infantry were not best suited
to operate so far from their bases in difficult wilderness conditions.
Even without fighting, their losses could have been heavy. All the
Americans would need to do would be retreat and ambush, and they
had the territory to work with. Sending troops to the Detroit Front
would have depleted the forces available to defend the really important points in Upper Canada, Niagara, York, and Kingston. Brock and
Procter, in contrast, saw different political and military needs and
opportunities, not least in terms of relations with the Native Americans. Brock's death led to less effective leadership and to disillusion-
ment among the Native Americans.

The failure to reconcile both strategies owed much to the pressure
of immediate commitments, both in the West and more widely, but
the eventual result was a confusion that ensured that Procter lacked
the necessary strength. This lack of strength made him more reliant
on the Native Americans, which encouraged him, first, to campaign
south of Lake Erie, and, later, to agree to stand on the Thames River;
the first without success and the second disastrously. Other instances
of the problems arising from a reliance on Native American support

included their unwillingness to take part in Procter's projected attack on the American naval base at Presque Isle (Erie) in Pennsylvania, because, with Fort Meigs in their rear, they did not wish to be separated from their families.[19]

Procter, however, was not to advance again. His options were dramatically reduced by Perry's victory on Lake Erie on 10 September 1813, a defeat that directly affected his strength as a quarter of his troops had been aboard the British flotilla, serving as gunners and marines. Procter was then to be defeated at the Battle of the Thames on 5 October.

To the west of Procter's sphere of operations, there had been a proposal for action from Thomas, 5th Earl of Selkirk, a proponent of assisted overseas settlement on Prince Edward Island, in Upper Canada, and for the forks of the Red River for Scottish farmers, many of them left destitute from the Clearances in Scotland. He suggested an expedition via Hudson Bay for the purpose of "operating a diversion on the Western frontier of the United States, by means of the Indians." Selkirk was told by Bathurst that British forces could not currently be spared, which led him to ask for arms and officers for the Hudson's Bay Company, in which he was the dominant shareholder, and for the company to be allowed to raise a force in Britain. The memorandum was endorsed "to be submitted for the favorable consideration of H.R.H. the Commander in Chief,"[20] Frederick, Duke of York. In the event, this had no effect of the War of 1812. Selkirk was able to send out cannon for the defense of the colony that had been established in the valley of the Red Valley, but his recently arrived colonists came into competition with the North West Company, a rival in the fur trade, leading, from June 1815, to armed conflict.

## Lake Ontario and the Niagara Front

Farther east, on Lake Ontario in 1813, the Americans took the initiative and, in an amphibious operation, York (now Toronto), the capital of Upper Canada, which then had a population of only seven hundred, was captured in a well-executed attack on 27 April by Dearborn—or, rather, by his competent subordinates, among them Commodore Issac Chauncey and Brigadier General Zebulon Pike, the latter a noted explorer of the American West. The fort and public buildings were burned down, leading to the destruction of a possibly significant quantity of British naval stores, although, partly due to the deliberate explosion of the main magazine by the British, the Americans lost more men than the defenders, who had been poorly prepared and led by Major General Sir Roger Shaeffe. American losses included the able Zebulon Pike. The attack on York was in part designed to hinder British naval shipbuilding on the lake, and this contributed to American success there later in the year. Moreover, the build-up of British matériel for Fort Amherstburg was badly hit.

The attack also, however, reflected the limitations of American warmaking. The Americans had earlier hoped to besiege Kingston, seeing its fall as the way to dislocate the supply system to Montréal and thus prepare for its capture. Influenced by inaccurate intelligence that the British had significantly reinforced Kingston, Dearborn reported that it was too difficult a target, and therefore the idea of a raid on weakly defended York was substituted as the first target. This raid, however, brought no long-term strategic benefit and, instead, as in 1775, the damage done by the American forces and the mistreatment of the civilian population helped underline the developing sense of Canadian alienation from the USA. This alienation was an important aspect of the political dimension of the conflict, and one that the self-absorbed American commanders and commentators did not appreciate. A similar failure to understand opposing perspectives can be seen in the case of British commanders, although they appreciated better the need to sap American popular support for the war.

Having attacked York, the Americans, backed by their warships, then advanced on the Niagara front in May, capturing Fort George at the mouth of the Niagara River. This fort had been Brock's headquarters the previous year, and it overlooked the mouth of the Niagara River, upstream from the American-held Fort Niagara which was on the eastern (American) shore of the river. On 27 May 1813, twenty-five hundred troops—a large force for Great Lakes amphibious operations—aboard thirteen ships and 180 *batteaux*, under Dearborn and Commodore Isaac Chauncey, landed on the shore of Lake Ontario to the west of Fort George. Larger American resources were crucial in this operation, and indicated what could be achieved with these resources provided they were well-handled, which involved employing them with care, so as to avoid problems that might arise if quality was lacking when resistance was encountered. Such care often entailed limiting goals, not least as a rapid advance could disorder forces.

Fort George was bombarded from Fort Niagara with twenty-five guns and mortars on 26 May. On the 27th Chauncey's squadron joined in with fifty-one naval guns. In contrast, Fort George had only eight cannon and two mortars, a force supported by five field pieces deployed in front of the fort. This contrast was important to the British defeat. The British made a stand in front of the fort, but were defeated by the larger American force which was supported by Chauncey's ships. The outnumbered one thousand-strong British force under Brigadier General John Vincent, the commander of the Center Division, then retreated, abandoning the fort and spiking its cannon. As with Procter's successful withdrawal, the escape of this force was a major blow to the Americans. Leaving an opponent in being gravely undercut the value of taking positions, although seizing these positions could indeed hit opposing supply systems hard. Vincent was able to march south to Queenston, and then west to Burlington Heights, a good defensive position, while the Americans, in contrast, moved cautiously.

In early June 1813, however, the Americans finally moved west from Fort George under Brigadier Generals John Chandler and William Winder. They were political appointees as brigadier generals, although Winder's background, with his strong interest in military matters, mistakenly suggested that he would make a good commander. In the event, when camped at Stoney Creek, they were defeated in a surprise pre-dawn British attack on 6 June. Stoney Creek was forty-six miles from Fort George and threatened the British position at Burlington Heights. Had Vincent withdrawn from there along Lake Ontario to York, he would have left the overland supply line to Procter in American hands; but, if he stood and fought, he could have been defeated. By attacking, Vincent regained control of the tempo of operations and, by the means of his attack—the surprise assault—he maximized American drawbacks. The actual attack was a confused affair in which both sides suffered losses, but, as was frequently the case with battles during this war, the result of the engagement was far more important than the actual clash. The American commanders, Chandler and Winder, were captured in the battle. At the close of the battle, the British pulled back and the demoralized Americans were left in control of their camp; but they then hastily retreated without burying their dead or taking their equipment. Such an abandonment of the field of battle was generally seen as a sign of defeat and was therefore an important point in the fighting.[21]

The British then moved toward Fort George. At Beaver Dams on 24 June, another American unit, again poorly commanded, was surrounded in the forest by Native Americans and, fearing massacre, surrendered. As with Hull's surrender at Detroit the previous year, this testified to potent American anxieties about the Native American style of warfare. Failure led to Dearborn being relieved of command on 6 July, a badly overdue move, and to American offensive plans being re-orientated from the Niagara front to the Champlain corridor. As the regulars were withdrawn accordingly, this left the American defense of the front demoralized and dependent on the militia. The failure of the Americans to achieve much on this front, and indeed to benefit from what they achieved, when they attacked there in greater force in 1814, suggests that the decision to shift priorities the previous year was a wise one.

In late 1813, thanks to these British successes, the American garrison in Fort George was cooped up and their patrols constrained by British forces. Following the ambush of a patrol by British forces and Ottawas on 8 July, the Americans complained that Lieutenant Joseph Eldridge had been killed after surrendering. The British questioned the Ottawa chief, Blackbird, whose answers, as translated by another chief, indicated the depth of Native American anger. Aside from claiming that Eldridge had refused to surrender, Blackbird accused the Americans of having cut up Native American corpses after battle, dug up Native American graves, and destroyed the corn in 1812. "The way they treat our killed," he added, "and the remains of those that are in their graves in the west, makes our people mad when they meet the Big Knives" [Americans].[22] Fear of these attitudes helped motivate American concern about engaging with Native Americans.

Meanwhile, the American position on Lake Ontario had been affected by the arrival, in May 1813, of a dynamic and effective commodore from the Royal Navy, Sir James Yeo, backed by 465 officers and sailors. Yeo took command of the Provincial Marine from Robert Herriot Barclay and challenged the Americans. On 18–19 May, a major amphibious attack on the American naval base at Sacket's Harbor, New York, inflicted considerable damage at the cost of 259 casualties, 28 per cent of the force.[23] Initial success was followed by an unsuccessful attempt to take Fort Tompkins, with the British, due to a lack of wind, unable to bring most of their naval firepower to bear in support. From Sacket's Harbor, the Americans could advance into the St. Lawrence as well as along the lake.

Isaac Chauncey, the American commander on Lake Ontario, was wary about exposing his flotilla to action, but, from the close of July, Chauncey and Yeo became more assertive in order to try to gain control of the lake and thus offset the struggle on the Niagara Peninsula. After several inconclusive clashes, Chauncey's failure to secure a decisive victory in the so-called Burlington's Races of 28 September 1813 not only denied him this control, but was also the last chance either side allowed the other to engage in a significant squadron action on Lake Ontario. Chauncey's success in forcing Yeo to run was not fully exploited because Yeo was able to take shelter in Burlington Bay, where Chauncey's concern about the depth of the water led him to decide not to press home the attack. He was also worried about operating close to British batteries on a shore that was stormy. Chauncey then withdrew.[24]

An opportunity to achieve a success comparable to that won by the Americans on Lake Erie eighteen days earlier was lost. Chauncey held back despite the fact that, aside from Perry's victory, several key naval battles over the previous century had been won in inshore battles, including the British successes over the French at Lagos (1759) and Quiberon Bay (1759), each of which were battles between fleets of ships of the line, as well as British victories at the Nile (1798), Copenhagen (1801), and Basque Roads (1809). Lake Ontario witnessed a shipbuilding contest for the remainder of the war, but no battle.[25]

## LAKE ERIE AND THE WESTERN FRONT

Farther west, naval operations were again linked with the conflict on land, as the generals sought dominance of Lake Erie so as to be able to transport troops and supplies safely. The Americans under Oliver Hazard Perry gained the initiative on the lake in August. The outnumbered British under Robert Herriot Barclay, a veteran of the battle of Trafalgar, who had arrived on 6 June 1813, blockaded Perry at the Presque Isle shipyard. On 29 July, however, Barclay broke off the blockade and sailed back to Long Point, the station at the mouth of the Detroit River, where he adopted a defensive position, although on

4 August he briefly threatened another attack on Presque Isle. Perry wisely decided not to force the British defensive position which he reconnoitred on 24 August and 1 September, but food shortages led Barclay to sail forth for a general action. As so often in the war, logistics proved a key element both operationally and tactically. In this case, and because of the importance of the supply route on the lake, logistics ensured not only problems for the British squadron, but also the need to fight the Americans. Owing to the destruction of naval and military supplies at York in May 1813, which was beyond his control, Prevost had failed to provide the necessary manpower and supplies. Prevost, who was arguably more adroit as an overall leader, not least in vigorously strengthening the defenses of Upper Canada, had pressed the British ministry for more sailors. Bathurst recorded in July 1813 that Prevost's aide-de-camp had brought dispatches, and also "a strong representation of the necessity for reinforcements, considering the great efforts made by the enemy. What he most presses for, as being essential for the protection of Upper Canada, is an additional number of seamen for the Lakes: and that they should be sent out before the River St. Lawrence is impractable." The aide thought that six hundred would do and said, "Upper Canada must fall, if a considerable reinforcement were not sent."[26]

In the event, however, this timetable was insufficiently tight, and, when it came to the crunch, the British had fewer ships and men and were short of gunpowder as well as seamen. Prevost demanded action from Barclay. In the battle, fought on 10 September 1813, the American broadside weight was 896 pounds and the British just 459. Barclay planned to stand off and use his long-range cannon, nullifying the strength of the heavier but short-range American carronades, but the wind shifted, giving the Americans the advantage. The American flagship, the *Lawrence*, took heavy damage and, with its guns disabled, the resolute Perry transferred to the brig *Niagara*. The British fleet, however, had also taken much damage, and powerful short-range carronade broadsides from the *Niagara* led to the surrender of all the British ships.[27] In the first squadron battle in American history, the Americans had won a major triumph. Perry famously reported to Harrison, "We have met the enemy and they are ours: two ships, two brigs, one schooner and one sloop. Yours, with great respect and esteem." To the secretary of the navy, William Jones, he wrote "It has pleased the Almighty to give the arms of the United

States a signal victory over their enemies on this lake," an echo of Horatio Nelson's report after his defeat of the French at the battle of the Nile in 1798, although that battle was on a very different scale: eleven of the thirteen French ships of the line present were lost.

The political dimension was important. Supporters of the war, such as Richard Rush, were delighted and saw Perry's victory as rallying popular morale. In January 1814, in a House debate on resolutions concerning American naval actions, Clay declared that "the Hero of Erie" showed what the Americans could do in squadron action:

> Imagine to yourself this valuable officer in the hour of peril, his vessel a wreck, her deck strewed with the mangled bodies of his dead and dying comrades—and admire, with me, the cool intrepidity and consummate skill with which he seized the propitious moment, changed his station, and, aided by his gallant second in command, and only second in merit, pressed forward to fame and victory.[28]

Not all comments have been so approving. Perry has been criticized for lacking skills and experience as the commander of a squadron, to go with his undoubted bravery, resolution, and skill in command of his own ships. His plan for the battle has been criticized as vague, he did not bring all his firepower to bear, and the failure to use signal flags has also been attacked.[29] Yet, the key point is that Perry won. He proved better able to respond to circumstances than Barclay and thus to shape the battle. At a very different scale, the quality of being a skillful improviser can also be seen with Napoleon[30] and, indeed, Nelson. By forcing a battle whose shape was unclear, both Napoleon and Nelson placed great reliance on the subsequent mêlée, which rewarded not only the original plan but also the fighting qualities of individual units and the initiative and skill of subordinates.

This defeat was a major blow to the British, as lake travel was crucial to the infrastructure and articulation of warfare in the region. As a result of the battle, the British supply links across Lake Erie were cut, which affected Native American support. The badly injured Barclay was exonerated by a court-martial, but did not receive another command until 1824. Barclay's defeat also meant that only one British warship remained on the Upper Great Lakes, the *Nancy*, a sixty-seven-ton schooner built at Detroit in 1789 which had been used as a troop transport in 1812–13. The loss of British bases ensured that she

wintered that year at the North West Company post on Michilimackinac Island.

After the battle, Procter, on 15 September 1813, proposed a retreat
from the Detroit front to Lake Ontario. This step was opposed by
Tecumseh, who correctly saw such a retreat as entailing the abandonment of the Native Americans. Such an abandonment threatened to
repeat what the Native Americans saw as earlier betrayals in 1783 and
1794, as well as to ignore Brock's promise of British support. Procter
compromised, at a meeting at Fort Amherstburg on 18 September
1813, by agreeing to retreat to the lower Thames River and stopping
there to engage the Americans, a decision that was to be shown to be a
mistake. Tecumseh offered to defend the fort while the British retreated, but Procter persuaded him to share in the retreat. Meanwhile,
Harrison was intent on exploiting the situation by mounting a hot
pursuit.

On 27 September, Harrison was able to benefit from American
naval strength in order to land below Fort Amherstburg. This landing
coincided with the start of the retreat by the British, and the Americans were able to capture the abandoned Fort Amherstburg that day.
As an indication of the contrast in numbers, Harrison landed five
thousand troops, while Procter retreated with six hundred as well as
fifteen hundred Native Americans. Harrison's Army of the Northwest consisted of regulars and Kentucky volunteers,[31] and his ability
to command regulars and citizen soldiers effectively was important.
It contrasted with much indifferent American generalship elsewhere.

Harrison pressed on with three thousand men to pursue Procter.
This pursuit involved skirmishing with Procter's rearguard, mostly
Native Americans, and part of the British ammunition supplies was
overtaken and captured on the morning of 5 October. Shadrach Byfield complained that the need to take Procter's baggage caused delay.
Benefiting from the rapid advance of mounted infantry, the Americans pressed on and forced battle on their exhausted opponents, leading to the defeat of the Anglo-Native American army at the Battle of
the Thames (or Moraviantown) near London, Ontario, on 5 October
1813. By this stage, Procter could field only 430 soldiers and 500 Native Americans. He drew up his regulars in two lines in a clearing in a
beech forest, with the left flanked by the River Thames, while the
right was covered by the Native Americans. This position, a classic
one for defending infantry formations, used for example by the En-

glish at Crécy (1346), was intended to counteract the greater American numbers by limiting their frontage and funnelling their approach toward the British firepower.

A key American unit was Colonel Richard Mentor Johnson's regiment, the Kentucky Mounted Volunteers, most of whom carried rifles, although some used muskets. Mounted Americans, under Johnson's brother James, charged through both British lines, disordering the outnumbered infantry in their thin formation and leading them to disperse or surrender despite the efforts of the officers to rally them. Byfield recorded, "After exchanging a few shots our men gave way." The only British piece of artillery, a 6-pounder, did not fire because its startled horses dragged the gun away. The Native Americans put up a fiercer resistance against the Americans under Richard Mentor Johnson. An Native American advance led by Tecumseh ended when he was killed, reputedly shot by Johnson; and, deploying more troops, the Americans wore down the resistance. Thirty-three Native Americans were found dead on the field, but other bodies were probably carried off. Byfield was told by the Native Americans that "they had beaten back the enemy on the right, but that their prophet was killed, and then they retreated."[32]

Although he was not without faults, there was no replacement for Tecumseh, and Johnson gained fame as a result of supposedly killing him. Johnson served in the Senate from 1819 to 1829 and as vice president from 1837 to 1841. In the election campaign in 1836, his killing of Tecumseh counted for more than the criticisms aimed at Johnson, on the basis of his dead black mistress, Julia Chinn, of being a "racial amalgamator." More generally, the victory came to play a key role in validating the military reputation of the American West.[33]

Like other battles of the period, the American victory at the Battle of the Thames reflected an improvement in fighting quality. In this case, the improvement was due to better training and tactical skill, and to a clearer understanding of Native American techniques and their limitations.[34] Greater numbers were also very important to American success as a relatively more numerous defending force could have used its firepower to disrupt the cavalry attack. Taking part in the usual pastime of shifting the blame, one that is all too frequent in military history, Procter, who narrowly escaped capture, argued that his difficulties owed something to the refusal by Major General Francis de Rottenburg, the commander in Upper Canada, to provide him with troops to help against Harrison. Procter can be faulted for not mounting a resistance to the American advance at Fort Amherstburg, as Tecumseh had urged on 18 September; instead, the position was abandoned. However, Procter's force was greatly outnumbered, he lacked food and munitions, and was liable to be completely surrounded. While Procter's retreat was poorly conducted, staying put was not a viable alternative.

The Battle of the Thames was one of the most important of the war and in this case Anglo-Native American cooperation had not delivered the necessary military verdict: this battle was a defeat in defense that matched the serious operational failure on the offensive against Fort Wayne in September 1812. It was also a defeat that had a consequence for the remainder of the war and, indeed, beyond. Yet there were also many examples of successful cooperation between British and Native American forces, for example the battles of Detroit, Queenston Heights, Beaver Dams, Châteauguay, and Crysler's Farm, a list that is far from exhaustive.

Maintaining his aversion to risk, Prevost ordered the evacuation of Upper Canada to Kingston at the eastern end of Lake Ontario. Procter, however, prevented such a debacle and, instead, on 17 October, led 235 troops, whom he had rallied, to Ancaster, which was near Burlington at the western end of Lake Ontario. Harrison did not advance on British positions to the east, doubtless because of issues of supplies, troop availability, expiring enlistments, and approaching winter.[35] At any event, the fighting on the Detroit/Lake Erie front was over, and this led to a reorganization of the British command structure in Canada, with the formerly separate Right and Center Divisions merged, becoming the Right Division responsible for the area west of Kingston.[36]

Procter's defeat led to a savage attack by Prevost who, ironically, had earlier praised him and been instrumental in his promotion. On 18 and 21 October 1813, Prevost issued very critical general orders, blaming Procter for the failure. In response, the understandably angry Procter demanded a hearing. The London authorities agreed, in 1814, that there should be a court-martial, but left it to Prevost to bring the charges. Due to the war, he had other things on his mind and there was no court-martial until 1815. Then, Procter was found guilty of lacking judgment and energy. He was sentenced to a suspension of rank and pay for six months, but the Prince Regent (the future George

IV) reduced this to a public reprimand only. Nevertheless, the verdict marked the end of Procter's career. Others, however, blamed his failure on Prevost, and Procter himself joined in the attack on the latter.[37]

Prevost was also displeased with Rottenburg who, in November 1813, was relegated to a subordinate position in Lower Canada. He was replaced in Upper Canada by Lieutenant General Gordon Drummond, a veteran of campaigning in the Low Countries, the West Indies, and the Mediterranean, and who had served before in Canada, from 1808 to 1811.[38] The opportunity was taken to alter commanders and command arrangements. Both Proctor and Major General John Vincent lost their commands, and the Right Division was placed under Major General Phineas Riall, who had distinguished himself in the capture of Martinique (1809), the Iles des Saintes (1809), and Guadeloupe (1810).

For the local population, the consequences of the battle were far bleaker. Initially, the American troops did not attack the Moravians, but their discovery of some of Procter's papers in one of the houses, combined with a ready indulgence for looting, led them to loot the village thoroughly and then to burn it down. As earlier in York, the destructiveness the Americans habitually applied to the Native Americans was readily extended to the European population. Their subsequent complaints about the fate of Washington at the hands of British troops in 1814 were totally hypocritical.

## THE NATIVE AMERICANS

Farther south, another major blow was struck at Native American power. Acute divisions among the Creek Nation in what is now the American Southeast, especially in Alabama, came to interact with the War of 1812. The Creek nation was divided with the Red Stick rebellion launched by the Creek National Council. A good number of the chiefs under attack by the Red Stick leaders were from the Upper Towns, but it is a mistake to see the war as between the Upper and Lower Towns, as most of the Lower Towns did not take part in the uprising, although some did. Opposition to whites, and specifically to American territorial expansion, was strongest among the Red Sticks, the name given to those Creeks who attacked what they saw as acculturation with the Americans. This opposition was encouraged by a visit in 1811 by Tecumseh, whose mother was probably one of the

Shawnees who, for a time, had settled among the Creeks. The Red Sticks became increasingly active in 1813, and also sought Spanish assistance. Had they waited until 1814, when the British made a major commitment to the Gulf, the Creeks would have been in a better position to resist the Americans. The Creeks, however, were not operating to an agenda coordinated with Britain, although American observers were convinced that hostile Creeks were influenced from the Great Lakes region, by British-allied Native Americans. The Creeks, instead, were affected by a sense of American pressure.

This feeling of being under pressure from American expansionism also influenced Spanish officials, and understandably so. In 1813, Major General James Wilkinson advanced from New Orleans, invading West Florida. The Americans had claimed for several years that the town of Mobile, the key Spanish position west of Pensacola, was in fact in American territory[39] and, in 1813, demanded that the commander of Fort Charlotte there withdraw his forces. Wilkinson, who thought that considerations of honor would lead to Spanish resistance, was surprised that he met instead with a ready compliance, not least as the fort was well-provided with artillery. This American advance, which fulfilled prewar goals, also strengthened their position in the War of 1812, particularly by bringing the Americans closer to Pensacola, a center of the British presence in Spanish North America,[40] and by lessening the possibility of British-Creek contact across Spanish territory.

At the same time, the American advance underlined Spanish concern about vulnerability, the willingness of the Americans to exploit this, and the question of how best for Spain to respond to Britain and her Native American allies, which was to become a more urgent issue in late 1814. Indeed, with strong backing from Georgia, there was considerable American interest in seizing East Florida.[41]

Boasting of magical powers that would enable them to overcome the threatening Americans, Creek prophets in 1813 became more influential in what Benjamin Hawkins, the agent to the Creeks, called "the sudden explosion of this fanaticism."[42] Creek action led to a response by American militia, but their surprise attack on the Red Sticks bringing supplies from the Spanish base of Pensacola was defeated in a counterattack at Burnt Corn Creek on 27 July 1813. Moreover, the poorly defended Fort Mims close to the Alabama River fell to the Red Stick Creeks on 30 August, leading to what was called the

Fort Mims massacre. The violence shown was designed to intimidate Native American opponents into submitting to the teachings of the prophets.[43]

Reports of this massacre helped rouse Tennessee to field enough troops to crush the Creeks. They were defeated at Tallasahatchee and Talladega on 3 and 9 November 1813 by Tennessee militia under John Coffee and Andrew Jackson respectively, while Ferdinand Claiborne captured the Creek town of Holy Ground on 23 December 1813. However, it proved difficult to exploit these advances because of differences among the American commanders, serious supply problems, and expiring terms of militia service. Jackson had to reorganize and resupply his force. These problems also hindered the campaign by the Georgia militia, which, having successfully captured the Creek town of Autosse on 29 November 1813, was attacked in camp at night on 27 January 1814 and forced to retreat.

These deficiencies and difficulties might sound like an indictment of the American military system, but there were numerous instances during the Napoleonic Wars in which European supply systems also broke down, and the distances in the American sphere of operations were great. A major problem with supply in the Creek War was that there were virtually no roads. Furthermore, there was always a problem with expiring enlistments when employing non-regulars. As part of a substantial American force eventually used in the Second Seminole War of 1835–42, regulars were to be deployed in the Southeast in far greater numbers, while others were used to enforce the compulsory movement of Creeks and Cherokees in 1836–39 in order to make way for American expansion; but, in 1813, there were too few regulars to spare for defeating the Creeks and, therefore, it was necessary to rely on militia. In addition, attempts were made to consolidate advances by building forts, such as Fort Mitchell, Fort Hull, and Fort Deposit.

The Creeks, in turn, suffered from serious divisions, a lack of military supplies, leadership of mixed quality, the greater numbers of the Americans, and the absence of reliable international support, from either Britain or Spain. To the British, they were a distant force, while Spain was weak. Earlier ideas that the British establish a presence in East Florida in order to develop links with the Creeks and that the latter be used as troops in the West Indies[44] had not been pursued.

Elsewhere, Native American society was also under serious pres-

sure. Anxious not to fight each other, the Iroquois, who had settlements in Canada and the USA, had agreed in 1812 that the Iroquois on
the Canadian side of the border would fight for the British, as they did
with particular affect at Queenston (1812)[45] and Beaver Dams (1813),
while their New York counterparts would be neutral. In July 1813,
however, a British raid on Black Rock, on the American shore of the
Niagara River, led the New York Iroquois to declare war on the British. That August, Iroquois fought Iroquois near Fort George and, in
December, the Canadian Iroquois burned the Tuscarora village on the
other bank. This attack drove the quest for revenge, so that, in July
1814, six hundred Iroquois joined the Americans crossing the Niagara
River. On 5 July, at the same time as the battle of Chippewa, and as
an extension of it, Iroquois fought each other. The casualties—over
eighty dead—led most Iroquois to end their role in the conflict.[46]

## The St. Lawrence Front

Meanwhile, in late 1813, as in November 1812, the Americans, focusing their military efforts on Canada, had prepared a bold step that was
designed to cut the St. Lawrence artery of British power. This would
have weakened, if not fatally undermined, the British position farther
west, both on the Niagara front and to the west of that. In the campaign, large numbers of troops were deployed, indeed the largest
number of regular troops in any American military operation prior to
the Civil War. A two-pronged offensive was planned. Major General
James Wilkinson, who, after his success at Mobile, had been called
north from the Gulf Coast to replace Dearborn, was to sail from Sacket's Harbor on Lake Ontario to the St. Lawrence and then to advance
on Montréal. This, however, was an operation that, after the initial
stages, the American squadron on Lake Ontario could do little to
assist. In these stages, Chauncey deployed his ships at the head of the
St. Lawrence, providing cover for the army transports sailing from
Lake Ontario.

Another force under Major General Wade Hampton was to move
from Plattsburg on Lake Champlain to the Chateaguay River and
then to the St. Lawrence where it would link up with Armstrong.
Hampton (1751–1835), a Virginian, had made his name (and promotion to colonel) during the War of Independence largely for bravery
and boldness, especially at the Battle of Eutaw Springs. He later

served as a Jeffersonian Republican in the House of Representatives for South Carolina (1795–1805) before rejoining the army in 1808. Based in New Orleans, however, he became a personal enemy of Wilkinson, whom he had been ordered to replace. In turn, Wilkinson superseded him as senior officer in 1813. Such tensions were all too frequent in the American forces, not that they did not strongly exist among their British rivals. It is unclear why Armstrong put in charge two generals who were known to be antagonistic towards each other, as this contributed greatly to the confusion underlying the American campaign against Montréal.

Hampton, who had not shown much activity earlier in the month, set off to invade Canada on 21 October 1813, only to discover that most of the New York militia refused to cross the Canadian border. This was one of the more important failures by militia during the war and, as with other instances of the same problem, indicates that their failures were not restricted to battle. On 25 October, the same day on which, in Europe, the British captured from the French the major Spanish fortress of Pamplona, Hampton's advancing column of four thousand regulars was stopped by log barricades. These had been constructed about thirty miles from Montréal across the road alongside the Châteaguay River and were flanked by difficult woods. Hampton determined to use one thousand troops to outflank the British position, which was held by about seventeen hundred Canadian militia, fencibles, *voltigeurs*, select embodied militia, and Native Americans. The fencibles and embodied militia were full-time units, trained like regulars and highly professional, not least in comparison with the American militia.[47] Once his outflanking force had got round the British, Hampton intended to launch a concerted attack in front and rear the following day. However, his morale was hit by the discovery that the secretary of war, John Armstrong, had decided that Hampton's winter quarters were to be south of the border, rather than near Montréal. This was a decision that undercut the value of any advance, and that reflected a more general failure in planning and maintaining morale. The difficulties of guiding operations from a distance were also amply revealed in this decision.

On 26 October, Hampton's tactics failed. As so often, a concerted attack, with all the complexity that entailed, did not work; in this case because the flanking force got lost. The well-led defending force under Lieutenant Colonel Charles-Michel de Salaberry, a veteran of campaigning in the West Indies and Low Countries, held off the

Americans, who did not continue the attack. They certainly did not make the sort of effort the British were to make in their unsuccessful attack at New Orleans in 1815, although the level of casualties the British suffered then scarcely suggests that this should be a point of criticism. Hampton's losses were small, but he fell back despite Wilkinson's orders to press on. In explaining his decision, Hampton drew attention to problems with logistics and disease, but his hatred of Wilkinson was probably more important. At any rate, Hampton failed to show the necessary determination. Once he fell back, Hampton's force lost cohesion, not least with the recall of the Vermont militia. Hampton resigned after the campaign. Wilkinson sought to blame him for its failure, and indeed tried to arrest him, although a review by Armstrong was to exonerate Hampton.

Wilkinson's force, eight thousand strong but poorly trained and inexperienced, and badly led by the demoralized and unwell Wilkinson, who freely used whisky and opium-based laudanum as palliatives, had meanwhile set off on 17 October from Sacket's Harbor. This was a key site in the strategy of the war on the Canadian frontier, as it provided a base not only for operations on Lake Ontario but also for an advance down the St. Lawrence, which was Wilkinson's intention. Some of the Americans died in a storm on the lake, but the expedition reached the St. Lawrence. They were shadowed, however, by eight hundred British regulars under Colonel Joseph Morrison. After the Americans camped near Crysler's Farm on 11 November, they tried to drive the British off. The Americans deployed a larger force under Brigadier General John Boyd, but their attack, launched in miserable rain, was not coordinated; the troops became disordered, and the superior fire discipline of the British regulars powerfully contributed to the failure of the American assault. The close-range rolling volleys from the British infantry was supplemented by cannon firing shrapnel shells. Wilkinson himself did not take the field. After suffering more than 400 casualties (compared to 180 British), the Americans drew back.

The wider significance of Crysler's Farm for the military history of the war is worthy of consideration. To the late David Chandler, for long the doyen of British military historians for the period, the battle established "the superiority of British linear tactics in the open against less well-trained opponents used to forest warfare" and was "a superb and salutary action."[48] This, in fact, is a questionable assessment as it is dangerous to read general conclusions about military quality from individual engagements, just as it is unhelpful to explain the result of such engagements by virtue of a supposed understanding of aggregate military quality. The last anyway is not a terribly helpful concept, however much it matches our tendency to adopt an ethnogenesis of military style and success, as in discussion of a supposed American or British way of war. Instead, it is necessary to give due weight to the circumstances of the day, to individual units, commanders, and terrain, and to their interaction. Crucial to this was the ability to respond more swiftly than opponents.

As far as Crysler's Farm was concerned, Morrison devised a well-balanced defense with troops in a line behind a log fence. This position was protected by woods to the left, in which Mohawks were positioned, and by the St. Lawrence to the right, and, along the road from Montréal that ran close to the river. Morrison placed more regulars along that road and, to the front, he put Canadian troops as a skirmish line designed to harry the American advance. Thus, the defense focused on the standard British linear position but, unlike that by Procter in the Battle of the Thames, was a defense in depth. The Americans advanced in three columns, but they were badly deployed, and the poor positioning of their artillery prevented its effective use. Inadequate command interacted with inexperienced troops.[49] The American units were fed into the battle without being in a coherent deployment, although their numbers were such that the British skirmishers were driven back by the weight of the American advance. The main American attack pressed the British but was repulsed, and Morrison followed with an effective advance that drove the Americans back. As a reminder of the contemporaneous range and effectiveness of their military power, the previous day, on 10 November, the British under Wellington in their invasion of southwest France had outflanked and stormed the French defenses on the River Nivelle.

Wilkinson's check did not help American morale but, as the British force had been to the American rear, the battle did not prevent Wilkinson from pressing on, and, on 12 November, the Americans passed the Long Sault rapids on the St. Lawrence River. Morrison, however, was still in Wilkinson's rear, although the British force remained heavily outnumbered. In the event, there was to be no second battle for, on 12 November, Wilkinson abandoned the offensive when it became clear that there was going to be no overwhelming concentration of American strength near Montréal. The news of Hampton's retreat led the sickly Wilkinson to decide to bring the campaign to a close, and he was to blame Hampton for the failure.

The most powerful American attempt to conquer Canada had therefore failed. The Americans indeed had made much less progress than when they invaded Canada in 1775–76, an invasion in which Québec had been besieged; but their opponents were now better prepared. The Americans in 1813 suffered from poor leadership and logistical problems, with Wilkinson's men lacking pay and winter clothing, and by the onset of bad weather; and their indecisive advances were stopped by firm resistance.[50] Had Wilkinson pressed on without Hampton's support, he would have been in a very difficult situation, with Morrison to his rear while Prevost had assembled a large force to defend Montréal, including five regular battalions. Moreover, the Canadian militia who had already thwarted Hampton were now available to focus on the new American threat and to block his advance on Montréal. Had there been such an advance, moreover, American numbers, far greater than in 1775, would have posed a serious logistical problem. Conversely, the American force would have ebbed away through disease and desertion, which would have hit morale.

Wilkinson was not strong enough to fight his way through to Montréal, to capture the city, and then to hold it against counterattack. Arguably a better general would have achieved more, as Winfield Scott did against Mexico City in 1847, defeating the Mexicans on several occasions and capturing the city. Wilkinson did not match the high-tempo campaigning of his former subordinate but, aside from respective logistical factors, Scott's campaign style reflected a conviction of American superiority over the Mexicans (which was certainly true in weaponry) that encouraged both operational and tactical boldness. This was not the case with regard to fighting the British during the War of 1812. Henry Clay, however, was not alone among American commentators in failing to understand why Montréal had not fallen.[51] There was a strong sense of disappointment which considerably lessened confidence in the likely outcome of the war. Wilkinson was to be punished in 1814, after a repeated failure when invading Canada anew, with the loss of his command, although the subsequent court-martial acquitted him. In contrast, Morrison received a medal and was voted thanks by the Assembly of Lower

Canada. He was to serve at the battle of Lundy's Lane in 1814 where he received severe wounds that ended his military service.

## THE NIAGARA FRONT, DECEMBER 1813

Wilkinson's failure was not the last of the American setbacks in 1813. Contrary to initial appearances, the victories by Perry and Harrison did not lead to the collapse of the British position in Upper Canada and, in fact, proved difficult to exploit, with Harrison soon falling back. Moreover, the Americans were driven back on the Niagara front that December. The British advanced on Fort George, which was weakly garrisoned under Brigadier General George McClure of the New York militia. The American regulars there who had been fit had all been moved to help Wilkinson's offensive farther east.

Vulnerable in the face of the British advance, McClure, on 10 December, abandoned Fort George without resisting attack. He also burned the 150 homes in the large nearby village of Newark to the ground, forcing the inhabitants to take what shelter they could find in the deep snow: Newark is now Niagara on the Lake, to distinguish it from Niagara Falls. McClure then crossed the river, denouncing the militia who, in turn, refused to serve under him. In falling back, he failed to demolish Fort George and Butler's barracks, the key military facilities.

The burning of Newark spurred the British to firm action. Lieutenant Colonel John Murray, who had occupied Fort George on 18 December, captured Fort Niagara on 19 December by a surprise night attack that benefited greatly from having discovered the countersign used in response to questions from the American sentinels. The British made extensive use of their bayonets and killed sixty-five Americans for only six lost. Major General Phineas Riall attacked American settlements on the Niagara, staging destructive raids on Buffalo, Lewiston, and Black Rock. Prevost issued a proclamation saying that the destruction was a reaction to that of Newark.[52]

The British held both Fort George and Fort Niagara for the remainder of the war, which gave them control over a key anchorage on Lake Ontario and thus denied the Americans under Chauncey the anchorage. This helped ensure that Chauncey would not be able to support land operations on the Niagara front in 1814, although poor coordination between him and the land commanders was also a serious issue in this failure and was seen in that light by the Americans. The capture of the two forts was an important British success in an area where there had hitherto been much conflict. The British sought to consolidate their position by constructing Fort Mississauga and Fort Drummond in 1814, the first to command the Niagara mouth, the latter Queenston Heights. Moreover, as a consequence of their offensive, the British were in force along the entire frontier except at Fort Amherstburg.

## THE CHESAPEAKE

As a precursor of what was to come in 1814, the British in 1813 not only sent more troops to Canada (where Prevost's command rose from about 7,700 men to about 13,700[53]), but also decided to use amphibious forces elsewhere in order to reduce American pressure on Canada. As in 1781, the Chesapeake was seen as vulnerable militarily, and as important to the American economy, being a key export zone for valuable agricultural products, especially tobacco, and thus for the capital that exports brought into the economy. The Chesapeake was also the base of the damaging Baltimore privateers. Moreover, the bay and its associated rivers provided the British with an opportunity to penetrate into the interior that was better than that offered by any other body of water in the United States, for example Long Island Sound and the Delaware. As well, the Chesapeake was closer to key naval bases in Britain and at Halifax than waterways farther south, such as those near Charleston.

Unlike in 1814, when there was to be a major offensive in the Chesapeake, there was still great pressure on the British military in Spain. When the 1813 offensive was launched, Wellington had not yet defeated the French in Spain at Vitoria, his crucial final major victory there (21 June 1813), and Napoleon had not yet been heavily defeated by Britain's key allies (Austria, Prussia, and Russia) at Leipzig (16–19 October 1813). This was the battle that led to the collapse of Napoleon's position in Germany, and thus cleared the way for the Allied invasion of eastern France.

As a consequence of this pressure on British resources, Admiral Sir John Borlase Warren, the commander of the fleet in North American waters, was only given twenty-four hundred troops in 1813. Their commander, Sir Thomas Sidney Beckwith, was a skilled leader of light troops with the sort of experience that American generals could not match. He had served on campaigns in India (1791–98), Denmark (1801), northern Germany and Denmark (1806–1807), and Iberia (1808–11). Looking ahead, one of his subordinates, Lieutenant Colonel Charles Napier, was to acquire great fame as the conqueror of Sind (in modern Pakistan) in 1843. This was a success achieved, like other British achievements in South Asia, in environments at least as difficult as those that faced them in North America, but with the major assistance of the troop numbers made available by operating in or near India. Beckwith's force, in contrast, was a small one, and Henry, 3rd Earl Bathurst, the secretary of state for war and the colonies, sensibly drew attention to this in issuing his instructions. These, indeed, were instructions that to some extent mirrored those given to Prevost in 1812:

> The number and description of the force placed under your command, as well as the object of the expedition itself, will point out to you that you are not to look to the permanent possession of any place, but to the reembarking the force as soon as the immediate object of each particular attack shall have been accomplished. . . . As the object of the expedition is to harass the enemy by different attacks, you will avoid the risk of a general action, unless it should become necessary to secure your retreat.[54]

The relationship between events on individual fronts and the wider struggle was not only indicated in such comments. Campaigning on particular fronts indeed affected options elsewhere. In 1812, for example, the failure of the American advance on Montréal owed something to the extent to which, due to the offensive success of Brock's British-Native American army earlier in the year, too many American resources had been devoted to the war farther west.

On 3 March 1813, the vigorous Rear Admiral George Cockburn arrived off Lynnhaven Bay, which was used as a base for operations in the Chesapeake in April. Without regulars, the Americans in the area had to rely on the local militia and on warships trapped in the Chesapeake. On land, the British met with mixed success. Craney Island in the Elizabeth River, protecting the approach to the port of Norfolk in Virginia, was unsuccessfully attacked on 22 June, a costly instance of both poor army-navy coordination and a failure of intelligence too often seen in British operations. It is easy to understand why the perceptive Napier, who took part in the expedition, felt that "We despise the Yankees too much." He also thought Cockburn's reliance on his luck misguided.[55] Moreover, Norfolk resisted successfully, although Hampton (close to Newport News) was seized.

The British also moved far up the bay and its tributary rivers, with Cockburn attacking Frenchtown (28 April), Havre-de-Grace (3 May) and Georgetown (5 May) on the Upper Chesapeake, and reaching Cedar and Maryland Points on the Potomac. Beyond this, he could not go because of shoals. In August 1813, the British squadron sailed up the Chesapeake again, attacking St. Michael's. To the east of Annapolis, a base was established on Kent Island off the Eastern Shore. Nevertheless, no blow was aimed directly at the major American towns in the region, Annapolis, Baltimore, and Washington, and the position on Kent Island was not maintained. The American forces in the Chesapeake were correctly felt to be so much larger than Beckwith's unit, while Warren was concerned about avoiding the hurricane season and with refitting his ships.

As a result, the British withdrew from the bay, although warships were left to blockade its entrance and occasional attacks were mounted on coastal towns. Moreover, the charts of the Chesapeake drawn up as a result of the 1813 expeditions were to aid the British operations there the following year. These operations were encouraged, furthermore, by the British sense of American vulnerability that was another legacy. Differences in fighting style were also revealed. Cockburn complained of the American defense of Havre-de-Grace: "No longer feeling themselves equal to a manly and open resistance, they commenced a teasing and irritating fire from behind their houses, walls, trees etc."[56] This remark looked back to unrealistic British comments during the War of Independence.

The cycle of reprisal seen on the Niagara front in December 1813 was to become increasingly apparent in the last year of the war. In part, it reflected mutual anger. In 1813, referring to the capture of Havre-de-Grace, Cockburn wrote about "setting fire to some of the houses to cause the proprietors (who had deserted them and formed part of the militia who had fled to the woods) to understand and feel what they were liable to bring upon themselves by building batteries and acting towards us with so much useless rancour."[57]

As a result of this destruction, and of that at Frederickstown and

Georgetown on the Sassafras River two days later, Madison sent a message to Congress that Britain had added to the "savage fury" of war on the Canadian frontier (a reference to the conflict involving the Native Americans), "a system of plunder and conflagration on the other." American destructiveness, in turn, was threatened in the Northwest. There, the concern of the secretary of war, John Armstrong, that the Battle of the Thames could be reversed and that, to counter the American position on Lake Erie, the British would use the land route along the River Thames, led him, on 29 December 1813, to instruct Harrison to destroy the settlements there. Madison, however, soon modified the order.[58]

## 1813 OVERALL

The intractability of the conflict was in part responsible for the growing anger that was seen in the destructiveness by both sides. This intractability also encouraged each government to consider peace negotiations. The prospect of a move to diplomacy, in turn, lent urgency to the attempt to secure advantages in the campaigning. Clay indeed argued, in December 1813, that "we must judge of the conditions of peace, when peace comes, not by the present state, but by that state of things which shall exist when it is negotiated."[59] The first major attempt to secure peace arose from the international context, with an initiative by Tsar Alexander I of Russia. He was keen that Britain should not spread her efforts by fighting the USA and, instead, wanted her to be able to focus on their mutual enemy, Napoleon, a goal Alexander shared with Wellington and other British leaders. Alexander also did not wish to bear the burden of the war with France while Britain was able to make transoceanic gains, a frequent theme from Britain's allies during successive wars, for example Frederick the Great of Prussia during the Seven Years' War.

In September 1812, Alexander, then the ruler of the leading power other than Britain fighting Napoleon, offered mediation. The news reached Washington on 24 February 1813 and, on 11 March, the American government responded positively, the Senate approving the step on 25 May.[60] Earlier, the government had been unenthusiastic about negotiations as they had not yet been informed of Napoleon's failure in Russia. Their new stance reflected not the fate of campaigning in North America but, instead, the marked decline in

American confidence since the previous year when, as Clay had declared in the House of Representatives on 4 December 1812, there had
been hope of Napoleon's success. The American government was
now aware of Napoleon's heavy defeat in Russia, although still optimistic about French pressure on the British forces under the command of Wellington in Spain.[61] The American failure to grasp the
extent of the deterioration in their position arose from a serious misjudgement of the fast-developing European situation. In December
1812, Alexander had decided to press on against France, which put the
latter's unwilling ally Prussia in the front line, forcing Prussia to a
demarche. In January 1813, Napoleon harshly rejected Prussian terms
for continued support and, in March, Prussia declared war on Napoleon. The British alliance system was thus becoming far stronger.
Napoleon was also facing growing difficulties within France.

Wellington warned his brother Henry, the ambassador to Spain,
in May 1813, that American support for Russian mediation posed a
problem: "The object of this offer must be to create a division between us and the Russians,"[62] and, due to European power politics,
this possibility was a key issue for Britain. Anglo-Russian relations
had been very varied over the previous quarter-century. Allied against
France in the Wars of the Second and Third Coalitions, Britain had
come very close to war with Russia in 1791 and 1801, while Alexander was allied with Napoleon from 1807 to 1812. In 1812–13, at the
same time that the mistrustful British government sought good relations with Russia, the government did not wish to be dependent on
Russian mediation, and indeed this was rejected. Moreover, a direct
approach for an armistice by Andrei Dashkov, the Russian envoy,
made to the British naval commanders, was also unsuccessful, with
the commanders being instructed from London that they had no authority to discuss the matter.[63]

Instead, on 4 November 1813, the British, who saw scant benefit
coming from a war they had never sought, offered direct negotiations
with the USA. The letter from Robert, Viscount Castlereagh, the foreign secretary, reached Annapolis on 30 December and on 5 January
1814, James Monroe, the secretary of state, accepted the proposal. By
then, not only had Wilkinson failed but the failure on the Niagara
front was also readily apparent. Moreover, any hope that the USA
would benefit from some sort of rough balance in Europe had collapsed. The end of any balance was due not only to French defeats at

the hands of Britain and her allies (and Madison was later to say he would not have backed war had he foreseen the French defeat[64]), but also to Napoleon's inability to negotiate a compromise peace, an inability that owed much to his refusal to accept that his position had deteriorated.

This international context is important because it tends to be underplayed as a result of the focus on Anglo-American negotiations or would-be negotiations. Such a focus, however, neglects a key context and, moreover, one that raises an important counterfactual or what-if; in this case, of Napoleon doing better. Counterfactuals are usually underplayed in scholarly works and some, indeed, are unhelpful, not least because each battle and campaign was specific to a particular context. It is possible, for example, that a large meteorite might have fallen into the North Atlantic, destroying much of the British fleet; but, as that was not considered by contemporaries, it was not worth discussion. In contrast, the relationship between the Anglo-American struggle and the wider international context was of relevance to contemporaries.

In 1813, Napoleon fought back hard in Germany, aided by concerns about Russian and Prussian intentions among the German rulers on whose support he counted, which included those of Bavaria, Saxony, and Württemberg. He rebuilt his army to a force of over four hundred thousand plus his artillery, but the new recruits were more like the inexperienced French troops of 1792 than the veterans of his earlier campaigns; and, unlike in 1792, at the outset of the French Revolutionary War, the forces of France's opponents were not outnumbered. In addition, Napoleon was unable to create a new cavalry to match the horses lost in Russia in 1812.

Nevertheless, there were positive signs from the perspective of an American observer who wanted France to remain strong. New levies, both French and German, helped Napoleon drive his opponents out of Saxony in May 1813, winning victories at Lützen (2 May) and Bautzen (20-21 May), and North Germany did not rise against him as had been anticipated. Saxony rallied to Napoleon in May, and Denmark in July. Concerned about the intentions of Russia and Prussia, not least their territorial ambitions in Poland and Germany, Austria, which (like Prussia) had supported Napoleon in his invasion of Russia in 1812, refused to join his enemies in early 1813. This was a major problem for them. Napoleon, however, was able to snatch defeat from the situation and to provoke the formation of a powerful coalition. Austria sought to mediate peace and proposed an independent central Europe, with Napoleon still in control of the left bank of the Rhine, and thus of the dockyards at Antwerp which posed a serious challenge to British naval power and, indeed, had been the target of the unsuccessful Walcheren expedition in 1809. The importance of Antwerp was underlined by the Viscount Castlereagh when he claimed, in November 1813, that "to leave it in the hands of France is little short of imposing upon Great Britain the charge of a perpetual war establishment."[65] Britain, indeed, was willing to return colonial conquests to France in order to get its way over Antwerp.

Austria also offered Napoleon non-interference over Spain, as well as diplomatic support over colonial concessions from Britain. These terms would have been a very helpful outcome from the French perspective, as Napoleon would have been able to concentrate on war with Britain in Iberia and overseas. Although that would not have made much of a difference at sea, the British army might have had to send more troops to Iberia to prevent the situation from deteriorating there. The course of the war in Iberia had shown that, when, as in 1810, Napoleon had no opponents elsewhere, the French could redeploy forces there so as to put serious pressure on Wellington's forces, although by 1813 even a (fragile) peace on his eastern flank would not have helped Napoleon much in the peninsula. Yet, such pressure on British resources would have affected Britain in its war with the USA.

Napoleon, however, rejected the Austrian suggestion, declared all France's annexations inalienable, and began military preparations against Austria. Defeat had not curbed his instinctive bellicosity, although, on the other hand, it is unclear how far the other powers were acting in good faith. Napoleon's refusal to negotiate peace, or to understand that it entailed compromise—a refusal delivered in person by an angry emperor to Count Wenzel Lothar Metternich, the influential Austrian foreign minister, in Dresden on 26 June—led Austria finally to join the anti-French camp: she declared war on 11 August. Sweden under Jean Bernadotte, a French marshal before, in 1810, he was elected heir to the throne of Sweden (he succeeded as Charles XIV in 1818), also joined in on the Allied side. This increased the forces deployed against Napoleon in Germany, and Bernadotte also put pressure on Napoleon's ally Denmark.

The French were now heavily outnumbered. Underlining the different scale of war on the two sides of the Atlantic, Austrian, Prussian, Russian, and Swedish forces in Germany exceeded 600,000 troops, while Napoleon deployed 370,000 men against them in the field. The French were defeated at Grossbeeren (23 August), on the Katzbach River (26 August), at Kulm (30 August), and at Dennewitz (6 September). By devoting too many units to trying to capture Berlin, and by failing to concentrate his forces during the campaign, Napoleon had allowed their attenuation, and this had preserved neither the territory under French control nor the strategic advantage.[66] Bavaria allied with Austria in October, while on 16–19 October the heavily outnumbered Napoleon was seriously defeated at Leipzig in the massive Battle of the Nations.[67] Saxony was then occupied by Russian and Prussian forces. Within France, Napoleon was affected by falling tax revenues, widespread draft avoidance, a serious shortage of arms and equipment, and a marked decline in the morale and efficiency of officials. The French economy was in a parlous state, as it was hit by British blockade and by the loss of Continental markets.

Both in late 1813 and in early 1814, Napoleon failed to offer terms that would divide his assailants. This failure came despite the fact that Austria distrusted Russia and Britain, and would have liked to retain a strong France, which, indeed, influenced the proposals made by Austria to Napoleon in November 1813; while the Russians sought a strong France in order to balance Britain. Such an agreement would have helped the Americans; but that was not a consideration for Europe's rulers, and indeed the Allied statesmen and military leaders on France's eastern front that winter made no mention of the conflict in North America.[68] Napoleon was instinctively unwilling to accept limits or half-measures. As a result, the possibility of Napoleon settling his differences with Austria and Russia and instead fighting Britain was not followed up. Earlier, in contrast, the victorious Napoleon had negotiated peace with Austria in 1805, and with Prussia and Russia in 1807, while continuing to fight Britain. These agreements had offered a possibility of France maintaining a stable order in Europe, successfully incorporating Iberia into Napoleon's system, and then fighting Britain or forcing her to terms that left France a major role outside Europe. Either of these scenarios would have given America more negotiating space with Britain or a relative advantage had she fought her. As a result of Napoleon's peace treaties in 1805–1807, Britain had been placed under severe pressure by France, especially after 1809 when Austria was defeated anew and accepted Napoleon's harsh terms. In contrast, there was no Austrian treaty with Napoleon in 1813 or 1814.

Another possible, but very different, close to the War of 1812 was envisaged by British hopes that the pressure of war and the pressures of this war would lead the Americans to abandon the struggle, which would result in a British victory. These hopes were a repetition of British expectations during the War of Independence, and it is important to discuss the idea as it underlay British strategy. As with the earlier conflict, it was impossible for Britain to conquer the United States but in 1812–14, starting from a very different territorial and political basis, it was hoped that pressure would lead to a fracturing of the American will; as indeed happened with France in 1814. This emphasis on cracking an opponent's will was also to be the Confederate hope in the Civil War (1861–65): it was impossible for the Confederacy to conquer the North and it did not contemplate doing so, but it was hoped that sufficient damage could be inflicted so that Union support for the struggle would ebb. This aspiration was linked to an assessment of the political situation, specifically the prospect that Abraham Lincoln's opponents would win the elections held in the North, particularly the 1864 presidential election.

Thus, in 1775-83, 1812–15, and 1861–65, it was hoped by one side, the political cohesion and constancy of which appeared stronger —at least to them—that victory could be won by exploiting the political weakness of the other side. This perception led to a possibility for integrating military with political perspectives, a possibility of an integrated strategy that is unduly neglected if these conflicts are treated simply, or even largely, as military episodes. In practice, moreover, the small size of British and American governments in the period 1775–1815 lessened the extent to which there might be an institutional barrier to outside pressure on either the military or the political process.

The plausibility of these contemporary assessments about winning sufficiently to lead the opponent to terms can be questioned. That they failed in each case, however, does not mean that they were without substance as a possible outcome. Moreover, these assessments could offer the best option, and one that might both make sense of the military situation and provide a strategy. During the War of 1812, British commanders proved sensitive to the nuances of American politics, not least widespread New England hostility to the war and suspicion there about the conduct of American operations.

Reports to this effect from elsewhere in the USA were also forwarded to London. Thus, in March 1813, Rear Admiral George Cockburn reported from Hampton Roads that "an intelligent merchant of Richmond," Virginia, had told him that, initially, the war had proved favorable to the local economy, not least through using British licences to continue to trade. This was an accurate assessment, but the merchant had continued:

> but the late measures of our government having (he said) not only put a stop to these advantageous prospects but having also thrown back into the country an immense quantity of last year's produce and caused an entire and complete stagnation of all commerce to succeed so immediately on the late scenes of activity and profit, had had a proportionate effect on the minds of the people, and there was now only to be heard from one end of the country to the other lamentations of individuals who were now beginning to suffer from the effects of the war. He also added with much apparent pleasure that Mr. Madison had lost all the latter measures he had proposed to Congress for prosecuting the war with rancor, and he assured me from the present state of the country the President would neither be enabled nor permitted to continue it.[69]

The sense that continued pressure might crack the Americans was difficult for the latter to counter, not least given the contentious nature of their politics, while the Americans could not bring comparable pressure to bear on Britain. Social problems and political radicalism there were largely unrelated to the war with America. Instead, the conquest of Canada was the only feasible American option, but it was unclear how far such a conquest would affect British policy. This policy would have been transformed had it been possible for the Americans to wage a successful war against British oceanic commerce. Despite American hopes, however, this was outside their capability, and increasingly so, as the British blockade became more effective. Whatever the role of American hopes of the conquest of Canada in the political build-up to the war, the conquest thus became the only strategic option left to the Americans.

At the operational level, the possible political impact of military moves was also different. Whereas the British could hope that the use of force would divide the Americans, the Americans were unable to bring comparable pressure to bear in Canada, let alone against the British Isles. The desired impact of British action was recorded by Cockburn, writing from the Chesapeake in May 1813:

> I had the satisfaction to find that what had passed at Havre, George Town, and Fredericstown had its effects, and led these people to understand that they have more to hope for from our generosity than from erecting batteries and opposing us by the means within their power. The inhabitants of this place having met me at landing to say that they had not permitted either guns or militia to be stationed there, and that whilst there I should not meet any opposition whatever, I therefore landed with the officers and a small guard only, and having ascertained that there was not any public property of any kind or warlike stores, and having allowed of such articles as we stood in need of being embarked in the boats on payment to the owners of their full value, I again re-embarked leaving the people of this place well pleased with the wisdom of their determination on their mode of receiving us. I also had a deputation from Charleston in the North East River, to assure me that that place is considered by them as at your mercy, and that neither guns nor militia men shall be suffered there.[70]

In part, however, this report was wishful thinking, a point that more generally underlines the difficulty of political analysis. Yet, despite such hopes, the British did not make the mistake of assuming that the loyalism seen in the War of Independence could be revived as a serious option. In addition to wishful thinking such as that by Cockburn, there was the problem, in assessing American war-weariness as well as operational success, of the British mistaking temporary advantage for permanent gain. Similarly, at the tactical level, when, earlier, there had been resistance, as at Havre-de-Grace, the British had pushed the American troops out, but had not followed the latter into the surrounding woods. This course brought them the advantage of taking the town and its supplies, but then they had to re-embark. Cockburn's report just cited indicated the hope that long-term military and political benefit could be gained by ending resistance. In part this was wrong, as American attitudes changed, and sensibly so, when British warships sailed away. In part, however, there was an accurate understanding in Britain that America was divided over the conflict, and that these divisions were not restricted to New England.

These divisions continued, moreover. With everything in the balance, the 1813 campaign had proved a serious disappointment for the Americans, for both government and public, and there was biting, and deserved, criticism of the secretary of war, John Armstrong. Wartime problems indeed exacerbated political divisions. These were serious, and not only between Republicans and Federalists, but also amongst the former, between pro-war and anti-war Republicans, and indeed among the pro-war Republicans. These divisions contributed to a growing sense of crisis.[71] The American national debt was rising, the public finances were in grave difficulties—not least with customs revenue hit by a collapse in imports—and the economy was increasingly under pressure from the more insistent British blockade. In 1813, it proved difficult to finance governmental needs, although the willingness of Stephen Girard, the country's wealthiest man, to lend $2.3 million in cash proved a crucial support,[72] as did news of the Russian readiness to mediate, a readiness that offered the better financial prospect of peace. In 1814, the British government was informed of American difficulties in raising money, of a shortage of specie, and of the danger of bank failures on a large scale if the war continued.[73] Financial problems helped explain why the payments promised to friendly Creek leaders were not made, much to the concern of Benjamin Hawkins, the adroit American agent to the Creeks.

Henry Clay had been confident in February 1812 that the nation would rise to the challenge politically and financially, as well as militarily: "Taxes are indispensably necessary in the event of hostilities . . . surely no man will hesitate to contribute his just *part* when *all* is at hazard."[74] Such hopes, however, were disappointed. In 1813, Clay had similarly been confident that opposition in New England to the war could be crushed. Again, he had been disappointed. The USA continued to be divided over the war, and the federal system ensured that these divisions were publicly displayed and institutionalized.[75] The dashing of hopes for the American navy contributed to disappointment and division.

There were also serious, and justified, questions about the quality of American leadership, and these were not restricted to the relevant secretaries. In September 1812, Richard Rush suggested to Madison that Monroe take command in the Northwest and that Jefferson replace him as secretary of state. Neither occurred, though the first was an option. Clay complained, three months later, that Madison was "wholly unfit" for war, being tardy, hesitant, and overly benevolent to lackluster colleagues.[76] The last was certainly true. Madison found himself in a situation that he could not control, and with a government and military he could not direct. Looked at differently, there was neither experience of wartime executive leadership by a presidential system nor a blueprint for one.[77] As a result of such problems, it was clear why hopes of peace were increasing on the American side.

In contrast to the War of Independence, the second year of the War of 1812 had not seen a major British offensive. Unlike in 1776, the British had major military commitments elsewhere, which gave the Americans an important second chance. If they were unable to benefit greatly in terms of successful offensive operations in 1813, they were able, at least, to consolidate and develop their military system without the acute pressure of 1776. Then American forces had been driven from Canada and defeated outside New York.[78] This contrast between the two conflicts is instructive in terms of the eventual outcome of the War of 1812. When, in 1777, the British had attacked anew, they had already gained the previous year the important advantages of a major base in the USA (New York City, and, to a lesser extent, Newport), as well as the initiative on the Canadian frontier; but the British enjoyed no such advantages in 1814.

# 4

# THE WAR AT SEA

Some time ago it was imagined on all hands that in the event of war with America, the first operation would be the destruction of her navy. What the fact had turned out to be, he was almost ashamed to mention. . . . Yet, if ever there was a contest where we ought to have been well prepared, where we had every advantage in regard to naval means, it was this contest with America."

Henry, 3rd Marquis of Lansdowne, opposition politician, House of Lords, 1813.[1]

The War of 1812 was a conflict between two very different naval powers, a pattern that is far more common in naval history than tends to be appreciated. Aside from a fundamental contrast in their strength, with Britain having the world's leading navy while the USA lacked a battle fleet, the two powers used their navies for very different purposes. Because there were no large-scale naval clashes on the high seas (which was a marked contrast with the situation between Britain and the USA on the inland lakes, at least insofar as the available forces made possible), it is all too easy to underrate the crucial strategic dimensions of naval power and their importance for the character and development of the war.

The USA had maritime, rather than naval, strength. The American mercantile marine had grown rapidly in size and importance after the War of Independence, and its range had greatly increased. Whaling and the profitable China trade, for example, had led the Americans into the Pacific. In 1784, the *Empress of China* made its first voyage to Canton, sailing via the Cape of Good Hope. However, there was no comparable expansion in American naval power because the new state, whose navy had not done well during the War of Independence, did not seek command of the sea nor transoceanic commercial or political dominion. Indeed, the last American warship was sold in 1785.

The American navy, however, was revived in the mid-1790s, albeit as a minor force. Work on three frigates began in 1793, initially in order to fight the privateering Barbary States of North Africa (Algiers, Tripoli, and Tunis), but then in response to French maritime pressure on American trade in the Quasi War of 1798 to 1800. War with France was not declared, despite a number of clashes between warships from the summer of 1798, the majority of which were successes for the Americans; but, that year, the military character of the American state was ratcheted up with the establishment of the Department of the Navy. As was the general pattern during the eighteenth century, there was also a significant reliance on free enterprise as it was necessary to commission privateers to act against the French at sea.

After Napoleon's seizure of power in late 1799 led to a change in French priorities, the USA was able to settle the Quasi War with France the following year. The American government then sought to improve the American position in the Mediterranean where, under treaties signed in 1795–98, annual payments of tribute to the Barbary States were made in order to prevent their privateering attacks on American commerce. This trade was no longer protected by the British navy as had been the case before independence. It was felt that paying tribute was humiliating and expensive, that operations in the Mediterranean would help train the navy, and that these operations would cost little more than retaining the fleet in home waters.

In 1801, Jefferson sent Commodore Richard Dale with three frigates and a schooner to the Mediterranean, while the bashaw of Tripoli (today, the capital of Libya) declared war. In what should have been an instructive lesson about misleading prewar hopes and expectations, the American blockade of Tripoli, however, proved difficult, in part because the deep-draft American ships were not suited for the blockade of shallow coastal waters. This difficulty of blockade prefigured the problems Britain was to have in bringing its naval power to bear against the USA. As a result, the blockade was abandoned in 1802 and Dale's successor, Commodore Richard Morris, instead, sailed in search of privateers. This unauthorized policy lacked the merit of success, and Morris was recalled and dismissed in 1803.

His replacement, Edward Preble, renewed the conflict. In October 1803 Preble was able to intimidate Sulayman, the sultan of Morocco, into settling his dispute with America, but the frigate *Philadelphia* ran aground on a reef off Tripoli and was captured. The crew was paraded through the streets of Tripoli. The following February, Stephen Decatur led a raid on the harbor in which the *Philadelphia* was seized and burned, thus removing a powerful image of American failure. The British naval hero Horatio Nelson called this feat "the most bold and daring act of the age." Later in 1804, fire attacks were made on Tripolitan ships off their base, while in April 1805 a force under William Eaton marched overland from Alexandria in Egypt and captured Derna. As with many successful interventions, this was effective in part because of the ability to exploit divisions among opponents; in this case, Eaton cooperated with the Bashaw's exiled brother, Hamet Karamanli. Two months later peace was negotiated with no annual tribute stipulated, although it was necessary to pay a ransom of $60,000 to obtain the release of the crew of the *Philadelphia*.[2] In certain respects, the conflict prefigured the War of 1812 in that it ended with an impression of American success which remained a strong afterglow that blotted out the reality of a far more difficult and, for long, intractable struggle.

The Tripoli war was not the limit of American naval experience. In 1806–10, gunboats based in New Orleans operated against French and Spanish privateers off the Mississippi Delta. The American navy in 1812 thus had experience, but it was on a totally different scale to the Royal Navy. The Americans had trained seamen to man their fleet as well as the most powerful frigates of the age, which they were to prove adept at handling in ship-to-ship actions. Yet, the Americans lacked sufficient sailors for all their commitments, while they had no ships of the line, unlike Britain which dominated in this sphere. The total American navy at the outset comprised only sixteen ships, seven of them frigates which had been built during the Federalist period. Aside from the seven operational frigates, there was another that never left port and one being cut down to a corvette. Oceangoing operational strength is difficult to determine and, due to issues of effectiveness, counting warships is a problematic way to do so; but, at any rate, the Americans lacked the capacity for fleet action.

This lack of capacity reflected the force structure and naval doctrine developed under Jefferson's agrarian republicanism,[3] each of which, in turn, was a product of an urgent political debate.[4] American republicanism was very different in its military results to the large fleets developed by the mercantile republics of the United Provinces and English Commonwealth in the seventeenth century. In part, concerns about the cost and likely effectiveness of such a fleet had encouraged opposition within the USA to its creation, while the Jeffersonian emphasis on gunboats conformed to a militia tradition; but, as discussed in chapter one, there was also political backing for a focus on an overland attack on Canada. A lack of Congressional and governmental support ensured that there was a shortage of expenditure on the navy in the late 1800s and early 1810s and, indeed, warships were laid up. The situation did not improve significantly as war approached. In early 1812, Congress rejected the request from Paul Hamilton, the secretary of the navy, for new ten frigates and twelve ships of the line. Instead, Congress was only willing to pay to refit three frigates and to spend money on dockyards.

Initially, the American war plan had been for a quick land offensive against Lower Canada up the Champlain Valley, which led to only limited interest in a strategic role for the navy. At the outbreak of the war, however, the Americans found it easier to act at sea than to strike on land where, for both military and political reasons, there were problems with mobilization.[5] The need to protect trade was also a key issue. Concern about safeguarding incoming merchantmen, with the crucial liquidity they offered, for both merchants and customs revenues, helped ensure a shift in attitude. As a result, warships were to be sent to sea, not only in order to convoy merchantmen, but also to destroy the British warships that might attack them. Commodore John Rodgers, the senior naval officer and a veteran of the Quasi War with France and the Barbary War, saw opportunities from taking the initiative, and a strong squadron of three frigates and two brigs under Rodgers left New York on 21 June. Rodgers searched for a large British convoy homeward bound from the West Indies, which he saw as a source of wealth for himself and the country. Although Rodgers was thwarted by poor weather, his cruise pushed the British onto the defensive and gave American merchantmen an opportunity to reach their ports.[6]

A naval emphasis accorded with the politics of both government and merchants who regarded the purpose of the war not as conquering Canada, but as putting pressure on Britain in order to end hostile commercial policies. The seizure of territory in Canada was also intended to further this objective, although, conversely, naval action was also seen as a possible way to put pressure on the British in Canada. Indeed, there was a common naval focus, because Canada was perceived as a key source of the naval resources, especially timber, needed by the British navy, and Madison was convinced that Napoleon would succeed in limiting British access to its other major source of naval stores, the Baltic, which would focus greater attention on Canada.[7] The latter indeed was a key source of timber for the navy.[8] Had Napoleon been successful in Russia, then Madison would have been proved correct.

It was easier, however, to plan than to execute. Naval operations and combat faced serious limitations during this period. Lacking, by modern standards, deep keels, sailing vessels suffered from limited seaworthiness, while the operational problems of working sailing ships for combat were very different from those that steam-powered vessels were to encounter later in the nineteenth century. The optimal conditions for sailing ships were to come from windward in a force 4–6 wind across a sea which was relatively flat, which is more often than not what it was like on the Great Lakes; it was more difficult to range guns in a swell. As a result, it was easier for untrained seamen to be effective on the lakes. Tactical practice tended to conform to theory even less at sea than on land, due in part to the impact of weather and wind on maneuverability. As a result of such factors, command at sea required considerable skill and success in naval engagements was particularly impressive.[9]

In 1812, Rodgers failed to find his convoy but, after American policy changed and the navy was split up into smaller squadrons and single ship units, the American frigates were more successful. The Americans captured three British frigates: *Guerrière*, *Macedonian*, and *Java* respectively fell victim to the *Constitution*,[10] the *United States*, and the *Constitution* again—frigates ably designed by Joshua Humphreys. With 24-pounder cannon, these ships, the pocket-battle-ships of their age, were, crucially, more heavily gunned than the British with their 18-pounders.[11] These successes provided an initially valuable boost to morale. Isaac Hull of the well-gunned *Constitution* received a gold medal from Congress for his capture of the *Guerrière* on 19 August. If the collisions between the two ships during the course of their battle suggested that Hull's seamanship was not what it should be, collisions were very hard to avoid, particularly in engagements like this when the rigging was so cut up. It should not necessarily color his reputation as a seaman. After the same ship captured the *Java* on 29 December, William Bainbridge, who had replaced Hull, also received a Congressional gold medal.[12]

Indeed, initially, although they were working with inherent disadvantages, the Americans did better at sea than had been anticipated by the British government; and, conversely, did worse on land, which made the victories at sea particularly worthwhile. The American sailors themselves had a great deal of faith in their own ability, and the British sailors knew the American sailors well, and everyone knew they had very good ships. These victories also helped cover the return of American merchantmen, and their cargoes and customs revenues contributed to the financing of the war. Clay, however, grumbled, "Brilliant as they are however they do not fill up the void created by our misfortunes on land."[13] Moveover, disputes within the naval officer corps over prize money led to litigation.

At sea, the British at first suffered from over-confidence as well as inaccurate gunnery, the latter a reflection on some ships of poor gun drill and a lack of recent combat experience. Their ships were simply less powerful (less strongly gunned) and less well-prepared than those of their opponents. The impact of luck was also important, as more often than not it was a lucky shot that dismasted a ship, but so also were tactics, as the Americans focused on this goal. The *Guerrière* was dismasted and its hull was repeatedly pierced by the *Constitution*, whose guns were double-shotted. Double-shotting ensured lower velocity and that the guns would fire slowly and the shot smash into the ship's sides (thus causing more casualties), rather than the shot going through the ship, the damage from which could quickly and easily be plugged. Indeed, the damage to the *Guerrière* was so acute that the Americans could not save their prize. The *Macedonian* was very heavily battered by the *United States* and was unable to sail for a fortnight.

In addition, the Royal Navy's North American station was not a key one in the war with Napoleon and, as a result, had been starved of resources. Many of the British ships were in a bad condition, as well as being short of sailors. The last was a problem for every navy but particularly for the Royal Navy, which had been over-committed for some time. It was a problem, moreover, that had helped to lead to war with America. Furthermore, the dockyards in Halifax and Bermuda lacked sufficient matériel and skilled shipwrights to ensure that the fleet remained seaworthy, and ships requiring major repairs had to be sent back to British dockyards.[14] This situation was the underside of being the world's leading naval power, although a problem for all navies. In contrast, the Americans could call on effective local dockyards, while good gunners and heavier guns helped their warships greatly, as with Stephen Decatur's capture of the *Macedonian* on 25 October 1812. It was only in June 1813, when the *Chesapeake* found the *Shannon*, that two frigates of equal strength fought. On that occasion, the British *Shannon* was victorious, which had a major impact on the morale of both sides.

Aside from the three frigates, the other British losses in 1812 were all of smaller vessels, such as the twenty-gun sloop *Alert* captured by the thirty-two-gun *Essex* on 13 August 1812: in this clash, the British guns were 18-pounders, the Americans 32-pounder carronades. On 17 October 1812, the eighteen-gun sloop *Wasp* captured the British eighteen-gun sloop *Frolic*, but was taken later that day by the British seventy-four-gun ship of the line *Poitiers*.

The American successes in the 1812 frigate clashes caused a furor in Britain, with much public soul-searching about fighting quality. But the minister who fell was Paul Hamilton, the American secretary of the navy, who resigned on 29 December 1812 after being attacked in Congress. He was rumored to be a drunk, while his command of the navy was poor and his instructions often vague. In Britain, on 18 February 1813, George Canning (a former treasurer of the navy and foreign secretary who was later, briefly, to be prime minister in 1827, but was not then in office) told the House of Commons that "the sacred spell of the invincibility of the British Navy was broken."[15] John Croker, the influential secretary to the Admiralty, who had been optimistic that the fleet would rapidly defeat its smaller American rival,[16] felt it necessary to publish the *Letter on the Subject of the Naval War with America* (1813) in defense of the government. In response to a sense of crisis, the Admiralty both built up its Halifax-based squadron and issued an order that it had not felt obliged to issue in the case of conflict with the French. On 10 July 1813, Croker informed Station Commanders in Chief that the Admiralty did

> not conceive that any of His Majesty's frigates should attempt to engage, single handed, the large class of American ships; which though they may be called frigates, are of a size, complement and weight of metal much beyond that class, and more resembling line of battle ships. In the event of one of His Majesty's frigates under your orders falling in with one of these ships, her captain should endeavor, in the first instance, to secure the retreat of His Majesty's ship, but if he finds that he has advantage in sailing, he should endeavor to maneuver, and keep company with her, without coming to action, in the hope of falling in with some other of His Majesty's ships with whose assistance the enemy might be attacked with a reasonable hope of success.[17]

Indeed, after the losses in 1812, the British did not lose a single frigate. Although they were not on the North American or West Indies stations at the outset of the war, the British also had some enormous frigates—known as "razees"—which were seventy-four- or sixty-four-gunners cut down to a single gun deck. More were ordered in response to the threat from the American frigates.

Caution was not only displayed by the British. Paul Hamilton's replacement as secretary of the navy, William Jones, a veteran of the Revolutionary War and an active trader, ordered his captains not to risk battle with larger British ships. With the American fleet heavily outnumbered at sea, Jones felt that conflict could not be afforded as it threatened not only losses but also the need for refitting. This was a strategy based on sustainability rather than conflict on the high seas, but by focusing on British trade, Jones, who understood the mechanics of trade, was able to force the Royal Navy onto the defensive. The dispatch of the brig *Argus* to British waters was also an important demonstration of the American ability to take war home to Britain. At the same time, Jones ordered his captains to destroy their prizes as the latter needed to be manned, and Jones wanted to keep American ships at sea.

On the British side, a sense of the enormity of the task, both convoy protection and taking the war to the Americans, led Admiral Sir John Borlase Warren, the highly experienced commander in chief of the combined North American and West Indian Station, to press, on 5 October and 29 December 1812,[18] for reinforcements. His argument, in January 1813, that these were necessary for defensive purposes captured a feeling that American potential and plans were unclear and therefore worrying

> in consequence of the enemy's privateers becoming daily more numerous, and the assembling of a force of three thousand men at Eastport on the frontiers of New Brunswick and menacing that province with attacks . . . the very many and serious applications made upon me for aid, and protection for the coasts of British America and the West Indies."[19]

Had there been an American invasion of New Brunswick it would, if successful, have threatened Nova Scotia and its crucial naval base at Halifax. But such an invasion was not likely given the problems facing the American war effort in New England. More generally, there was no serious American pressure on British naval strength. Overall economic capability and institutional experience gave the British a considerable advantage at sea. By 1812, the victualing system of the British navy was feeding 145,000 men daily (aside from prisoners), and it was eventually possible to mount a formidable effort in North America.

Yet, most of the British navy was involved in operations against France. These included the best commanders, for example William Hoste, a protégé of Nelson and a master of frigate operations, who held the Adriatic in awe in 1812–14. Napoleon had rebuilt his fleet after its heavy defeat at Trafalgar in 1805, and the British had to devote much effort to blockading French ports and to supporting land operations in Europe, especially in Iberia. There was great concern about the French Mediterranean fleet which was based in Toulon. The British fleet was stretched, and there was particular anxiety about sorties from Toulon in 1811 and 1812; although in 1812 a sortie was turned back. It was not only in the Mediterranean that British naval resources were stretched.[20]

Nevertheless, the capture of French overseas bases in the West Indies and the Indian Ocean in 1809–10 had lessened the ability of the French navy to challenge the British, and thus made it possible to build up British strength in American waters. War in 1806 or 1807 would have been more serious as the network of French bases was still largely intact then. Moreover, funding for the British navy rose, reaching a peak of £20,096,709 in 1813.[21] In addition, in December 1812, the British navy was strengthened when, as a consequence of Napoleon's invasion of France, fifteen Russian ships of the line and seven frigates reached England, improving the equation of naval power with France. It is not easy to answer the question of the percentage of the Royal Navy devoted to the conflict with the Americans because warships could do double service: both blockading the French fleet and chasing down American frigates. Nevertheless, at the same time that the largest British fleet was deployed in the Mediterranean, the percentage of warships committed to North American waters or to increased convoy duty rose from about fifteen in 1812 to thirty to forty in 1813.

American successes in individual clashes did not prevent the implementation of a British blockade of most of the USA, a blockade that gave effect to the Order in Council of 13 October 1812 authorizing "general reprisals" against American ships and goods. The blockade initially applied, from 26 December 1812, to the Chesapeake and Delaware, but it was progressively expanded. The British blockade, moreover, transformed the naval situation by lessening American options whatever American politicians decided in terms of naval investment and deployment. Indeed, Croker wrote to Warren in January 1813:

> As it is of the highest importance to the character and interests of the country that the naval force of the enemy, should be quickly and completely disposed of, my Lords [of the Admiralty] have thought themselves justified at this moment in withdrawing ships from other important services for the purpose of placing under your orders a force with which you cannot fail to bring the naval war to a termination, either by the capture of the American national vessels, or by strictly blockading them in their own waters.[22]

Blockade was seen as the way to deal with American privateering as well as to attack American trade. In March 1813, Warren was ordered to blockade New York City, Charleston, Port Royal, Savannah, and New Orleans. Robert, 2nd Viscount Melville, who had become the first lord of the Admiralty in March 1812, wrote to Warren:

We do not intend this as a mere *paper* blockade, but as a complete stop to all trade and intercourse by sea with those ports, as far as the wind and weather, and the continual presence of a sufficient armed force, will permit and ensure. If you find that this cannot be done without abandoning for a time the interruption which you appear to be giving to the internal navigation of the Chesapeake, the latter object must be given up, and you must be content with blockading its entrance and sending in occasionally your cruisers for the purpose of harassing and annoyance.[23]

Thus, blockade was seen as more important than raiding the Chesapeake, an instructive indication of the importance of economic warfare, and one that is important to bear in mind when considering British operations. The blockade drew together the military, political, and economic dimensions of the war, but studies of the conflict (as of both world wars) tend to devote insufficient attention to the blockade. In some respects, the blockade was the counterpart to the policy of essentially resting on the defensive recommended for Canada in 1812–13; although the blockade had far more capacity to bite. In November 1813, indeed, the blockade was strengthened, with an attempt to stop trade from Long Island Sound southwards. The same month, Warren was recalled. His command was broken into three commands, the North American, Leeward, and Jamaica stations, the way it had been before his appointment. Vice Admiral Sir Alexander Cochrane was appointed to take command of the North American station, which he did in April 1814.

Whoever was in command, blockade was far from easy, and there were serious deficiencies with the British blockade during this war.[24] There were different types of blockade. Close blockade was designed to stop an enemy naval force from emerging; open blockade was intended to catch an enemy naval force as it emerged; and maritime blockade was to stop trade and to have a direct economic impact on the opponent's society, an aspect that can be related to more recent notions of total war. Blockaders, however, could be driven off station by wind and weather, and the exposure of warships to this battering placed a major strain on the fleet. Fog was also a problem as, like darkness, it could cover American shipping and prove a hazard to British warships, not least due to the poorly chartered nature of in-

shore waters. Shoals were also a problem when attacking enemy warships sheltering in coastal waters. Reliance on the wind alone also
made inshore naval operations very chancy. Warren noted, in December 1813, that the blockade of the Chesapeake was not fully effective:

> Several large clipper schooners of from two to three hundred
> tons, strongly manned and armed have run through the block-
> ade in the Chesapeake, in spite of every endeavor and of the
> most vigilant attention of our ships to prevent their getting
> out, nor can any thing stop these vessels escaping to sea in
> dark nights and strong winds.[25]

That month, the *Constitution* was able to evade the blockade off
Boston, while in late 1813 the frigate *President* did so from Newport
and made open sea. The success of the blockade in 1813 was mixed.
No warship sailing from Boston was stopped except the *Chesapeake*
and it sailed to fight the *Shannon* and did not try to avoid her. The
sailings from New York (failure of the *United States, Macedonian,*
and *Hornet*) and Norfolk (failure of the *Constellation*) proved more
difficult. Once at sea, there were several successful cruises in 1813,
including very disruptive ones by the *President* and the *Argus*, but
operations did not lead to the overall effects to the level the government hoped for.

The blockade was still evaded in 1814, with several small warships sailing from various ports early in 1814. *Trewman's Exeter
Flying-Post* of 1 December 1814 reported, "Letters received from the
American coast . . . state that the *Constitution* and *Guerrière* frigates
had been victualed for twelve months, and were waiting for an opportunity to slip out to sea—which it was expected a dark night whilst our
ships were blown from the coast by the gales, would present to them."
The *Constitution* actually sailed from Boston that December and, on
20 February 1815, off Madeira captured the British light frigate *Cyane*
and the corvette *Levant*. There was a cruising order for *Guerrière*, but
she did not sail. In January 1815, however, the eighteen-gun sloops
*Hornet* and *Peacock* were able to evade the British blockade of New
York City en route for the South Atlantic, although the *President* was
battered into surrender, while the frigate *Constellation* failed to
breach the Chesapeake blockade. The frigate *Congress* was ready for
sea, but its crew was sent to Lake Ontario and it did not sail. The
American attempt to operate in squadron strength thus failed. A

squadron might have been powerful enough to overcome a British convoy. Indeed, in November and December 1814, the Admiralty Office sent instructions on how British commanders should react should the Americans send their ships of the line to attack.[26]

There were also serious limitations in the surveillance, and command and control, capabilities of British naval power. These made it very difficult to "see" or control in any operational sense, and certainly limited the value of any blockade. It was generally possible for a lookout to see only about fifteen miles from the top of the main mast in fine weather. However, fleets used a series of frigates stationed just over the horizon, and they signalled using their sails, which were much bigger than flags and, because the masts were so tall, could be seen at some distance over the horizon. This was an example of how the operational and tactical constraints on naval power were tested by skill and improvements. Given a tendency to dismiss the British as rigid, a tendency to which their tactics and defeat at New Orleans (see Chapter 5) contributes, it is important to note a willingness to push limits and to improvise. For example, the 1814 Chesapeake campaign showed that the British could operate successfully in shallow waters, as did the victory over American gunboats on Lake Borgne near New Orleans on 14 December 1814.

British gunnery, moreover, improved during the war as, more generally, did their naval effectiveness, both in Atlantic waters and on the Great Lakes. This improvement can be seen in the fate of American warships and commanders. Stephen Decatur, already a hero for seizing and burning the captured *Philadelphia* in Tripoli harbor in 1804, captured the frigate *Macedonian* in October 1812 off the Azores when he was in command of the *United States*. Yet, in January 1815, he surrendered the *President* when he tried to run the British blockade of New York, and this failure compromised his reputation. The forty-four-gun frigate slipped out of New York on the night of 14 January 1815, but sustained severe damage when her pilot ran her aground on the Sandy Hook. Chased by blockaders the next day, the *President*, although slowed as a result of the damage she had suffered, shot the sails from the yards of the forty-two-gun frigate *Endymion*. When *Pomone* (thirty-eight guns) and *Tenedos* later caught up with Decatur, *Pomone* was able to launch two broadsides, which Decatur did not return. He then surrendered. The two British ships were mostly armed with 18-pounders, whereas the *President* had more powerful guns. In Theodore Roosevelt's estimation, Decatur "acted rather tamely, certainly not heroically" in not fighting it out: "At least it was well worth trying."[27]

Larger British naval forces were also effective against individual ships further afield. In the frigate *Essex*, David Porter had success-fully attacked British commerce in the South Atlantic and the South Pacific, capturing twelve whalers and their valuable cargo off the Galapagos Islands in 1813, and claiming the island of Nuku Hiva in the Marquesas Islands in the Eastern Pacific for the USA. (The annex-ation of what Essex named Madison's Island was never acknowledged by the American government and the islands became a French colony in 1842. They are still part of French Polynesia.) The voyage of the *Essex* was part of a major extension in American trade warfare, but Porter was forced to surrender by two British warships off Valparaiso in Chile in February 1814 after they cannonaded his disabled ship from a distance. Although the British suffered far more casualties when they attacked the privateer *General Armstrong* in the Azores in September 1814, the Americans eventually scuttled and burned the ship.

In addition, the British were successful in conflicts between indi-vidual ships. On 1 June 1813, in an encounter between single ships, the *Shannon* beat the American *Chesapeake* off Boston in a clash fought at close range in which a lack of preparedness on the part of the American commander was a key element.[28] The British won this clash because of very good gunnery and the fact that the bosun of the *Chesapeake* had omitted to secure the foretopsail, so that when one single piece of rigging was hit the foretopsail came down and the ship luffed up and was easily raked by the *Shannon*. This instance of the role chance played in combat can be interpreted as either incompe-tence or over-confidence: exactly what the British were suffering from at the start of the war. Now the Americans had caught the bug from too many and too easy successes.

On 14 August 1813, the *Argus* was captured off Wales by the similarly gunned *Pelican* after the British gunners proved superior.[29] By 1814, indeed, there were very few American warships able to oper-ate for any length of time. Most American warships sailed between December 1813 and April 1814 including two frigates and a number of smaller vessels, some on two cruises, but loss rates for the small vessels were very high. Moreover, the *Decatur*, the largest privateer to sail from Charleston, which had boarded and seized the British sloop *Dominica* in August 1813, was captured by the British frigate *Le Rhin* in 1814. Yet as a reminder of continued American capability, on 20 February 1815, off Madeira, the *Constitution* outmaneuvered and captured the outgunned frigate *Cyane* and the sloop *Levant*: the *Constitution*'s thirty-two long 24-pounders proved a key advantage. A subsequent attempt by British frigates to catch the *Constitution* failed, and she was able to return to New York. On 26 February 1815, the Baltimore privateer *Chausseur* captured the outgunned *St. Lawrence* in the West Indies.[30]

Newspapers frequently reported desperate struggles on the high seas. Thus, Plymouth and Falmouth items in *Trewman's Exeter Flying-Post* of 14 July 1814 detailed clashes with American ships. The former noted the capture of the British brig *Reindeer* by the well-designed American naval sloop *Wasp*: "The *Reindeer* immediately laid the enemy alongside, and in the most gallant style attempted to carry her opponent by boarding; but after a most desperate and sanguinary battle, which lasted about half an hour, she was overpowered by superior numbers, and obliged to strike." Both warships were eighteen-gunners, but the *Wasp* displaced nearly twice the *Reindeer* and should have been a twenty-two-gun ship. On 1 September 1814, the *Wasp* sank the *Avon*, another eighteen-gun brig, but the *Wasp* was lost at sea with all hands the following month.[31] As an unwilling testimony to British success, over five thousand American prisoners from the naval war were sent to Dartmoor Prison on the bleak granite moorland of Devon, joining the numerous French prisoners already there. The food was reasonable, but the prison, though new, was damp and cold.

By late 1814, the USA was facing severe economic problems, limiting the ability to deploy ships. When warships went to sea, it also seemed that the British were more effective at engaging them. A small force of two frigates and two sloops that went to sea that winter could distract attention from the extent to which the remainder of the navy remained blockaded, some to the point that they were not even manned and considered for active operations.

Overall, American privateers and small warships had only a limited impact on the British merchant marine. Whereas American trade fell greatly (exports falling from $45 million in 1811 to $7 million in 1814), British trade was higher in 1814 than in 1811, ensuring that the costs of the alliance against Napoleon could be underwritten,[32] which was a fundamental bar to American success. Nevertheless, across the world, it was necessary for British traders to face the risk of attack from American privateers, most successfully the fourteen-gun *Yankee* from Bristol, Rhode Island, which took forty prizes. The risk of attack affected the practice and profitability of British trade.[33] Privateers rather than American warships captured most merchantmen. According to Lloyd's, the British lost 1,175 merchantmen of which only 373 were recaptured, and insurance rates rose in some particular trades; although overall marine insurance rates were no higher and the British were able to take counter-measures, including increasing both convoy escorts and the number of warships on the North American coast.[34] In reality it is difficult to determine down to the exact number how many ships were taken due to lapses in accounting, the burning of captures, as well as the war with France which was going on during much of this time. Yet, the losses showed that even a modest American fleet had been "able to enforce high protection costs on Britain."[35]

If, by strengthening their blockade, the British lessened the inroads of American privateers and warships that captured over 150 merchantmen in the first four months of the war, nevertheless the Americans thought it worthwhile pushing ahead with naval construction. This decision reflected both a political and public conviction, drawing on the euphoria arising from victories, that naval power was worthwhile and a more specific awareness that it had indeed brought advantages.

The consequences, however, are not always easy to assess. In 1812 and 1813, Wellington complained that the Royal Navy was unable to stop American privateers from attacking the supply route from Britain to his forces in Portugal. In practice, these complaints were overblown. First, the British already had to cope with French privateers, operating from nearby bases in western France and northern Spain that challenged the supply routes. Second, the Royal Navy escorted convoys and the Americans lacked the strength to challenge these convoys.

Ironically, the supply of American grain to Wellington's army was a crucial feature in America's prewar trade, and remained important for part of the war. As a result, it was thought that British permission to export grain could be a key element in affecting American attitudes. Licensed trade was permitted to American ships under an

Order in Council of April 1812, with many licences being given to enable the movement of grain to Iberia. The issue of new licences was, however, stopped on 14 November, although existing ones were honored until they ran out. Moreover, the American Licence Act of July 1813 blocked the use of British licences for American trade.[36] By 1813, the British were turning to the Barbary States of North Africa for supplies for the peninsula, so that they should not have to purchase from the USA. The British harvest was also better after the poor 1812 one, making possible supplies from Ireland to the peninsula. Issues focused on the supply of grain are yet another reminder of the need to approach the War of 1812 in terms of its multiple international contexts.

Aside from the struggle on the oceans, the Americans had also shown an important ability to develop naval capability on the Great Lakes, which provided an important attack component as well as a major cover for the defense. There had already been clashes between the British and French in the Seven Years' War, but there was no institutional continuity. On 6 February 1813, Madison instructed Dearborn on the need to out-build the British on the Great Lakes: "If they build two ships, we should build four. If they build thirty or 40 gun ships, we should build them of 50 or 60 guns. The command of those waters is the hinge on which the war will essentially turn according to the probable course of it."[37]

In 1812, Isaac Chauncey, commandant of the navy yard at New York, built up a force that established a powerful presence on Lake Ontario, while in 1813 Oliver Perry built nine ships, reversing the situation on Lake Erie. In 1814, however, the British recovered their position above the Detroit River on Lake Huron, using small boats.[38] Albeit with serious delays they were also able to construct HMS *St. Lawrence*, a 102-gun three-decker ship at Kingston on Lake Ontario,[39] while the Americans worked on a ship of the line, the *New Orleans*, at Sacket's Harbor. In practice, there would have been major problems with manning such ships, although, finally launched on 10 September 1814 and ready to sail by mid-October, the *St. Lawrence* sailed out three times with the Lake Ontario squadron that autumn. It was intended to follow this with two more ships each mounting more than one hundred guns The naval forces deployed on the Great Lakes rose greatly, from twelve American and six British ships in 1812 to thirty-four and seventeen in 1813, and thirty and twenty-eight in 1814. The number of cannon increased from 84 American and 78 British in 1812, to 221 and 144 in 1813, and 347 and 417 in 1814.

The benefit gained from these ships has to be set, however, against the formidable logistical challenge posed by the requirements of building up these forces. Some ships were carried overland and rebuilt at the lakes, and the British had to move equipment from Québec and Halifax in order to fit out the frigates they built on Lake Ontario.[40] Nevertheless, despite such difficulties, logistical requirements limited the prospects for land operations at the same time that success on the Great Lakes made them a more likely prospect. Aside from gaining amphibious capability and logistical flexibility, winning such success forced opponents to rely on the slower prospect of movement by land. Indeed, Wellington, who had, from his command in the Peninsular War, experience of combined operations and the benefits of command of the sea, advised Liverpool in November 1814 that, without dominating the lakes, "it is impossible . . . to keep the enemy out of the whole frontier (with Canada), much less to make conquest."[41] He added, the following month, "I have told the Ministers repeatedly that a naval superiority on the lakes is a *sine qua non* of success in war on the frontier of Canada, even if our object should be solely defensive."[42]

British superiority on the Great Lakes provided a key opportunity for successful action in the first campaign of the war, not least for responding to William Hull's advance at the west of Lake Erie. This British success led Henry Clay, in December 1812, to claim that American neglect of the command of the lakes had been responsible for much that had gone wrong.[43] He was far from alone in this view, and it was suggested that earlier preparation would have provided the necessary shipping,[44] although it would still have been necessary to support such a fleet with sailors, cannon, and matériel, as well as to ensure safe anchorages.

Alfred Thayer Mahan, president of the Naval War College from 1886 to 1889 and in 1892–93, and the most influential American writer on naval warfare, was a key advocate of American deep-sea naval power later in the century. In his book *Sea Power in its Relations to the War of 1812*, he also wrote that "the victories on Lake Erie and Lake Champlain[45] do illustrate, in a distinguished manner, his principal thesis, the controlling influence upon events of naval power, even when trans-

ferred to an inland body of fresh water."⁴⁶ At the same time, such
superiority, while important around the lakes, did not provide much of
an advantage farther afield. More generally, the American 1813 campaign around the lakes also indicated the problems of sustaining and
exploiting advantages. Nevertheless, during the war American gunboats gave a good account of themselves in several naval actions, especially on Lakes Erie and Champlain. They also resisted British warships
in the Chesapeake.⁴⁷ The Americans encountered problems, however,
in raising sufficient sailors. In 1814, it proved impossible to raise the
sailors necessary for the campaign on the Great Lakes, and, instead, as
in 1813, they had to be taken from the blue-water (oceanic) fleet. That
fleet itself had lost sailors in 1812 because British sailors left American
service: they would have risked being treated as traitors had they been
captured. More generally, in April 1814, Chauncey was very disappointed at the unprepared state of the Lake Ontario squadron.⁴⁸

The situation on the Great Lakes lacked the strategic significance
of deep-sea naval capability. As the Americans could not match the
British, or even mount a sustained challenge, this gave the British
major advantages in the Atlantic. Blockade greatly harmed the American economy,⁴⁹ and it became more effective from 1813, restricting
American raids as well as trade. Thus, from the spring of 1813, the
blockade was tight across the Chesapeake, hindering both trade and
privateering. The American navy was not in a position to break the
blockade. Moreover, when the British navy moved into the Chesapeake in force in 1814, the blockade there was transformed, with
American ships trapped in harbors, such as Baltimore and Norfolk, or
tributaries: Barney's flotilla was stuck in the Patuxent.

British privateering also made major inroads on American trade,
as well as bringing prosperity to the British possessions of Nova
Scotia, New Brunswick, and Bermuda, where privateers were based.
These privateers faced fewer obstacles from American warships than
their counterparts did from the British fleet, and this was a measure of
the success of the British navy and its blockade.⁵⁰ It was also possible
for Britain to send reinforcements to Canada and, although this required convoy protection, the Royal Navy could provide it.⁵¹ Had it
been necessary, the navy could have provided direct assistance to
Québec (while the St. Lawrence was free from ice) or Halifax, had
they been attacked. If the Americans could not capture these positions, Canada could not be taken.

British amphibious capability was also of concern to the Americans, and became more so as the war continued. In September 1812, William Duane, the editor of the *Aurora*, the Jeffersonian Philadelphia newspaper, informed Madison about his concern that the British would land a force between New York City and New Hampshire or destroy the former by bombardment.[52] Indeed, the defense problems of New England were linked to opposition there to the war.[53] A bitter critic of British impressments, Duane himself was an armchair general who was made an adjutant general after the war started.

Raids on the American coast were launched from the start of the war, the damage they inflicted in part testifying to a willingness to make civilians suffer.[54] British commanders, however, took measures to limit this suffering, as in 1814 when Stonington, Connecticut, was attacked.[55] The Americans had no control over whether raids could escalate into large-scale amphibious attacks, and they were vulnerable to the latter. In 1812, as an aspect of the failure of the gunboat ideology associated with Jefferson, America's ports lacked adequately integrated defenses, and there was also a widespread absence of planning for such attacks.[56] American concern about amphibious attacks led, in July 1813, to the creation of a Corps of Sea Fencibles for the "defense of ports and harbors of the United States." They were to play a role in the defense of Fort McHenry against the British in 1814.

In June 1813, Admiral Warren first attacked Craney Island and Hampton, Virginia. The following month, Rear Admiral George Cockburn was sent to destroy American shipping at Ocracoke Island, North Carolina. A night attack was attempted, but Cockburn's report indicated the difficulties of such operations:

> The whole moved from the ships towards the shore about 2 o'clock this morning, but owing to the great distance from the Bar to the Harbor, and the heavy swell which was running, it was considerably after daylight before the advanced division turned a projecting shoal point, behind which the vessels lay . . . the enemy therefore had some little time to prepare for defense, which he did not fail to avail himself of, and immediately the boats doubled this point a heavy fire was opened on them from a brig [*Anaconda*] and a schooner [*Atlas*] . . . Lieutenant Westphal therefore with his Division

pulled [rowed] directly and resolutely for these, under cover of some rockets which were thrown by Captain Russell with admirable precision."

As the British approached, the Americans surrendered. Lighter American vessels successfully fled as the pursuing British were thwarted by frequently grounding on the shoals. The British then landed and purchased food.[57] They had less success raiding on the eastern shore of the Chesapeake, as at Caulk's Field on 30 August 1814, when an attack by a large shore party (124 men) on a prepared force of Maryland militia led to its repulse and the mortal wounding of the British commander, Sir Peter Parker, and the death of thirteen others.

British amphibious capability, however, was retained to the end. On 11 February 1815, Vice Admiral Sir Alexander Cochrane and Major General John Lambert captured Fort Bowyer, which protected Mobile.[58] When hostilities ceased, the capture of first Savannah and then Charleston was planned. Both were already blockaded, which was seen as a way to benefit from Cockburn's operations in the region. Landing on Cumberland Island, Georgia, in early January, he used it as a base to mount raids on the Georgia coast, capturing St. Mary's and Brunswick, and seizing supplies and recruiting runaway slaves, before menacing Savannah.[59] Indeed, a report from HMS *Ceylon* off Georgia indicated that Cockburn was threatening to attack New York City.[60]

In contrast, the American idea of a small squadron cruising off Nova Scotia and the St. Lawrence to intercept British supply ships was not realized, and in large part due to the British blockade of American ports. Alongside the key factor of the unpopularity of the war in New England, naval weakness also ensured that the Americans could not repeat the policy, seen in earlier wars with France, of mounting amphibious attacks on Maritime Canada. In 1690, Port Royal (now Annapolis Royal) in Acadia (Nova Scotia) had been captured by an expedition from Massachusetts, although an attempt from there later that year against Québec had failed. In 1707, in the next Anglo-French war, Port Royal successfully resisted a New England attack, although, in 1709, it fell to four thousand British marines joined with fifteen hundred militia. In 1711, an attack on Québec mounted by British regulars and New England militia failed, but in 1745, Louisbourg on Cape Breton Island fell to three thousand Massachusetts volunteers supported by British warships; and in 1755, 2,000 American volunteers joined 250 British regulars in capturing Fort Beauséjour.

There was no equivalent to such expeditions in the War of 1812, as there was no naval protection available—which meant, for example, that there was no interruption to the export of Canadian timber to Britain. Nor did the British need to deploy large numbers of troops to reply to or block such attacks. Had it been necessary, this deployment would have made it very difficult to respond adequately to American attacks in the interior. This lack of American capability for a naval dimension to the attack on Canada was an instance of the wider strategic and operational weakness of the Americans.

Amphibious capability was seen at the opposite end of the continent, but again it was enjoyed by the British. It was not much use for the Americans, after the Lewis and Clark expedition of 1804–1806, to boast of their ability to cross North America, or to see this as a basis for American claims for ownership of the far Northwest[61] if, once they arrived, or sailed there, they were vulnerable to British naval power. On 30 November 1813, Fort Astoria, the base on the south bank of the Columbia River established in 1811 by the *Tonquin*, a ship belonging to John Jacob Astor's Pacific Fur Company, was successfully captured by HMS *Racoon* and renamed Fort George. The fort had, in fact, already been sold on 7 October to the Canadian-based North West Company. John McTavish, a company trader, had explained to the Astorians that a British frigate was en route and had successfully suggested such a purchase, but its captain, William Black, insisted on going through the motions of seizing the position. Moreover, other Pacific Fur Company bases were taken by the British, including Forts Okanagan and Spokane in 1813.[62]

Aside from on the Great Lakes, the Americans were unable to alter the arithmetic or parameters of naval power. In addition to significant construction of frigates and sloops, they built ships of the line during the war: at its close they had three, but none was ready for operations, although one was nearly so. The *Independence,* a seventy-four-gun ship, was launched at Charlestown, Massachusetts, in June 1814, while, four months later, the *Washington*, another seventy-four-gunner, was completed at Portsmouth, New Hampshire. Construction of the latter had begun in the spring of 1813, which showed how long it took to build up naval strength. This lack of readiness for operations was just as well in light of British numerical superiority, as the British would probably have sunk the ships. Indeed, this prospect led to a refusal to allow the frigate *Constitution* to sail. Instead, it was kept at Norfolk serving as part of the port's defenses.

As an augury of the future, the American Robert Fulton, who had already successfully experimented with underwater warfare (especially mines), tried to make major advances during the War of 1812, not least with submarines, spar torpedoes, underwater guns, and steam vessels such as the proposed *Fulton I*. Moreover, Elijah Mix experimented with torpedoes, and although, due to a premature detonation, he failed to sink HMS *Plantagenet* in July 1813, a British schooner had the previous month fallen victim to a torpedo, "a diabolical and cowardly contrivance," according to Admiral Warren. What became known as the Torpedo Act, passed by Congress in March 1813, encouraged such action by promising any citizen who destroyed a British warship half its value.[63]

Fulton was successful with steam vessels, but only after peace was signed. His *Demologus*, a steam-powered floating battery for New York Harbor, was completed too late for war service. It was renamed *Fulton* after his death on 24 February 1815. His work on torpedoes had been criticized as inhumane by the Federalists and the British press. Even had Fulton been more successful, there were serious limits to what the Americans could have achieved with their economic capability. Fulton had argued in 1806 that "it does not require much depth of thought to trace that science, by discovering gunpowder, changed the whole art of war by land and sea; and by future combination may sweep military marines from the ocean."[64] The last was a fundamental threat to the British navy. As yet, however, this was not an option. No more steamships were launched for the American navy until 1837. Four years later, however, two paddlewheel cruisers were launched that were then the largest steam warships in the world.

The War of 1812 was not a success for America as a naval power, but it was a triumph for its naval reputation, and still plays a major part in modern concepts of America as a global naval power. The USS *Constitution*, now preserved as a museum ship, is a national institution. The ability to win naval duels in 1812 created a lasting impression and helped make the navy more popular than the army, challenging earlier

British assumptions of inherent superiority.[65] The American navy had also been more successful in this light than in the War of Independence. In 1816, Congress agreed to finance a plan for nine new ships of the line and nine large frigates: four and two respectively had been launched by 1826.

On the other hand, emphasising this popularity detracts from the realist perspective that, on the high seas, American power after 1815 remained dependent on British acceptance. Britain had had 152 ships of the line and 183 frigates in 1810. The loss of several frigates and more smaller vessels was humiliating. Indeed, while the American captains, in order to get more prize money, did not concede that they were engaging weaker British warships, the British responded to their humiliation by exaggerating the strength of the American warships and underplaying those of the British ships. For example, William James, in his *A Full and Correct Account of the Chief Naval Occurrences of the Late War between Great Britain and the United States of America* (1817), stated that the American frigates were built on the same scantlings, i.e., frame size, started as ships-of-the-line and that many of the crew were British. The American ships were certainly exceptionally well armed and very large by traditional frigate standards, but they were not ships of the line. In *The Naval War of 1812* (1882), Theodore Roosevelt was to write what was deliberately presented as a reply to James's partisan account.

The loss of the British frigates, however, was no real qualification of British maritime power. The British ultimately drove most of the American "super frigates" into port, blockade largely achieving what ship-to-ship duels could not. At the end of the war, the *President* had recently been captured, snared in the blockade off New York. The *United States* was blockaded in New London, and the *Constitution* was at sea. Although their operational tempo decreased after 1812, the "super frigates" thus remained a factor not least in ensuring that the Royal Navy had to fear meeting ships that were more powerful than the privateers, but the American warships could not set the tempo of naval operations. The War of 1812 was no triumph for Britain's naval reputation, but it underlined the extent of Britain's naval power and indicated what this offered in terms of blockade and amphibious capability.

# 5

# THE EMPIRE STRIKES BACK, 1814–15

"I saw the flag of my country waving over a city—the strength and pride of my native state—a city devoted to plunder and desolution by its assailants. I witnessed the preparation for its assaults, and I saw the array of its enemies as they advanced to the attack. I heard the sound of battle; the noise of the conflict fell upon my listening ear, and told me that 'the brave and the free' had met the invaders."

Francis Scott Key recounting his observation of the bombardment of Fort McHenry, 1814

"Echo from the cannonade and musketry was so tremendous in the forests, that the vibration seemed as if the earth was cracking and tumbling to pieces. . . . And the flashes of fire looked as if coming out of the bowels of the Earth, so little above its surface were the batteries of the Americans."

Captain John Cooke on battle of New Orleans, 1815[1]

Napoleon's defeat in early 1814, and his unconditional abdication on 11 April 1814,[2] enabled the British to send more warships and naval personnel and far more troops to North America than in 1812 or 1813. Unexpectedly, Napoleon was to return on 1 March 1815 from exile on the Mediterranean island of Elba and to regain power, but he was defeated anew at Waterloo on 18 June and obliged to abdicate a second time on 22 June. This account, however, is a bland summary that throws no light on the range of possible develop-

ments in Europe. This was a range, moreover, that was very important from the perspective of the War of 1812 and of Anglo-American
relations. The key element was Napoleon's failure in 1813–14 to respond to the possibilities for peace, let alone to shape negotiations. If
his ability to do the latter was very limited, Charles Maurice Talleyrand, the foreign minister, was subsequently to do better for France at
the Congress of Vienna, despite having a weak hand. In early 1814,
the Allies invaded France, with Austrian and Prussian forces playing
the key role in eastern France. Initially successful—so that Napoleon
discovered a willingness to negotiate, abandoning his earlier demands for a Rhine frontier and to retain much of Italy—the Allies
were checked in mid-February as Napoleon maneuvered with skill in
order to destroy the most exposed Austro-Prussian units. The Prussians were defeated at Brienne on 29 January and a Russian force at
Champaubert on 10 February. Instead of taking the opportunity to
negotiate peace, Napoleon then returned to his unrealistic demands
of the start of the year. These, however, were unacceptable, not only
to Britain, Prussia, and Russia, but also to Austria, the power most
willing to negotiate and to leave Napoleon in power.

The Allies' sincerity is unclear, but it was Napoleon's attitude to
diplomacy that ruined the chance to use the negotiations at Châtillon
in February to bring peace. After this, the Allies, on 1 March, agreed at
Chaumont not to conclude any separate agreement with Napoleon
and, instead, both to continue the war and then to join in maintaining
the peace; the agreement was announced on 9 March. On 15 March
1814, Napoleon's counter-proposal to the Châtillon offer was presented. This counter-proposal would have left France with her colonies, the left bank of the Rhine, and much of Italy, but such unrealistic
responses ensured a determination to remove Napoleon. Austria
therefore rallied to its allies.

After defeating a French force at La-Fère-Champenoise on 25
March, the Austrians and Prussians marched on Paris, ignoring Napoleon's position on their flank. As the Allies advanced, the control of
the outnumbered Napoleon over both regime and army crumbled. Its
defenders were driven back in the Paris suburbs on 30 March, and
negotiations began the next day. A provisional French government
deposed Napoleon and, with his marshals unwilling to fight on, Napoleon abdicated. This was a step that worried Jefferson, who readily
understood its implications for the USA. An armistice was signed on

23 April and Louis XVIII, the Bourbon claimant to the French throne, who had for many years taken shelter in Britain, returned to France the following day, entering Paris on 3 May. Americans were hopeful that what they saw as the traditional antipathy between France and Britain would re-emerge, but they appreciated that this would take a while, not least as Louis XVIII had been influenced by his years in Britain.[3]

The fall of Napoleon ended the logic of the war in terms of Britain's trading position, as it was no longer necessary for Britain to stop neutral trade with France, nor to press American sailors in order to man British warships—which, indeed, were no longer required to blockade French ports. Yet, although both logic and need for the war were less, it was now possible to focus military efforts on the USA. About six thousand British troops had been sent to North America in 1813, but more had been dispatched to Spain. In 1814, without the need to send troops to Spain, more could be shipped to North America. They included some of the veterans of the Duke of Wellington's campaigns against the French in Portugal and Spain, some embarking directly for the Chesapeake from the Gironde estuary in southwest France to which they had advanced after clearing Spain. Peter Bowlby of the 4th Regiment of Foot marched from Bayonne, which he had been besieging, to Bordeaux, and embarked at Pauliac for Bermuda and the Chesapeake. On 14 April 1814, Colonel Henry Torrens, the military secretary of Frederick, Duke of York, the commander in chief of the army, wrote, "The government have [sic] determined to give Jonathan [the nickname for Americans] a good drubbing, and orders have been sent to Lord Wellington to prepare a corps of 12,000 infantry and a small detachment of cavalry to be sent to America."[4] In the event, 16,300 troops were sent.[5] Many of this force were not, however, as is sometimes claimed, peninsular veterans.

These reinforcements led to a far more wide-ranging British campaign in 1814. It included operations in the Chesapeake, as well as a focus on the conquest of American territory, especially in the Lake Champlain corridor and in Maine. There was a common goal in terms of securing Canada for Britain. The Chesapeake campaign was a diversion intended to reduce pressure on Canada, both by diverting American forces and by making the Americans aware of the dangers of fighting on. Furthermore, American territory was to be conquered in order to improve Britain's negotiating position in the eventual

peace talks. Thus, Canada was the strategic focus.[6] Its protection was
necessary strategically, but also politically. Talk of ceding Gibraltar
to Spain as part of the peace settlement at the close of the War of
Independence had led to criticism in Parliament in December 1782.
This indicated that, whatever might be agreed in a treaty, winning
parliamentary approval for the cession of territory was problematic.[7]
Moreover, the protection of Canada was a sensitive issue.

The British were hopeful that news of their success in Europe
would affect American opinion. In its issue of 23 June 1814, *Trewman's Exeter Flying-Post* noted:

> By another arrival from America we are informed that intel-
> ligence has arrived of the Allies having entered Paris. . . . The
> effect of this intelligence upon the American government
> may well be conceived. It had sunk their spirits, lowered their
> tone and produced infinite confusion and dismay. Nor was
> this dismay diminished by the arrival of another document,
> viz. the Proclamation of our Admiral, declaring the whole
> coast of America in a state of blockade.

A fortnight later, the paper carried a London report of 2 July,
noting the news there that an armistice had been signed in North
America, news that was in fact inaccurate. Albert Gallatin, formerly
secretary of the Treasury and, in 1814, an American peace commissioner, wrote that April:

> A well organized and large [British] army is at once liberated
> from any European employment, and ready, together with a
> superabundant naval force, to act immediately against us.
> How ill-prepared we are to meet it in a proper manner . . .
> above all our own divisions and the hostile attitude of the
> Eastern States give room to apprehend that a continuance of
> the war might prove fatal to the United States."[8]

At first in 1814, however, the Americans took the initiative. They
benefited from improvements in organization and performance that
reflected experience of the first two years of the war, as well as from
promoting younger commanders in place of discredited senior figures.[9]
Both were aspects of the learning curve. Not needing, as the British did,
to send units from Europe, with the delay and unpredictability this
entailed, the Americans were encouraged by the availability of their

strike forces near the zone of operations, and by a correct sense that they had to act more resolutely in order to make gains. Military needs and political requirements combined to this end.

Far to the west of the main sphere of conflict, this combination was indicated by the expansionism of William Clark, superintendent of Indian affairs for the Louisiana Territory from 1807 and the governor of the Missouri Territory from 1813. He had pressed the establishment of blockhouses and the construction of gunboats in the Mississippi and Missouri valleys, although Fort Madison, built in 1809 at the confluence of the Mississippi and the Des Moines Rivers, had to be evacuated in November 1813 because Clark deemed it indefensible. In May 1814, Clark led an expedition from St. Louis to capture the undefended British trading base at Prairie du Chien at the confluence of the Wisconsin and Mississippi Rivers (now in Wisconsin).[10]

Fort Shelby was hastily constructed there, but a 650-strong British-Native American force under Captain William McKay from Fort Mackinac recaptured the position having travelled across Lake Michigan. Fort Shelby with its garrison of sixty-five men was supported by *Governor Clark*, an American gunboat but, under the fire of the attackers' sole cannon, the crew proved irresolute. As the British prepared their attack, the fort soon after surrendered on 20 July. Moreover, an American force seeking to relieve the fort was successfully blocked by a larger Native American force at the Rock Island Rapids (between modern Davenport, Iowa, and Rock Island, Illinois), while another force under Major Zachary Taylor was surprised and defeated by a larger Native American-British force at the Rock River Rapids, and then retreated down the Mississippi to the Des Moines River where Taylor erected Fort Johnson (in modern Iowa). This, however, was a weak position from which he retreated further in October to protect St. Louis.

Farther north, on 23 July, an American raid on Mackinac Island destroyed the base of the North West Company. This was done in order to hit the fur trade and thus the Native Americans linked to the British. The company's schooner *Perseverance* was also captured.[11] On 4 August, however, the continued effectiveness of Anglo-Native American cooperation was shown at Fort Mackinac on Mackinac Island when its British commander, Colonel Robert McDouall, deployed 350 Native Americans on the wooded flanks of his position. The seven hundred-strong Americans under George Croghan, the commander of the expedition sent to capture the position, tried to out-flank McDouall by advancing through the trees, only for one column to be ambushed by the Native Americans (the other column was lost) after which the Americans retreated.[12]

As an instance of the respective numbers involved and of the great importance of the Native Americans in the Northwest, McDouall had only 140 British troops. He and most of his men had undertaken a lengthy journey from Kingston the previous February–May, travelling via Lake Simcoe and the Nottawasaga River route. Winter conditions had affected the options for both sides, but an American attack as soon as the ice had melted would have found the British less well prepared. The contrast between American failure and Croghan's success at Fort Stephenson the previous year, when attacked by Procter (see Chapter 3), indicated the greater command difficulties of offensive warfare. These difficulties were a problem that affected both sides during the war. In this operation, Croghan lacked skill and he totally failed to direct the tempo of the operation and battle.

Having failed against Fort Mackinac, the Americans sought to destroy the *Nancy*, the only British warship on the upper lakes. Its capture or destruction would have broken the communication route between Fort Mackinac and the Nottawasaga River and thus to Kingston. On 13 August, three American warships arrived off the mouth of the river and, the following day, they destroyed both the British blockhouse and the *Nancy*. They then used felled trees to block the river mouth. However, travelling in bateaux and a canoe, the *Nancy*'s commander, Miller Worsley, and his crew, escaped and reached Fort Mackinac.

From there, with the support of troops, four small boats under Worsley set off on 1 September to attack the American warships, two of which were in Georgian Bay. During the night on 3 September, the *Tigress* was taken in a surprise attack. In order to surprise the *Scorpion*, the American flag was left flying and the red jackets of the British troops were covered. At dawn on 6 September, fire was opened on the unsuspecting *Scorpion* from a distance of only twelve yards, and the boat was stormed and captured. This left the British in control of Lake Huron, and the supply lines to Fort Mackinac and beyond, until the end of the war.[13] It is an instructive comparison of the role of public myth in the coverage of the war that had the fortitude and boldness shown by Worsley and his men been displayed by Americans it would have attracted far more attention. Instead, although the episode is covered in most Canadian accounts of the war, it is largely ignored in their American counterparts. Coming late in the war is not the issue, as that is also true of prominent episodes in the conflict, most obviously the defense of Fort McHenry and the Battle of New Orleans.

Earlier in 1814, the first engagement in what the Americans saw as the key front, the Champlain corridor, occurred in March. At winter quarters at French Mills, the American army had suffered greatly from insufficient food and inadequate accommodation, but it was along the Champlain corridor that the Americans intended to advance toward Montréal. As a prelude, in response to the fortifying by the British of a position at La Colle Mill, Major General James Wilkinson, in his last command of the war and his career, led four thousand troops across the Canadian border on 30 March. The British had a strong defensive position at the mill for their twenty-five hundred troops, which the Americans approached that afternoon. American bombardment had little impact, not least because the mill had strong stone walls, although the Americans in turn blocked British advances across La Colle Creek toward the American battery. As so often in the battles during this war, the importance of features on which batteries could be sited was significant, both for the deployment of forces and for the flow of the fighting. Having suffered 254 casualties to the British 61, Wilkinson withdrew. He had not proved up to the task. Bad weather had not helped, but he can also be faulted both for inadequate preparation and for failing to shape the flow of the battle.

Although regulars were crucial to the British defense of Canada, the British were also helped by Canadian resolve. "An Appeal to the British Public," issued in July 1814, declared:

The defenseless situation of the province of Upper Canada on the sudden and totally unexpected declaration of war against Great Britain by the United States of America, instead of dispiriting its brave inhabitants animated them with the most determined courage. Consisting chiefly of Loyalists driven from their native homes during the American rebellion, they beheld with indignation their old enemy envying them, their new habitations won from the wilderness, and again thirsting

for their blood . . . they volunteered their services with ac-
clamation. . . . Theirs was not the enthusiasm of the moment,
it still burns with unabated vigor . . . enables a raw militia to
suffer with patience the greatest privations [and] to face death
with astonishing intrepidity . . . united with the small body of
regulars . . . they have been enabled to take or destroy every
enemy that has had the temerity to pass the borders.

This determination extended to the French Canadians, many of
whom fought, and fought well, in the *Voltigeurs Canadiens*, helping
to secure Lower Canada, in which they were the majority population,
against American invasion. Most of the officers in the *Voltigeurs*
were farmers; although, alongside the French Canadians, many of the
officers were English-speakers.[14] The Americans were seen as a challenge to French Canadian culture, which was perceived as protected
by British rule, a perception that was a major success for the incorporating nature of the British Empire. The Catholic clergy worried
about the Protestant zeal of the Americans, the peasantry and seig-
neurial landowners about the American eagerness for land, and the
urban middling order was anxious about a challenge to their position.
This support for British rule was far more apparent than in 1775–76,
and was a key aspect of the political context of the conflict. Prevost's
political policies helped significantly to win French Canadian support for the war effort. In addition, recent immigrants from the
United States into Upper Canada failed to rise against the British, as
the Americans had hoped.

Nevertheless, support for Britain was more limited and condi-
tional than was to be suggested in retrospect. In Upper Canada, there
was also considerable reluctance to fight for Britain, especially among
the later Loyalist settlements.[15] Moreover, the strain of the war, especially its destructiveness, proved a great burden. Support for Britain
did not greatly increase until the 1830s.[16] These political factors affected the extent of Canadian military support, although its quality,
especially that of the Canadian regulars, was high.

## THE NIAGARA FRONT

The Americans did not coordinate Wilkinson's advance with operations on the Niagara front. Instead, it was only later in 1814 that the

Americans under Major General Jacob Brown crossed the Niagara River, but, when they did so, they quickly seized Fort Erie on 3 July, the outnumbered garrison speedily surrendering in a display of lack of resolve. This advance was to be an important operation because the campaign and the officers who made their reputations during it would have a decisive impact on the kind of regular army that developed in the USA between 1815 and 1846. The American plan was for an advance along the Niagara River to Lake Ontario, before moving west to challenge the British position in Upper Canada. Misinterpreting his orders, Brown had earlier moved his troops from Sacket's Harbor to Buffalo, weakening the possibility of a renewed advance on Montréal from Lake Ontario and, instead, ensuring that the Americans focused on the Niagara peninsula.

There, in July, the British had two thousand troops under Major General Phineas Riall, the Americans forty-eight hundred, a superiority that would have proved greater had it been possible to concentrate more of the militia. Having moved south from Fort George in response to the American crossing, Riall drew up his men behind the Chippawa River, but, rather than resting on the defensive, on 5 July he ordered an advance on the Americans. This reflected the value of gaining the initiative, but a scrambled American response proved effective, with the defensive firepower of Winfield Scott's 1st Brigade causing sufficient British casualties to lead Riall to retreat. He was impressed by the Americans' tactical skill. Moreover, earlier that year Scott had trained his brigade to stand up to British troops without breaking in the face of a firefight or a British advance. The British suffered 478 casualties, against 318 American ones. The British lost heavily to the American use of canister shot which helped lead them to retreat.

As with many of the battles of the war, however, Chippawa can be seen in different lights. Despite their numerical superiority, and the fact that the British had abandoned their defensive position in order to mount an attack, exposing themselves to the risk of conflict, the Americans were unable to inflict a decisive blow. This failure was not least in the final section of the battle when Brown could not convert his checking of the British into a successful pursuit. A more decisive success would have left the British in a far weaker position during the subsequent campaign, but it was difficult to convert defensive successes into victorious attacks.

This was a problem for both sides during the war, in part due to the problems of reconfiguring formations and gaining tempo in the midst of a battle. Despite Brown's inability to inflict a decisive blow, the success of the American regulars at Chippawa, using conventional tactics, standing up to British regulars, and turning their flanks, helped improve American morale. Riall's comment on Scott's men, "Those are Regulars, by God!," was to be much quoted, although no contemporary eyewitness recounts this exclamation and its origins have been traced to early nineteenth-century secondary accounts. The American success also showed the British that the lesson of the battle of Bunker Hill in 1775 was still true: a bold British advance would not necessarily lead to victory.[17]

The Americans failed to exploit Chippawa. Riall's men success- fully withdrew, while the Americans besieged Fort George, but only on 20 July and only loosely. Without the support and supplies of Chaun- cey's squadron, and concerned about British plans, the Americans then retreated behind the Chippawa River, intending to move on Burlington Bay. This led to the night battle of Lundy's Lane (25 July), which, like Monmouth Courthouse in 1778—Washington's last maneuver battle— is a controversial engagement in that both sides claimed victory and produced conflicting contemporary accounts. The engagement was a contact one, with Scott's brigade running into British troops advancing south from Fort George at Lundy's Lane to the west of Niagara Falls. In the initial clash, Scott advanced on the outnumbered British under Riall, leading the latter to order a retreat, but Drummond arrived with reinforcements, countermanded the order, and firmed up the British position. In turn, Scott was reinforced by Brown, whose men marched toward the sound of the guns. The battle was fought to defeat the opponent, rather than in order to gain particular territory, but tactically it was a struggle for advantage over a hill on which the British had deployed their cannon. Drummond, the resolute British commander, regarded the command of this hill as key to success in the battle.

Indeed, this battle was one in which the placing of cannon was seen as crucial, and their role underlines the more general importance of artillery on the battlefield and in force structures.[18] As the British posi- tion was better, their 24-pounder and 6-pounder cannon did more dam- age, both to the American troops and to their cannon, which could not elevate sufficiently to provide adequate counter-battery fire. As a re- sult, the Americans repeatedly attacked the hill. After flank attacks achieved some success, a series of frontal attacks finally gained the position, although that simply led to British counterattacks.

Three British counterattacks were checked in close-quarter fighting which showed American fighting quality; but American attacks were also defeated, and the Americans were under acute pressure and facing shortages of ammunition and water, which led them to withdraw. At the end of the fighting, the Americans had held the contested ground, but they had lost a higher percentage of the men engaged, and the battle ended because they abandoned the ground. In the bloodiest battle of the war on the Canadian frontier, the British lost 84 killed, 559 wounded, and 193 missing; the Americans 173 killed, 571 wounded, and 117 missing. The wounding of generals, Jacob Brown and Winfield Scott on the American side, and Phineas Riall and Gordon Drummond on the British, indicated the risks to which commanders were exposed, risks that were to be clearly shown in the British defeat at New Orleans in 1815. Riall, who, once wounded, was captured, had his left arm amputated. He convalesced in the same room as Scott, who did not fight again during that war.[19] The aftermath of the battle was grim, although the need for life to go on was reflected in the journal of Lieutenant John Le Couteur of the 104th Foot, "A great camp kettle of thick chocolate revived us surprisingly, though we devoured it among dead bodies in all directions."[20]

Lieutenant General Eleazer Ripley, the senior American officer after Brown and Scott were wounded, did not carry out orders to regroup the troops and attack again the following morning. Whatever the tactical conclusion, the battle was an operational success for the British, as the Americans no longer held the Chippawa River nor most of the western shore of the Niagara valley, and, instead, fell back on Fort Erie; although this retreat was not harried by a British pursuit. From Fort Erie, the Americans were no longer threatening the British army or positions, for the Americans had lost the initiative.

The battles in this campaign revealed the difficulties of controlling engagements, both from a distance and on the ground, as well as the role of risk. Commanders took the chance of battle, but found it difficult to control its flow and tempo, not least because of the difficulty of coordinating forces, and of creating and then using reserves. Poor visibility was one reason why it was difficult to maneuver units on the battlefield, especially once they were engaged. Even in clear weather, there was a limit to what could be seen with the naked eye or with the telescope. This situation was exacerbated by the general absence of detailed maps and the limitations of topographical mapping. With no facilities for aerial reconnaissance (the French use of balloons in the 1790s was not sustained due to the difficulties of employing them),[21] generals had very limited knowledge of the terrain and of the position or movements of opposing forces, and many battles revolved around the surprise deployment of units. As a result, the ability to understand the lie of the land and to assess possible military consequences was a very important aspect of generalship.

Aside from a lack of information, tactical flexibility was also lessened by poor battlefield communication, a problem accentuated at night. It was particularly difficult to keep units in touch, which was necessary in order to prevent gaps that could be exploited by opponents, not least by mounting flank attacks. A good deal of the battle of Lundy's Lane was fought in the dark of night, and this factor, combined with both sides' exhaustion, ended the fighting.

Far from returning to the offensive on the Niagara front after Lundy's Lane, the Americans fell back to the frontier, although they retained Fort Erie against British siege, repulsing a night British attack on 15 August. Drummond's attack plan was overly complex and lacked surprise. Four columns attacked. Two, aimed at the new part of the fort, were repulsed, but the troops from the other two, which had merged, managed to gain one of the bastions. Yet, they could not exploit this success as the entrance into the fort itself was well covered. The British then brought up a cannon, but the powder magazine under the bastion blew up, with heavy British casualties. Already, prior to this explosion, the commanders of the two columns, Lieutenant Colonel Hercules Scott and then William Drummond, the nephew of the general, had been killed, William Drummond having allegedly told his men to give no quarter. After the explosion, the British then withdrew.

After this costly failure, the British then skirmished actively and mounted persistent artillery bombardments of Fort Erie. In response, Brown staged a successful night sortie on 17 September, which led, in heavy rain, to the capture of two of the three British batteries and the spiking of many of the British cannon. Pointless without artillery superiority, the siege was lifted four days later. At this stage, the defense of Fort Erie could be seen as one of a series of successful American defensive operations that year.

The Americans, however, failed to exploit this success, despite moving four thousand troops to this front from the Plattsburg positions. Major General George Izard, the senior American general on the Canadian frontier, had built large-scale fortifications at Plattsburg in order to thwart a likely British invasion, but despite news of Prevost's preparations to march on Plattsburg, Izard was ordered by John Armstrong, the secretary of war, to take four thousand men to support Fort Erie. This move involved a lengthy and difficult journey, especially the first stage over the hills to Sacket's Harbor, and, as with all such route marches, was a debilitating one. Once arrived on the Niagara front, on 12 October, Izard commanded a combined force of seven thousand troops, but he proved unwilling to attack Drummond's defensive position. On 18–19 October, a clash between an American brigade, sent to capture a British grain store at Cook's Mills, and a smaller British force led to the American capture of the position, but the outnumbered Drummond did not rise to the bait and Izard withdrew to the American shore of the Niagara River. This withdrawal involved the abandonment of Fort Erie, whose garrison was affected by sickness and desertion, and the Americans evacuated the position on 5 November, destroying the fortress.[22] American options were affected by the extent to which Britain by then had a powerful naval presence on Lake Ontario.

Izard's campaign was an instance of the many might-have-beens of the campaign. Seven thousand troops was a reasonable force, and more than many that achieved important successes in the war. Yet, advancing would entail tying up troops in garrisoning captured positions, as well as in masking Fort George. The British had naval superiority on Lake Ontario, and to attack York in the absence of naval support, such as that enjoyed by the Americans in April 1813, would have been foolish. Furthermore, thanks to Harrison's success at the Battle of the Thames in 1813, the need to cut British supply lines to Detroit and Fort Amherstburg was no more. Drummond himself was seeking a new alignment, with a road to Lake Huron that could help move troops and supplies to Fort Mackinac, and the Americans were not in a position to attack this route. Izard had too few troops to exploit his opportunities and it was late in the year. Yet, he proved a lackluster commander, angering Jacob Brown by his inaction, and his failure to do more contributed to the less-than-distinguished record of American offensive operations that year.

Farther west, American options were constrained by greater difficulties in getting the militia system to work.[23] These difficulties
were a product of war weariness but also of a sense of a balance of
threat: with the real danger to the USA ended, but no prospect of
conquering Canada to encourage commitment. For example, in Kentucky there was a feeling that the state had done enough. When one
thousand militia were requested for Detroit, Isaac Shelby, the governor, who had in 1813 taken part in the Battle of the Thames at the
head of the Kentucky volunteers, refused to send the militia unless
the War Department undertook to provide the pay. This episode was a
key indicator of the military problems caused by shared sovereignty
in a federal system. Moreover, angered by the transfer of most of the
regular troops farther east and by Armstrong's treatment of him, Harrison resigned in May 1814.

Meanwhile, the defeat of the allied Native Americans had ended
the option of British operations against Detroit and, with the British
regulars withdrawn, the defense of the southwestern part of Upper
Canada was essentially left to the militia, who were put under pressure
in 1814 from frequent American raids. In May, American troops burned
residents' buildings from Port Dover to Turkey Point, and further raids
in July, August, and September saw homes, barns, mills and crops,
burned in western Upper Canada. The last American raid, an attack on
the Thames River settlements by seven hundred mounted troops under
Brigadier General Duncan McArthur, led to a total American victory at
Malcolm's Mills on 6 November, but had no operational or strategic
consequences.[24] By the end of that year, American officers at Amherstburg were talking about depopulating the territory. These destructive
raids were part of the context for British operations in the Chesapeake
area, as well as having the effect in Upper Canada of leaving a legacy of
strong anti-American feeling.

THE CHAMPLAIN FRONT

For the British forces in Canada, there was a choice about where to
invade the USA, an invasion intended to gain bargaining counters for
the peace talks and to seize bases that might otherwise be used for an
American invasion of Canada. Operating against Detroit or Sacket's
Harbor or on the Niagara front were all options, but also faced significant logistical and military drawbacks. The supply of the troops to be

deployed in 1814 was a more serious issue than earlier in the war because of the greater size of these forces, and this encouraged a British focus on the Champlain corridor as it would be possible there to use supplies purchased from New England and also brought from Britain. Moreover, supply routes from Lake Ontario west appeared vulnerable to American naval power on the Great Lakes.

As it turned out, the campaign in the Champlain corridor was finally also to hinge on naval power. Indeed, the role of local naval superiority was demonstrated when a British advance along the western shore of Lake Champlain was abandoned when the British squadron on the lake was defeated on 11 September 1814. This was after the burning of Washington (24 August), but before the British advance on Baltimore was thwarted (13–14 September). About ten thousand British troops, the largest force ever to invade the USA, had crossed the Canadian border on 1 September, the same day on which another force seized Castine on the coast of Maine. Advancing from the Canadian border, they reached Plattsburg five days later, having pushed back an American delaying force at Beekmantown earlier in the day; but they then waited five days for the naval battle which would determine whether the British could use the lake to move their supplies.

The American squadron under Thomas Macdonough was well positioned and prepared and, on 11 September, it fought well. Excellent American seamanship, good command decisions, and the strength of the short-range American cannonades enabled the Americans to compensate for British strength in long-range gunnery and to thwart the British anticipation of naval superiority on the lake. In the event, all the major British ships were sunk or captured and the commander, Captain George Downie, was killed by an American cannonball.[25]

The caution of the lackluster British commander, Sir George Prevost, the governor-general of North America, who was unwilling to sustain his attack on the American positions on land, let alone move beyond Plattsburg, without command of Lake Champlain, also played an important role. He thus failed to exploit the opportunity created by the failure of John Armstrong, the American secretary of war, to anticipate the main direction of British attack. Assuming that this would center on the Niagara front, Armstrong had instructed Major General George Izard, despite the latter's protests, to move more than half the American force on the Champlain front toward Sacket's Harbor.

The south bank of the Saranac River south of Plattsburg, as a result, was held by Brigadier General Alexander Macomb. Born in Detroit in 1782, he was a talented young commander who was not, unlike many other American generals, a veteran of the War of Independence, Macomb was part of a new generation of generals. Initially in command of only thirty-four hundred troops, he benefited from the arrival of the Vermont militia, which was a significant step as Vermont had hitherto been reluctant to support the war effort. Prevost's delay in mounting the attack gave the Vermonters the opportunity to arrive. Thanks to his defensive preparations, Macomb deterred British advances on bridges across the Saranac prior to the naval clash. These preparations included removing the planks from the bridges. On the day of the battle on Lake Champlain, the British mounted another assault. While one brigade attacked the bridges, a larger column under Major General Frederick Robinson was able to cross the Saranac by a ford three miles up-river from Plattsburg. Prevost, however, ordered a recall once he saw that the British squadron had been lost on the lake. His angry subordinates, who felt that victory was within their grasp, complained without success, and Prevost retreated into Canada. Despite having nearly eight thousand troops available at Plattsburg, the opportunity to inflict a major defeat on the American army had been lost.[26]

Again, the balance of judgment is difficult. Prevost can be criticized for caution, as Sir Guy Carleton, advancing south from Canada in late 1776 can also be, not least for his failure to attack Ticonderoga that October despite the advice of some of his officers. However, General John Burgoyne's surrender at Saratoga in October 1777 was widely seen as the product of rashness in similar circumstances, although, in fact, Burgoyne moved far farther south than Carleton or Prevost and with far fewer troops than Prevost. Unlike Prevost, moreover, Burgoyne was outnumbered. In 1814, the key issue was logistics, as well as Prevost's concern that his route back to Canada would be cut. Both were seen to depend on control of the lake. The defeat on the lake was also a pointed reminder of the risks of an advance, although, on his retreat, he did not lose the large number of troops to desertion that was to be alleged. Indeed, Prevost lost only 234 men in the campaign. In retreating, however, he abandoned some of his stores, taking considerable losses in provisions and ammunition. Prevost had failed, and was to be bitterly criticized in the British press as well as by Wellington, who recommended his removal. Prevost was recalled to Britain to respond to the criticism, but died in January 1816, shortly before a court-martial was due to be held. In contrast, Alexander Macomb was promoted to Major General, and was commanding general of the American army from 1828 to 1841. Prevost's career in Canada raises the issue of the applicability of the thesis advanced in the 1970s by Norman Dixon, in his *The Psychology of Military Incompetence* (1976), that those promoted for peacetime purposes lack the personality necessary for wartime success. It is interesting, however, to note that Wellington had tempered his comments by December 1814, writing from Paris: "I admire all that has been done by the military in America, as far as I understand it generally. Whether Sir George Prevost was right or wrong in his decision at Lake Champlain, is more than I can tell; but of this I am very certain, he must equally have retired to Kingston after our fleet was beaten, and I am inclined to believe he was right."[27]

In America, there was no equivalent to the large-scale military support Wellington had received from Portugal and Spain during the Peninsular War. Moreover, in the attack on Sacket's Harbor in May 1813, Prevost was in the forefront of the action, and he acted decisively when he ordered the retreat. Prevost was replaced by Drummond, who had the vigor and resolution his predecessor lacked, but his task was only to oversee the peace, and he left for Britain in 1816.

Despite their defensive success on Lake Champlain, the Americans in 1814, as in 1812–13, had failed to make gains in Canada, which was serious as it was their sole area of offensive operations, and it was only in Canada that they could hope to compensate for British conquests elsewhere. This failure invites some comparison with the more successful impression of American military proficiency created by the War of Independence. In essence, both conflicts showed that the American military system was more appropriate for defense than for conquest (a situation that had changed by the Mexican-American War of 1846–8) and, to that extent, the failure to conquer Canada in both conflicts is the most appropriate point of comparison.

Yet, the failure to conquer Canada in the War of 1812 was more important than that in 1775–83, as America already had gained independence, so that this was not the goal in the War of 1812. Moreover, due to British naval power, Canada was the sole sphere in which the Americans could take the initiative and strike directly at the British.

Conversely, because the attacks on Canada played a far greater role in the War of 1812, it is easy to imply from their failure that American military capability had declined since the War of Independence. But this is misleading, for the 1775–76 failure in Canada showed the difficulty of the task.

### Amphibious Attacks

War in Canada, moreover, seemed less relevant in 1814 as British attacks refocused concerns across much of coastal America, and urgently so. British attacks on America's East Coast were more dramatic than campaigning on the Canadian frontier, not least because they hit at or threatened the centers of American power. Furthermore, it was there that the British were able to apply their naval power, amphibious capability, and reinforcements from the British Isles. The resulting pressure was employed in a number of ways, each designed to make the Americans feel the fact of British power. In 1814, the blockade was extended, greatly hitting American imports and exports. In addition, that same year a major effort was made in order to apply British strength more directly. In part, this effort was designed to help defend Canada by diverting American strength, the policy outlined in January 1808 by Archibald Robertson, an army engineer who had served in the War of Independence and had been asked for advice by Henry, 1st Viscount Melville:

> In the case of an American war taking place, I do not doubt but that a flying squadron with some troops in transport, threatening either the Chesapeake or Delaware Rivers might alarm and impede any intended movement of the enemy against Canada, without (on our part) any particular attempt to land in any place, but only threatening particular points thought of consequence by the enemy and after attracting their attention to one point shift the ground and threaten some other.[28]

The use of amphibious power faced more problems than such a proposal might suggest, and effective control and coordination of deployment and operations was not possible from across the Atlantic.[29] But such power was a key aspect of the British way of war. The British had sent a squadron into the Chesapeake in 1813 (see Chapter 3), in order to stop it becoming a base for naval and privateering activity, as well as to divert American forces from the Canadian frontier, and to mount raids that would emphasize American vulnerability and lessen support for the war.[30] Prior to 1814, the policy had had mixed success. American naval and privateering activity had been hit, but the attempt to drive it home by seizing Norfolk, a major port, had failed, both in the battle of nearby Craney Island on 22 June 1813 and thereafter. Instead, the British fleet had had to anchor at Lynnhaven Bay and thus to depend on distant dockyards. The diversionary purpose had not succeeded, as American troops sent north against Canada were not recalled and, instead, militia were used for local defense. Furthermore, despite British hopes, the raids failed to sap American support for the war and, instead, led to greater hostility to Britain.

In the summer of 1814, with troops and ships no longer required for action against France, British pressure was more insistent and wide-ranging. Indeed, forty-eight thousand troops were deployed in North America in 1814, more than the number of British troops at the Battle of Waterloo the following year. Unlike in America, however, there were other allied forces, German and Dutch, at Waterloo, and they made a key contribution there. Moreover, although the number of British troops in North America in 1814 was large, the range of British commitments there stemming from the far-flung nature of the War of 1812 ensured that there was no major concentration of this force.

## MAINE

British pressure was a matter not only of the strength of the navy, but also of its capacity for amphibious operations. A longstanding border dispute over the Maine district of Massachusetts was the basis for the British government's decision to try to seize much of Maine in order to ensure a safe overland route between Nova Scotia and Québec, which would provide an all-weather route, whereas the St. Lawrence was blocked by winter ice. In a little-known expedition, Admiral Sir Thomas Masterman Hardy, the "Kiss me Hardy" of Horatio Nelson's dying words at the battle of Trafalgar, carried one thousand troops to Eastport on Moose Island near New Brunswick on 11 July 1814. The heavily outnumbered garrison of Fort Sullivan surrendered and Hardy claimed the region for Britain. The fort was renamed Fort Sherbrooke

after Lieutenant General Sir John Sherbrooke, the lieutenant governor of Nova Scotia. On 9–12 August, in order to show what could be
done, Hardy also bombarded the small port of Stonington, Connecticut, although his concern to restrict civilian hardship helped ensure
that the damage was limited.

On 1 September 1814, an expedition with about twenty-five hundred troops under Major General Gerard Gosselin and Rear Admiral
Edward Griffith captured Castine, which was defended by only 140
troops, who fled. On the coast of Maine, Castine, unlike Eastport, was
not close to Nova Scotia. It had also been the target of a successful
British amphibious operation during the War of Independence. In
1814, marching inland up the Penobscot River from Castine, the British captured Frankfort on 2 September, before seizing Hampden in
the face of weak resistance on 3 September. The British, at the cost of
one dead and eight wounded, dispersed fourteen hundred dispirited
and inexperienced militia at Hampden and captured twenty cannon
from the *Adams*.[31] This American frigate had run aground and barely
made it into the Penobscot several days earlier. Under repair, it was
trapped at Hampden. The British use of Congreve rockets helped
wreck American morale. To prevent its capture, the *Adams* was
burned by her captain, Charles Morris, on 3 September. Having captured Bangor, the British received the surrender of the local militia.
Another British force overran Buck's Harbor and Machias to the east.
By 11 September, all of Maine east of the Penobscot River had been
conquered. Local forces mounted no serious resistance, while the
people proved willing to take an oath of allegiance to George III. Unsurprisingly, this does not feature in standard American texts, but it
indicated the potentially plastic character of the Canadian frontier.
People on Moose Island (which Britain claimed) were required to take
an oath, as were those who wished to trade with the British.[32]

Rejecting, at the close of 1814, the federal government's plan for
the reconquest of the lost territory, Governor Caleb Strong of Massachusetts instead focused on protecting Boston from the threat of
attack. Hit hard by the war-induced recession, Massachusetts lacked
money, while Strong was advised that an American offensive would
fail without naval control of Penobscot Bay, and there was no prospect of such control. Indeed, in response to the British threat, New
Englanders pressed the federal government to end the war, and also
decided on an emergency meeting at Hartford, Connecticut. British

control of the initiative had been amply demonstrated. Wellington, however, was sceptical about the value of using the gains in Maine in any peace negotiations, writing to the Earl of Liverpool: "It is evidently only temporary, and till a larger force will drive away the few companies he [Sherbrooke] has left there; and an officer might as well claim the sovereignty of the ground on which his piquets stand, or over which his patrols pass."[33]

## THE CHESAPEAKE

Farther south, the British had mounted a larger effort in August. In "compliance with . . . instructions to attract the attention of the government of the United States and to cause a diversion in favor of the army in Canada" (which were also the basis of the attack on Maine), a fleet under Vice Admiral Sir Alexander Cochrane (1758–1832), who had replaced Warren, entered the Chesapeake. The impact of intelligence information is unclear, as more generally during the war, but in 1820 Philip Mores, an American then living in London, wrote to Wellington claiming that he had acted as a spy in the campaign, not least in the reconnaissance of Baltimore.[34]

Although the bulk of American population, industry, and purchasing power were concentrated in and close to the coast, the defense nevertheless had depth as a result of "country" space. New Orleans' distance from the coast was important to its successful defense in 1815, while the extent of country space proved valuable in operations round the Chesapeake in 1814. As a result, the British could not only take Washington without fatal effects to the American war effort (as had also been the case with the then-capital, Philadelphia, in 1777); but, in addition, the Americans had the opportunity to withdraw from Washington without losing their capacity to maintain their forces. Furthermore, although the coast and nearby areas were exposed to assault, it would be mistaken to argue that such attack was therefore easy or bound to succeed.

Once in the Chesapeake, the British were able to exert pressure in a number of directions, the combination of naval power with the broad rivers that flow into the bay, such as the James, Patuscent, and Potomac, offering them considerable flexibility. This had also been the case in 1780–81, until Cornwallis surrendered that flexibility by basing himself at Yorktown and failing, subsequently, to abandon the

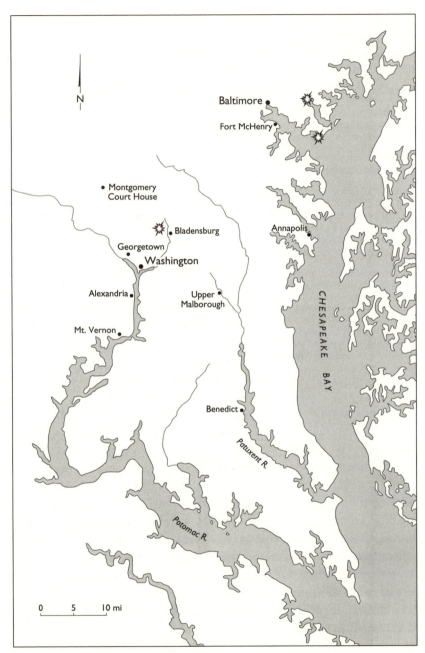

**Chesapeake Theater**

position before it was blockaded. From April 1814, British raids in the Chesapeake increased, and soon became a more persistent pressure than that seen the previous year. For example, in June 1814 there were attacks along the shores of the Patuxent River; at the same time Cockburn, arguing that American morale was poor and its government weak, pressed for an attack on Washington. In July and early August he raided the shores of the Potomac River.

The key operation was mounted in mid-August. A squadron under Captain James Gordon, an experienced officer who had lost a leg and an arm fighting the French, mounted a successful secondary attack, although it was delayed by the need to navigate round the shoals in the Potomac. Gordon, nevertheless, forced his way up the river, seized Fort Washington without a fight, captured an undefended Alexandria, Virginia, on 28 August, and returned with a rich haul of merchantmen and prize goods, along the way outfiring American shore batteries at White House Bluff and Indian Head under David Porter and Oliver Hazard Perry respectively.[35] Having left Alexandria on 1 September, Gordon rejoined the British fleet on 9 September.

The main expedition was a force of forty-seven hundred troops, many Peninsular War veterans, but also including a marine battalion. The commander, Major General Robert Ross (1766–1814), was an highly experienced soldier, a veteran of service in Holland, Egypt, Italy, Portugal, and Spain. On 19 August, he landed without opposition at Benedict on the Patuxent River, fifty miles from Washington, a move that enabled the British not to expose their main force to fire from the Potomac batteries if advancing along that river. Ross was fortunate that the landing was not opposed, because amphibious operations were very difficult. First, naval fire support had serious limitations. Ships were large targets, whereas guns fired from land did so from a stable platform. Secondly, the assault craft were powered by naval oarsmen and an auxiliary sail, which made it difficult to move rapidly. Inshore navigation was a problem, and it was particularly hard to land horses.[36] The processes of approach to shore and disembarkation were often slow and difficult, and once troops were ashore they lost the advantage of maritime mobility. Instead, they were frequently vulnerable to attack. Amphibious forces also had a lopsided force structure. Ross wrote of the "serious disadvantage being experienced from the want of cavalry."[37] On the other hand, the British had considerable experience of amphibious operations, more so than any other power.

On 20 August, Ross advanced on Washington. He was joined at Upper Marlboro by a detachment from the navy, but a lack of artillery horses ensured that the cannon had to be manhandled and only one 6-pounder gun and two 3-pounders supported the British, a key weakness given American numbers. The lack of artillery was another instance of the problems the British encountered when they moved from the firepower and mobility provided by the navy to operations ashore.

At Bladensburg on 24 August, Ross found sixty-five hundred Americans, mostly militia, drawn up under Brigadier General William Winder behind a branch of the Potomac River. Despite being outnumbered, without cavalry, and heavily outgunned by five effectively used 18-pounder naval guns under Commodore Joshua Barney, the British attacked. They were boldly led by Ross, who bravely commanded from the front. The British troops advanced across the river and attacked the Americans in the front and flanks, defeating them after three hours of combat. As at Hampden in Maine on 3 September, the inexperienced and badly led American militia did not fight well: many fled, terrified by the shock of combat and frightened by the British rockets. Winder was forced to rely on his few regulars, who were, in turn, defeated when the American position under Barney was flanked. Ross reported that "the enemy was discovered strongly posted on very commanding heights. . . . [A] position which was carefully defended by artillery and riflemen." Thanks to a good attack, however, "This first line giving way was driven on the second which yielding to the irresistible attack of the bayonet and the well-directed discharge of rockets got into confusion and fled leaving the British masters of the field," and having captured ten cannon.[38] The young Peter Bowlby (1792–1877), who had become an ensign in the 4th Regiment of Foot in 1808 and was already a veteran of the Walcheren expedition and the peninsula, recorded:

> The weather was dreadfully hot and the road deep in sand. . . .
> Arrived at Bleydensburg [sic] we saw the American army marching from Washington to a position a mile in front. We had to pass the stream by a wooden bridge in single file. Fortunately it was covered from the American position by a turn

in the road under the wood. As soon as the leading regiment, the 85th, cleared this, they extended to the right and advanced in light infantry order over a tolerably open country, the 4th regiment doing the same to the left. In front we had a wood occupied by the Americans and some high ground to the right of the wood occupied also by columns of the Americans and some field artillery, Commodore Barney and his guns playing down the high road. The 85th first reached him and all his men were cut down at their guns. The American army then retreated in great haste on Washington. On approaching the wood I received a shot in the shin which splintered the bone but did not break it. I tied a handkerchief round it and marched with the regiment to Washington.[39]

John Threlkeld, an American, recorded that "we were expecting the enemy one way when news arrived of their approach on a different route. The whole army had then to run three miles to gain this situation and not time to take regular positions." He was scathing about the militia: "perhaps none ever saw a gun pointed at a man to kill in their lives."[40] Barney's presence in the battle ensured that there is an instructive American account in the otherwise somewhat unlikely source of *The Naval War of 1812: A Documentary History*. As with most battle reports, this was very much an account by one participant, and one that substantially reflected his position and commitments; but, as Barney held a key position, this is valuable. He described deploying his cannon and awaiting the British arrival:

During this period the engagement continued the enemy advancing, our own army retreating before them apparently in much disorder, at length the enemy made his appearance on the main road, in force, and in front of my battery, and on seeing us made a halt. I reserved our fire. In a few minutes the enemy again advanced, when I ordered an 18 lb to be fired, which completely cleared the road, shortly after a second and a third attempt was made by the enemy to come forward but all were destroyed. The enemy then crossed over into an open field and attempted to flank our right. He was there met by three twelve pounders, the marines under Captain Miller and my men acting as infantry, and again was totally cut up. By this time not a vestige of the American army remained except a body of 5 or 600 posted on a height on my right from whom I expected much support, from their fine situation. The enemy from this period never appeared in force in front of us. They pushed forward their sharp shooters, one of which shot my horse under me, who fell dead between two of my guns. The enemy who had been kept in check by our fire for nearly half an hour now began to outflank us on the right, our guns were turned that way. He pushed up the hill, about 2 or 300 towards the corps of Americans stationed as above described, who, to my great mortification made no resistance, giving a fire or two and retired. In this situation we had the whole army of the enemy to contend with; our ammunition, wagons had gone off in the general panic. At this time I received a severe wound in my thigh. . . . to the honor of my officers and men, as fast as their companions and mess mates fell at the guns they were instantly replaced. . . . Finding the enemy now completely in our rear, and no means of defense I gave orders to my officers and men to retire.

Captured, Barney was treated well, as was the norm—especially for officers—during this war as far as American and British forces were concerned: the situation was different for, and from, the Native Americans. Barney was then paroled.[41] The battle was to be remembered as a humiliation, indeed as the "Bladensburg Races" to critics appalled by the American flight.

The battle is a reminder that the standard impression of British tactics, in terms of linear defensive firepower, is no guide to the overall range of British tactical doctrine and practice. The well-timed bayonet charge, launched when opponents were disorganized by British fire (and sometimes by their having advanced on the British), was as effective as the volley. Medical records and other sources on casualties suggest that the bayonet was essentially a psychological weapon. Firepower caused more casualties, and was therefore crucial to the decision of the battle. However, the bayonet charge permitted exploitation of the advantage. Such a charge, preceded by a volley, had become a standard British tactic from the late 1750s, and was used with great effect in the War of Independence. In the War of 1812, as earlier in Egypt against the French in 1801, in India against the Marathas in 1803, and at Salamanca in Spain against the French in 1812, the British attacked with alacrity. This British tactic expanded the range of tactical problems and possibilities that American units could anticipate.

After the battle, Ross entered nearby Washington that night without resistance, as the American forces had retreated beyond Georgetown. There was to be no street fighting comparable to that which the Austrians faced in Genoa in 1746 and Brussels in 1789, the British encountered in Buenos Aires in Argentina and Rosetta in Egypt in 1807, the Russians at Leipzig in 1813, and the Dutch in Brussels in 1830. In each of these cases bar Leipzig, where the Russians' opponents were French regulars, the army named was unsuccessful. The British failure at Buenos Aires is particularly instructive, as, prior to 1814, it was the last British deployment against a city in the New World. The entire campaign indicated the problems of British expeditionary power, problems that are suggestive for the possible fate of an attempt to storm Baltimore later in 1814 or, indeed, Charleston or New York City had the war continued. In July 1806, in an unauthorized expedition that took advantage of the presence of sizeable British forces in Cape Town (which had been recently captured from the Dutch), Buenos Aires fell to a force of about twelve hundred troops, apparently opening up a vast new sphere for imperial expansion. Hopes for freeing Spanish South America for British trade, and of spreading power by means of expeditions to Chile and Mexico, spread throughout Britain. In the meantime, however, the small British garrison was forced to surrender in August in the face of a major popular rising. After a larger British force was sent to capture Buenos Aires anew, the smaller city of Montevideo was successfully stormed in February 1807. On 5 July, however, when about eight thousand troops attacked Buenos Aires, they found the town strongly defended. The attacking columns were isolated in the barricaded streets and, having suffered three thousand casualties, the commander agreed to an exchange of prisoners and to the evacuation of the Plate estuary, including Montevideo.[42]

This failure provided an important indicator of the limitations of seaborne power. The British in 1807 deployed a substantial force, larger than that sent against Washington and Baltimore in 1814; enjoyed, as in 1814, good naval support; and, as in the Chesapeake, did not face an ecosystem as hostile as that in the West Indies; but they were confronted by a hostile population that did not want to exchange Spanish rule for foreign and Protestant control. The attitude of the local populace was crucial to the battle in Buenos Aires, and even had the British captured the city, they would have faced a sullen population and been obliged to use large numbers of troops to extend and maintain control. In Washington, however, there was no attempt to mount resistance in the aftermath of defeat in 1814. There was not the time to prepare resistance, but it was also not a tradition in North American conflict. In Boston in 1775–1806, New York in 1776, and Philadelphia in 1777, the British had been opposed outside the town. They had not faced the need to fight their way into it nor, subsequently, insurrection within it.

In Washington, in 1814, the public buildings were destroyed by the British troops in retaliation for American destructiveness at York in 1813, an attempt at equivalence not generally mentioned in American public history where the emphasis, instead, is on damage by the British. The military facilities were also destroyed. Ross reported:

> Having rested the army for a short time, I determined to march upon Washington and reached that city at 8 o'clock that night. Judging it of consequence to complete the destruction of the public buildings with the least possible delay so that the army might retire without loss of time the following buildings were set fire to and consumed—the Capital including the Senate House and House of Representatives, the Arsenal, the Dockyard, Treasury, War Office, Presidents Palace, Rope Walk, and the Great Bridge across the Potomac, in the dockyard a frigate nearly ready to be launched and a ship of war were consumed.

Bowlby recorded: "On entering Washington with General Ross at the head of the Light troops, a volley was fired from a corner house killing his horse. The house was immediately burned, its garrison having escaped. The army was now halted and fatigue parties sent into the town to set fire to the public buildings and dock yards which burned all night."[43]

William Kirke, of the King's Own Rifles, who had fought at Bladensburg, "a smart engagement," emphasized the destruction of munitions in Washington: "[We] burned down the city of Washington. Destroyed 20,000 stand of small arms, 200 pieces of cannon, large stores, one frigate, a sloop of war and a great number of gun boats, but in short we totally destroyed that part of the United States of America."[44]

The whitewashing to cover evidence of the fire of the rebuilt president's house encouraged its being called the White House, although there are references to it as the White House before the war as it had been whitewashed earlier. The correspondence of Madison's wife Dolly leaves no doubt of the haste, uncertainty, and disruption of the flight.[45] Some of the destruction, however, was by the Americans, who were determined in particular to prevent the navy yard and its stores from being seized by the British. As a result, Thomas Tingey, the navy yard's commandant, had it burned down. The destruction in Washington led to talk of moving the capital to Philadelphia.

In the crisis caused by this defeat, the American leadership proved divided and poor, with John Armstrong, the secretary of war, being especially unhelpful, which led to complaints by militia units. A convenient scapegoat, Armstrong was forced to resign by Madison on 3 September: a result, first, of the burning of Washington, which demonstrated the folly of his earlier insistence that there was no threat to the city; and, second, of the militia complaints.[46] Armstrong, however, was not the only inadequate leader. Although he was not forced to resign, James Monroe, the secretary of state, had meddled in the dispositions of the force at Bladensburg, and to disastrous effect.

Ross's orders that private property in Washington should not be destroyed were respected, with the exception of the few buildings from which resistance was offered. Looting was punished with floggings. There was no comparison to the excesses of the Russians in Warsaw in 1794, nor that of the British in Ciudad Rodrigo and Badajoz in Spain after they had been stormed them in 1812—although, in each case, there had been firm resistance that had cost many British casualties. Nevertheless, despite the relative care shown by the British, Madison felt able, in a proclamation of 1 September 1814, to urge his fellow citizens to expel invaders who had displayed "a deliberate disregard of the principles of humanity and the rules of civilized warfare."

This theme, of a British use of terror against civilians as a tool of war, was to pass into American mythology. It contrasted with the far more measured practice, and indeed limited goals, of the British, but the Americans habitually lacked any ability to contextualize their own experience and Madison's proclamations were consistently misleading. More significantly as far as the War of 1812 was concerned, the American government had left Washington and left behind no one to negotiate with the British. This compared with Russian conduct toward Napoleon in 1812—not that the British were anticipating the response Napoleon had envisaged. Ross was not prepared for negotiations.

After the destruction at Washington, Ross's force then returned to the fleet, re-embarking on 30 August. Ross reported: "The object of the expedition being accomplished I determined before any greater force of the enemy could be assembled to withdraw the troops and accordingly commenced retiring on the night of the 25th."[47] His dispatch of the 30th, published in a *London Gazette Extraordinary* of 27 September, praised his men's morale: "cheerfulness in undergoing fatigue and anxiety for the accomplishment of the object were conspicuous in all ranks." For a few days, Ross and Cochrane remained off the Patuxent River, waiting for the return of the detached forces, principally Gordon's squadron from its expedition up the Potomac River.

Ross then struck further up the Chesapeake at Baltimore. This was one of America's leading ports and the commercial center of the Chesapeake region, a city of a little over forty thousand people (a large number for the period) that was far more important than Washington as an economic target. It was also a keenly Republican city, where the *Federal Republican*, an antiwar Federalist newspaper, had its offices destroyed by rioters on 22 June 1812. Six days later, fresh Republican mob violence led to the brutalizing of prominent Federalists, including the killing of James Lingan, a seventy-year-old Revolutionary War general, and the crippling of Henry "Lighthorse Harry" Lee, another veteran, and of Alexander Hanson, the editor of the *Federal Republican*. The city authorities refused to stop the mob or to take responsibility for the protection of the Federalists.[48] With its deep harbor and major shipyards, Baltimore, a key port for the new country, was also the leading center of privateering, with successful ships such as *Comet* and *Chasseur*. Their captain, Thomas Byle, declared the British Isles under blockade on 30 August 1814. A significant percentage of Baltimore's population, not least some who were not wealthy, had a financial stake in the wartime privateering,[49] which was encouraged by the problems the war posed for Chesapeake trade. On 11 September 1814, Cochrane's fleet dropped anchor at the mouth of the Patapsco River, thirteen miles below Baltimore.

Baltimore, however, had had its fortifications enhanced since the summer of 1813 with extensive breastworks, an effort that reflected the wealth and civic determination of the city, because the federal government was not really up to the task of ensuring adequate defenses. Major General Samuel Smith, a Republican Senator who was an opponent of Madison, was the key figure. The commander of the Baltimore militia and a wealthy merchant, he helped ensure that preparations of the city's defenses were pressed forward. The preparations included repairs to Fort McHenry as well as the construction of new fortifications, especially defense lines on Hampstead Hill to provide protection by land, and the improvement of militia effectiveness through drill and training. Funds were raised by a popular subscription, loans administered by a local committee, and many citizens worked on the defenses. The garrison of Fort McHenry was strengthened with artillery companies and the fort's armament by the removal of guns from a French warship in the harbor. By the spring of 1814, close to sixty cannon were mounted at Fort McHenry. Furnaces to heat the cannonballs were also provided, making the projectiles more deadly against shipping, which of course was constructed of, and equipped with, combustibles. The defeat of Maryland militia at Bladensburg was not encouraging, but Baltimore's determination was increased by Washington's fiery fate.

In 1813, the British lacked the numbers for an attack on Baltimore. In 1814, they had more troops, but were still seriously outnumbered, while the defenses had become stronger. Ross, nevertheless, landed with forty-seven hundred troops at North Point, ten miles from Baltimore, on 12 September 1814. A force of American militia, the 3rd Brigade of Maryland militia under Brigadier General John Stricker, was deployed to block the British advance. Stricker had a protecting screen of about 290 men. A British advance force of about fifty troops, under Cockburn and Ross, encountered them and attacked in order to appear to be in overwhelming strength and gain the initiative. The Americans retreated, but at the close of the exchange of fire Ross himself received a mortal shot.

This hit British morale, but the British pressed on to engage Stricker's main force. Colonel Arthur Brooke, a veteran of operations in the Low Countries, the West Indies, Egypt, and Spain, who replaced Ross, reported of the operation that the Americans had abandoned their first position on the British advance, but "about two miles beyond this post our advance became engaged. The country was here closely wooded and the enemy's riflemen were enabled to conceal themselves." Brooke continued that, despite the loss of Ross, "our advance continuing to press forward, the enemy's light troops were pushed to within five miles of Baltimore," where, he reported, he found about six thousand men drawn up. The British launched a general attack, Brooke recording, "In less than fifteen minutes the enemy's force being utterly broken and dispersed, fled in every direction over the country, leaving on the field 2 pieces of cannon . . . this short but brilliant affair." Bowlby noted: "The American troops soon gave way leaving in the lurch the men in the trees who were shot from their perches at leisure." Brooke added that, had his force included cavalry, American casualties on the retreat would have been far higher, a point certainly true of several battles in the American Revolution. From the American perspective, however, Brooke grossly overstated what happened at an outpost line, and this is a reminder of the need to consider more than one perspective. That day, the British suffered forty-six fatalities, including Rose, the Americans twenty-four; 295 and 139 men respectively were wounded.[50]

On 13 September 1814, Brooke advanced and occupied a position one and a half miles from Baltimore, around which city the Americans "had constructed a chain of pallisaded redoubts connected by a small breast work."[51] As at Plattsburg on 11 September, the British troops then halted to await the naval action that was regarded as crucial to British success, a halt that reflected the role of combined operations in the ethos as well as the practicalities of British operations. As the bulk of the Americans were undefeated, this halt was sensible. There was no comparison to the situation with Long Island/New York City in 1776 and Brandywine/Philadelphia in 1777, or at Bladensburg in 1814: no major American defeats followed by the unopposed British capture of a city.

Supporting warships under Cochrane moved up the Patapsco River and bombarded Fort McHenry from dawn on 13 September. The fort barred the access to Baltimore harbor, which was also hindered by the shallow character of the river and the sinking of merchantmen to block it. The British, however, were unable to destroy the fort. In part, this failure reflected the long range of the British bombardment, which was mounted from beyond the range of the American guns in the fort. The vulnerability of ships to fortresses had been demonstrated on 2 June 1813 when the American sloops *Growler* and *Eagle* had been captured in a gunboat engagement under the guns of the British fortress of Isle aux Noix south of Montréal. Against Fort Mc-Henry, the British used a rocket ship, HMS *Erebus*, and five bomb ketches, *Devastation, Etna, Meteor, Terror*, and *Volcano*. These each carried a 13-inch eight thousand-pound sea mortar, the range of which was greater than the American shore guns. The mortars could, in theory, fire a 194-pound cast-iron bomb (shell) two and a half miles. However, when the British ships moved closer on the afternoon of 13 September, they came within range and took damage before they pulled back out of range, a situation that was to be repeated in January 1815 in the unsuccessful British attack on Fort St. Phillip.

About fifteen hundred to two thousand rockets and bombs were fired, of which the rockets were particularly dramatic. The British mathematician and gunnery expert Benjamin Robins read papers to the Royal Society on rockets in 1749 and 1750, but the key impetus was an attempt to develop an Asian innovation. The inspiration was Indian, especially the use of war rockets by Mysore forces against the British at their capital, Seringapatam, in 1799, although this use had not prevented the British from successfully storming the fortress. Rocketry was taken forward by William Congreve (1772–1828), who, in 1791, was attached to the Royal Laboratory at Woolwich and who spent his own money on his research. Congreve argued that "the rocket is, in fact, nothing more than a mode of using the projectile force of gunpowder by continuation instead of by impulse; it is obtaining the impetus of the cartridge without the cylinder, it is ammunition without ordnance, and its force is exerted without reaction or recoil upon the fulcrum from whence it originates." A planned British attack by boat-mounted rockets on the French invasion port of Boulogne was thwarted by adverse winds in 1805, but by then Congreve's rockets had a range of two thousand yards, and five hundred could be discharged at one time from ten launchers. By 1806, Congreve was making larger rockets, which were used in attacks on Boulogne (1806) and Copenhagen (1807). Congreve rockets caused extensive fires and panic when the French-occupied Dutch port of Flushing was attacked by a British amphibious force in 1809. Congreve was then making 32-pounder rockets with a range of three thousand yards, considerably greater than that of field artillery; and, in 1810, the more mobile twelve-pounder rocket was produced. He also oversaw the fitting out of HMS *Erebus* in 1814. Wellington was skeptical about the value of rockets because of the difficulty of controlling their flight, but Commodore Sir Home Popham, who operated on the Biscayan coast in 1812 in the Peninsular War, pressed for them, declaring that "they are admirable . . . the Spaniards are quite astonished." Congreve was permitted to raise two rocket companies, one of which served at the battle of Leipzig (1813). It impressed Alexander I of Russia, but caused fear rather than damage. Congreve's rockets were, nevertheless, expensive to produce, as well as inaccurate. In 1819, Thomas Cochrane, then head of the Chilean navy, found rockets useless when he attacked Spanish-held Callao in Peru. Both the French and the Saxons also used rockets during the Napoleonic Wars.[52]

Rockets therefore represented the potential of military change, as well as the flexibility of the British military, but they did not bring victory at Baltimore. Despite the rockets and the very heavy shelling, the defenders of Fort McHenry in 1814 suffered few casualties: only four dead and twenty-four injured. Moreover, a British attempt on the night of 13–14 September under Lieutenant Charles Napier to capture the fort by means of an amphibious attack via the branch of the river to the west of the fort failed. The boats lost their way in the fog and were fired on by American batteries, alerted by the noise, before the troops could land. Abandoning the attempt, Napier retreated under heavy fire.

The British warships bombarded Fort McHenry until 7:30 in the morning on 14 September, but without success. The resolute resistance was to be a key source of inspiration for the early republic, and a valuable one because it was not prone to interpretation in terms of sectional interests. The bombardment was to be depicted in many paintings, and the flag resolutely flying amidst the British rockets and shells was a dramatic symbol of American determination, captured, for example, by John Bower in his *A View of the Bombardment of Fort McHenry* (1816) and Alfred Jacob Miller in his *Bombardment of Fort McHenry* (c. 1837). The episode also inspired the poem *The Star Spangled Banner* by Francis Scott Key, an observer of the action, and indeed he was depicted watching the bombardment in Edward Percy Moran's painting *Dawn's Early Light* (1912). Born in 1779, Key was a successful lawyer who had served as a volunteer at Bladensburg. An elderly friend, Dr. William Beanes, had been seized by the British for having imprisoned British soldiers, which was seen as a breach of Beanes' earlier promise of neutrality. He was taken aboard HMS *Tonnant*. Key visited the fleet and was able to obtain a promise of his friend's release, but they were detained while the British made preparations for their attack on the fort, and watched the bombardment from the principal British anchorage. Their uncertainty about whether the position had fallen was answered on the 14th, as the American flag still flew, while the fifes and drums played "Yankee Doodle." This resilience prompted Key to write his poem, which he finished on 16 September. Printed as a handbill, "Defense of Fort McHenry," on 17 September, and in a newspaper three days later, the title was swiftly changed to "The Star-Spangled Banner." In March 1931 the poem became the national anthem:

> O say can you see by the dawn's early light. . . .
> And the rockets' red glare, the bombs bursting in air,
> Gave proof through the night that our flag was still there;
> O say, does that star-spangled banner yet wave
> O'er the land of the free and the home of the brave?[53]

Thus, Fort McHenry's defense was by the 1930s an appropriate symbol for a country proclaiming freedom. Maryland, in contrast, had had a more ambiguous reputation during the Civil War (1861–65), with opinion divided over supporting the Union, leading, in Baltimore in 1861, to the Pratt Street Riot, with Union troops firing on demonstrators. During the war, Fort McHenry, indeed, served as a prison for Confederate soldiers, as well as for civilian sympathizers, including Key's grandson. In contrast, in 1914 a statue to Major George Armistead, the fort's commander a century earlier, was erected; and in 1922 this was followed by a statue of Orpheus, the poet of Classical Greece. This was paid for by Congress as a memorial to Key and the defenders of Baltimore. The largest free-standing bronze statue in the country, the statue of Orpheus was dedicated by President William Harding in a live, nationwide, radio broadcast.[54] Four years later, at Plattsburg, a 135-foot tall memorial to the American victory on Lake Champlain was dedicated. On the Canadian side, Brock had already been commemorated with a monument on Queenston Heights beneath which he was buried in 1824. Blown up by an Irish American in 1840, it was replaced by a tall column carrying Brock's statue.

In 1814, the strength of Baltimore's defenses led to the abandonment of the British expedition on 14 September, with the fleet moving downriver by 9:00 AM. Brooke reported that he had planned a night attack on the defenses on the 13–14th in order to counter American artillery superiority, but that the navy was unable to cooperate because the Americans had sunk over twenty ships and thus blocked the advance of the British warships on Baltimore. Brooke, who lacked Ross's dynamism, decided "that the capture of the town would not have been a sufficient equivalent to the loss which might probably be sustained in storming the heights." He therefore responded to Cochrane's advice and withdrew on the 14th. The far more junior William Kirke presented the operation as a success thwarted by American strength: "Landed on the 12 September near Baltimore. In a few hours after we engaged and defeated them. They retreated towards Baltimore and got a fresh reinforcement which occasioned us to reimbark."[55]

There was an instructive contrast with the expeditionary force sent against Denmark in 1807. The British then had deployed a larger force, eighteen thousand troops, and had moved more swiftly. Landing on the island of Zealand on 16 August, eight miles north of Copenhagen, they besieged the city the following day. On 29 August, Wellington routed an attempt by a larger Danish militia force to relieve the city. In this battle, at Kjöge, the combination of a quick charge and a single volley brought victory. A destructive artillery bombardment of a weakly defended Copenhagen that began on 2 September caused heavy casualties and led the Danes to seek terms on 5 September. The Danes were forced in the resulting agreement to hand over their fleet, the major purpose of the expedition, but the British government's hopes of retaining control of Zealand ended when the generals advised that it would be difficult to do so.[56] In 1814, in contrast, it was impossible to bring comparable force against Baltimore, either in terms of the concentration of men outside the city or of artillery able to mount a bombardment.

As the American forces did not pursue the retreating British forces, Brooke did not have the chance to fight again. Having reembarked at North Point on 15 September,[57] the British troops then sailed down the Chesapeake. Landing parties were put ashore in order to obtain supplies. Bowlby recorded that his regiment landed on the south side of the bay, marching "for a place called the Northumberland Court House which we never reached, for finding the army had an ambuscade prepared we retraced our steps, and re-embarked without losing a man, the principal object having been to give the troops a little exercise."[58]

The army then set off for Jamaica, from where they would be available for operations in the Gulf of Mexico. The American press was concerned that the British warships might end up in the Delaware or at the Head of the Elk from where the troops might disembark and march on Philadelphia,[59] as Howe had done in 1777. In practice, the onset of autumnal weather made further operations on the American Atlantic Coast unlikely. Conversely, the hurricane season was ending in the Caribbean. Thus, the Gulf Coast was to be a seasonal alternative to the Atlantic Coast, as the West Indies had been for the French fleet during the War of Independence.

The boldness of British naval command is also an issue. Vice Admiral Alexander Cochrane had had command of a frigate on the North American station in the 1790s and, aside from operations in Europe, had held responsible positions in the West Indies. He had been commander in chief in the Leeward Islands, was second in command at the battle of St. Domingo (1806), and was governor of Guadeloupe after its capture in 1810. His North American command was his last active one until 1821 when he was appointed commander in chief at Plymouth. This career, which was far from atypical, was not, however, the best background for the energy required against America. In the West Indies, the British had enjoyed the clear superiority over the French fleet that was required to cover amphibious attacks and to thwart privateers. In many senses, the same was even more true off America in 1814, but the Americans were not isolated garrisons on vulnerable islands, as the French had been at Martinique in 1809 and Guadeloupe in 1810.

A more vigorous style would have been offered by Cochrane's nephew, Thomas, who had an excellent reputation as a determined commander well able to harry his opponents, although he was very junior at the time. In 1808, for example, as captain of the frigate *Impérieuse*, Thomas Cochrane attacked positions on the coasts of southern France and Catalonia, destroying semaphore stations, fortifications, lighthouses, batteries, and bridges. Subsequently, as commander of the Chilean navy from 1818 to 1822, Cochrane played a key role in driving the Spaniards from Chile and Peru before going on to command the Brazilian navy in 1823–25 and that of Greece in

1827. Cochrane was nominated his uncle's flag captain in 1814, but due to his probably unwitting involvement in a stock market swindle, was imprisoned and dismissed from the navy. Thus, he was not available for service in North America. Another vigorous naval commander skilled in amphibious action, Vice Admiral Thomas Freemantle, was also busy elsewhere, albeit more honorably. In 1812–14, operating in the Adriatic, he drove the French from much of the coast of Dalmatia, playing a major role in the capture of the ports of Fiume and Trieste in 1813 and 1814 respectively.

Thus, it can be suggested that different commanders would have led to a much more favorable result, a view that Cochrane would doubtless have shared. Despite criticisms, such a counterfactual, or what-if scenario, is not a worthless exercise[60] as it raises the question of the possibility of British success in the war, and thus mirrors that concerning whether the Americans could have conquered Canada. These questions provide a way to gauge military effectiveness and the plausibility of plans, and thus the purpose of the war. In the specific case of Cochrane, however, the skills required to organize a fleet such as that off North America and to overcome the complexities of the American war were not necessarily those of an energetic frigate commander, which was the forte he was again to display in South America.

Moreover, the task confronting the British in North America in 1814 was very different to that facing Freemantle in the Adriatic or Cochrane later in South America and Greece. There was no question of working with an active insurrection against an unpopular imperial power, nor indeed of benefiting from, and encouraging, the collapse of this power. Some British commentators hoped that this might be the case, but even if the British were able to benefit from extensive support by Native Americans and blacks, the latter lacked the strength, not to mention the means and circumstances—i.e., freedom—to be of importance other than in marginal parts of the country. In particular, this indirect approach could not provide a formula to defeat the Americans from Massachusetts to North Carolina.

This point also raises the question of the contrast between victory in battle and in war. In command in North America, Thomas Cochrane might have provided more of the former, but would that have secured the latter? Here, it is useful to look ahead to Cochrane's service in Chile. There, at the head of amphibious forces, he successfully stormed Valdivia in 1819 and overawed Lima in 1821.[61] The contrast with the British failures at Baltimore and New Orleans in 1814–15 is readily apparent, but circumstances were different: abler and vigorous command could only achieve so much, and it is unclear that more operational success would have been strategically decisive in the War of 1812. Conversely, one of the arguments of this book is that the political consequences of the war were more significant than its military events and results. Had Cochrane, or another naval commander, had greater success in 1814–15, then the terms of peace might have been similar, but the impression of victory would have been very different.

Similarly, the marginal nature in (European) American society of the Native Americans and blacks, whom some British commanders and commentators saw as crucial aids, might have proved far more consequential as an issue if, thanks to more successes, Britain had been able to pursue an outcome of partial victory. Indeed, in 1815 Lieutenant Colonel Edward Nicolls unsuccessfully sought to use the threat of British power in order to prevent postwar American encroachments on the Native Americans in Spanish-ruled west Florida. An agreement that left the Native Americans in a better position, however, would have been at best a tentative one given the dynamism, growth, and expansionism of (European) American society. Moreover, it was not viable to imagine that the British in North America could have matched the situation in Europe where, in the postwar settlement devised at the Congress of Vienna in 1814–15, they built up their allies, particularly the Netherlands (formerly United Provinces) and Piedmont, to block French *revanche*: Belgium, until 1792 the Austrian Netherlands, was joined to the former United Provinces, both as the United Netherlands, to be under the King of the Netherlands, while the former Republic of Genoa was given to Piedmont. These were decisions by the Congress, but the British played the key role. In subsequent years, the British acted to prevent aggression by others in Europe, mostly by diplomacy but also by force, as in 1823, when troops were sent to Portugal in the face of a Spanish-supported insurrection; or in 1849, when a fleet was sent to provide the Ottomans (Turks) with a demonstration of support against Austro-Russian pressure.

This use of British power, however, was not an option as far as North America was concerned. The basis of a system to protect against American expansion was lacking: Spain, the Native Americans, and Mexico were too weak and divided, and Britain could not devote the necessary long-term attention. The bold British hopes that had not been realized included the proposal sent in May 1814 to Henry, Viscount Sidmouth, prime minister from 1801 to 1804 and home secretary from 1812 to 1822, that the British change the politics of America by turning to the slaves:

> From the great armed force now on service, abounding in military skill and judgement, arising from their own glorious establishment I venture to suggest the sending an over-whelming military force into the Chesapeake—say, not less than 25,000 men—to land in such parts of Virginia and Mary-land, as may be thought most advisable. Terms . . . to be sent to the American Executive; which, if not speedily complied with; then, Proclamations to be issued, declaring Virginia and Maryland as conquered countries, with consequent eman-cipation from slavery to all of its inhabitants, under such regulations etc. as may be considered politically advisable, leaving the other American states to make their own peace, and settle into any kind of government they may prefer . . . the great body of Negroes (surpassing that of the white inhabi-tants) rejoicing in their liberation from slavery might soon be embodied as a military force, in aid of our own, if wanted.
>
> Distributing among the emancipated slaves, one third or one half of that land, whereon they had been treated as slaves; in order to afford them a future maintenance, may be consid-ered moral, as well as political justice, and independent of this future free labor, to be paid them by their employer, as it might be on the portion of land left with the proprietor, if he chose to remain and occupy it under a new system of govern-ment established for Virginia and Maryland. Or for work per-formed for any other employer.
>
> The establishing of Virginia and Maryland into a separate government would operate on the other states in making them more peaceably disposed towards this country, and the bulk of the inhabitants being black, or people of color, would (under the protection of Great Britain) secure it from again becoming united to the other states.
>
> It would operate in effecting a valuable and strengthening

connection with Canada from the back lands of Virginia, and would open the navigation of the Ohio and Mississippi.

All this and much more might be thus achieved to the great and lasting benefit of this country, if the present crisis or favorable moment is embraced, while so large a disposable force is afloat to strike a death blow to Mr. Madison's politics, which aimed at taking a most base and cowardly advantage of our situation.

Our numerous gallant officers and soldiers could not be sent a finer climate and country for support, when connected with Canada, or ultimately be provided for better than by permitting them to settle therein that chose it as a conquered country like unto Canada, instead of being disbanded and difficult to find a maintenance at home.[62]

Such an existential prospect for the conflict did not materialize. Similarly, although in 1812 Napoleon, as he moved into Russia, considered proclaiming the freedom of the Russian serfs (peasants subject to labor under servile conditions), he did not do so. Such a move did not accord with Napoleon's limited goal of forcing Alexander I to re-enter the Continental system directed at excluding British trade.[63]

The British operations in the Chesapeake led to no gains that were retained at the close of the war, although they influenced the peace negotiations at Ghent. The British had sent too few troops to do more than raid, and there was criticism in Britain that, instead of dispatching forces to the Chesapeake, more troops should have been sent to Canada where they might have played a major role in strengthening the British position on the Niagara front or in the Lake Champlain corridor. In practice, however, aside from the wider strategic question of how could the British win this war, as opposed to avoiding losing it, there were operational issues. In particular, such a reinforcement would have strained logistical capacity. Moreover, it is unclear that Prevost's indifferent generalship at Plattsburg, or the prospects for his expedition, would have been transformed by additional troops. Furthermore, it would have taken longer to deploy the troops on the Niagara front or even along Lake Champlain than it took in the Chesapeake.

Whatever the operational and strategic disappointments or mistakes, the Chesapeake expedition had demonstrated British amphib-

ious capability, and the threat of further attacks on America remained. Clay complained from the peace talks at Ghent, "What does
wound me to the very soul is that a set of pirates and incendiaries
should have been permitted to pollute our soil, conflagrate our capital
and return to their ships."[64] He also warned of the need to plan for the
failure of the peace talks.[65] The course of the 1814 campaign had
made the repetition of British attacks apparently more, not less,
likely, and it was unclear what the Americans could do to stop them.
Indeed, in October 1814 the Senate was told by James Monroe (from
September, secretary of war as well as for state) that New York City
was at risk. Until the following February, when news of the Treaty of
Ghent arrived, he pressed for an expansion of the regular army from
sixty-two thousand to one hundred thousand troops, to be achieved
by recruiting and by drafts from the militia. Much of this planned
force was designed to protect the coast, but supporting it would have
been a major burden on American public finances, as well as on the
economy and society. The threat of British attack meant that it was
not acceptable to rely solely on the militia to protect the coast and
indeed the interior, although that call was very important. For example, in 1814 camps of Pennsylvania militia and volunteers were established southeast and southwest of Philadelphia to protect the city
from the possibility of British attack. As the campaign of 1777 had
shown, the city was vulnerable to an advance from the Chesapeake. It
was necessary, moreover, to use some regulars to defend the Atlantic
coast, which affected the number of regulars who could be sent into
Canada; although this did not prevent the government from planning
to dispatch a large number there.

American finances, however, were already in a parlous state. In
September 1814, Alexander Dallas, the newly appointed secretary of
the treasury, found not only no money but also an inability to meet
the interest payments on the national debt. Dallas indeed had to sus-
pend the payments, while his reports led Congress to increase taxes.
In practice, despite Monroe's hopes in October 1814, there were only
about forty-nine thousand men in the army at the close of the war.
Nevertheless, this reflected an important expansion in the size of the
army over the course of the war. The resulting strains included not
only financial difficulties, but also a major issue with desertion. As a
result, most of the 205 American soldiers executed during the war
were killed in 1814 when there was a major attempt to address this

growing problem.[66] As in the War of Independence, high rates of desertion were an aspect of American warmaking that was overlooked in the public myth of national resolution.

Instead of a focus on the Niagara frontier, Monroe planned an 1815 campaign that would finally gain Montréal, with a main advance up the Richelieu valley,[67] although there was every reason to believe that this would have been no more successful than the earlier attacks. Indeed, the international and military situations, as well as the drift of American politics, suggested that this would very much be the case. There was no sign that Britain would give up the struggle and, instead, British confidence was riding high after the defeat and overthrow of Napoleon. The USA lacked allies and, despite British anger that American privateers were still able to take shelter in French ports, there was no sign that that would change. Moreover, the disaffection and opposition to the war expressed by the secret meetings of New England delegates in the Hartford Convention, which met from 15 December 1814 to January 1815,[68] could be expected to encourage British hopes about American divisions and warweariness, and to undermine American operations against Montréal. Indeed, the Federalists were delighted by Napoleon's fall, which they hoped would lead to the end to war in North America.[69]

The defeat of Napoleon had also transformed Britain's commercial position, while economic pressure on the USA became more intense in 1814. The downfall of the Napoleonic empire progressively opened Europe to British trade. This opening ensured that there was less need for American goods in Continental Europe or Britain with, crucially, Baltic grain replacing American supplies, and also provided opportunities for British exporters and, thus, the British economy. Conversely, American exports were hit by the strengthening of the British blockade, by British operations in the Chesapeake, and by a lack of interest in American grain exports, which fell greatly: to a little over 41,000 barrels in 1814, in comparison to 972,000 in 1813.[70]

The British government and press were buoyed by reports of American divisions, which were a factor in leading Britain to press on, and in encouraging the attack on New Orleans in the winter of 1814–15. It would have been possible to close campaigning in 1814 without such an enterprise and without launching the all-year-round operations that it appeared to announce, but the British intended to mount a continual pressure that the Americans could not match. A

London report of 4 October 1814, printed in *Trewman's Exeter Flying-Post* of two days later, noted: "The American people are dissatisfied to the highest degree with the misconduct of Madison, and it is expected he will be compelled to relinquish his government. Mr. Rufus King, who is a Federalist, it is thought will be appointed Minister for Foreign Affairs, and some of the American papers assert that it is very probable he will supercede Mr. Madison in the Presidentship."

On 8 November, the *Star*, a leading London newspaper, reported: "Debates, it seems, in Congress are carried on with remarkable virulence. . . . a change in the Administration is the first thing looked for." *Trewman's Exeter Flying-Post* of 3 November carried the headline, "Vigorous Prosecution of the War in America," and the article noted "all our disposable force will, without loss of time, be sent out to America." The speech by George, the Prince Regent, opening the parliamentary session on 8 November, a speech written by ministers as was the norm, declared that Britain wanted peace but could win the war:

> It would have given me great satisfaction to have been enabled to communicate to you the termination of the war between this country and the USA.
>
> Although this war originated in the most unprovoked aggression on the part of the government of the US, and was calculated to promote the designs of the common enemy of Europe [Napoleon], against the rights and independence of all other nations, I never have ceased to entertain a sincere design to bring it to a conclusion. . . .
>
> The operations of His Majesty's forces by sea and land in the Chesapeake, in the course of the present year, have been attended with the utmost brilliant and successful results. . . . Notwithstanding the reverse which appears to have occurred on Lake Champlain, I entertain the most confident expectation, as well from the amount as from the description of the British force now serving in Canada, that the ascendancy of His Majesty's arms throughout that part of North America, will be effectually established."

## THE SOUTH

British failure at Lake Champlain only encouraged more of an effort in the Gulf of Mexico. 1815 was to see not an American invasion of Canada, but a British drive on New Orleans, which was regarded as the crucial point in America's presence in the South and the key, economically, to the American position in trans-Appalachia, as indeed it was. In 1800, Henry Dundas, the secretary of state for war, later 1st Viscount Melville, had pressed for an expedition to seize New Orleans from Spain, then France's ally; but none was mounted and, instead, Napoleon gained Louisiana from Spain that year by the Treaty of San Ildefonso. New Orleans then had been acquired by the USA with the Louisiana Purchase from France in 1803. Louisiana itself had been organized as a territory in 1804 and admitted as a state eight years later. The latter indeed was an aspect of the expansionism that led, two months later, to the declaration of war on the British.

Some 150 miles to the north of the Gulf, New Orleans was America's sole naval base in the Gulf region, which had been an area of American concern from the start of the war, with particular anxiety about the possibility of British cooperation with the Creeks. In the event, this cooperation did not materialize, and the Creeks suffered from going to war with the Americans before British help could be arranged. Liverpool was urged, in September 1812, to consider the conquest and retention of Louisiana. Two months later Lieutenant James Stirling, the commander of the sloop *Brazen*, which had cruised off the Mississippi delta, suggested a blockade of New Orleans, and Bathurst's papers for 1813 included details of how best to attack New Orleans, approaching from Lake Borgne,[71] the route eventually taken in 1814–15. However, it was only in 1814 that the British were able to plan for significant action in the region, Colonel Henry Bunbury, the military under-secretary at the Ministry for War and the Colonies, warned against the New Orleans expedition,[72] but there was interest in Britain in using the city as a counter in peace talks: to be returned to ensure gains elsewhere, or to be kept.

Before they could bring their force to bear to cooperate with the British, the Creeks had been defeated by Andrew Jackson in 1814. The Creeks had put Jackson under pressure at Emuckfau Creek (22 January) and Enitachopco Creek (24 January), but thanks in part to support by Cherokees and friendly Creeks, Jackson was to take and

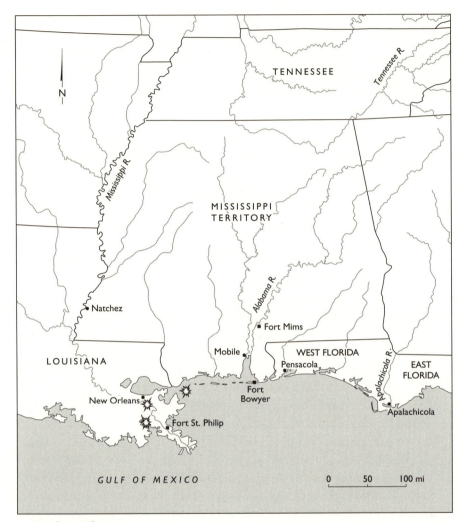

**Southern Theater**

hold the initiative thereafter. On 27 March 1814, with a total force of three thousand, he attacked the center of Creek power, storming their fortified camp at Horseshoe Bend on the Tallapoosa River. Far from relying solely on militia and regulars, Jackson also benefited from the support of about six hundred Cherokees and Creeks. Cherokees and American cavalry under Coffee attacked the Creek base from the rear, while Jackson mounted a frontal attack. The 39th U.S. Regiment, a regular unit, played the most significant role in storming the barricade at Horseshoe Bend. Jackson was astute not only in his tactics, especially his envelopment of Native American forces, but also in his response to the topography and possibilities of particular battlefields. Nine hundred out of a force of one thousand Native Americans died at Horseshoe Bend, the largest Native American number of fatalities in any battle with American forces, and one in which the defeated Creeks were slaughtered.[73]

The war ended on 9 August 1814 when Jackson, by the Treaty of Fort Jackson, imposed the cession of 23 million acres, half the Creek lands, including three-fifths of modern Alabama and one-fifth of Georgia. This was a punitive peace at the end of a devastating war for the Creeks, one in which Jackson's strategy was to destroy the Creek nation.[74] Jackson had benefited from the debilitating Creek divisions. The faction of Creeks that opposed assimilation and supported a return to native culture was referred to by its enemies as Red Sticks, the name probably deriving from the red war club the warriors wielded against their enemies. The Upper Creek towns were farthest away from American settlement and appear to have been most susceptible to Red Stick recruiting efforts, though there were Red Sticks in the Lower towns as well. There were also many non-Red Sticks in the Upper towns. The opponents of the Red Sticks sided, for the most part, with the American invaders. The Creeks were also greatly dependent on trade with the Americans.

As early as November 1812, the British had thought of using the Native Americans of the South as a diversionary aid. The following January, Benjamin Hawkins warned of "an invasion of British and West Indian Blacks, several regiments of which are actually concentrated at Jamaica."[75] Bathurst had opposed any encouragement to a slave rising, but the British expedition sent to the Gulf of Mexico in 1814 carried "a number of rifles, carbines, and an adequate quantity of ammunition for the purpose of arming the friendly Indians," and Cochrane counted on support in the New Orleans expedition from "some thousand Indians and by their assistance after the fall of the city to drive the Americans out of Louisiana beyond the Spanish boundary."[76] Moreover, in early September 1814, the Baratarian pirates under Jean Laffite, based at Barataria sixty miles southwest of New Orleans, were unsuccessfully approached for cooperation,[77] while there was also interest in recruiting African American support. In 1814, Cochrane, who set up a corps of colonial marines composed of escaped slaves, also proposed that "about one thousand men, half black troops, ought to be employed upon the coast of South Carolina and Georgia—that possession be taken of Cumberland Island . . . a force so situated acting upon the flanks of the enemy on their southern boundary will operate much in favor of the Indians and oblige the Georgians to keep troops for home defense."[78]

The defeat of the Creeks, however, obliged the British to rely on their own efforts. They developed bases on the Apalachicola River and, in August, in Pensacola; but an effort to capture Fort Bowyer at the mouth of Mobile Bay on 16 September failed: the fort held off an attack by British warships bombarding HMS *Hermes*, a 22-gunner, so heavily that it grounded and had to be destroyed. This robust defense ended the prospect of a successful attack on the fort, and the British retreated, having lost thirty-two killed to the American four. The Americans under Wilkinson, in contrast, had easily captured Mobile from the Spaniards in April 1813, following on from the seizure of the Baton Rouge area in October 1810: the seizure of Mobile was intended to pre-empt the British from doing so and succeeded in this goal. Nevertheless, looked at more positively, a handful of British marines, with the aid of Native Americans and escaped slaves, managed to mount an effective guerrilla war from Spanish Florida against the states of Georgia and Mississippi, tying down thousands of American troops. The issue of a slave force had been underlined by the Aponte Rebellion on Cuba in 1812,[79] while Cockburn's operations in the Chesapeake in 1813 were assisted by escaped slaves.[80]

A larger-scale British effort in the Gulf of Mexico was planned for the winter of 1814–15. This was to be made with the forces from the Chesapeake, once they had completed their campaign, and they were to be joined to fresh units from Europe. The latter, however, were delayed by preparations and the weather. Joseph Hutchison, a young officer in the 7th Royal Fusiliers who had served extensively in the peninsula, embarked with his regiment at Portsmouth on 6 October. Rapidly reaching Plymouth, the fusiliers were joined by the 43rd Regiment but delayed by contrary winds until 26 October. The commander of the expedition, Major General Sir Edward Pakenham, was Wellington's protégé and brother-in-law (Wellington married his sister), and a decorated veteran of the conflict with French forces in Portugal and Spain. He had been a successful divisional commander at Salamanca. Despite the delays, Pakenham's force made its way across the Atlantic to the West Indies, being deployed to the Gulf via Jamaica. Nevertheless, the contrary winds were a crucial background to, and limitation of, what was to be a large-scale use of amphibious power.[81]

Meanwhile Jackson, who bore the scar of British mistreatment during the War of Independence, advanced on Pensacola, the capital of West Florida. He demanded that its Spanish rulers force the British out, and Spanish refusal led Jackson to attack Pensacola against only limited opposition: the local Spanish and British forces were weak and the fortifications were neglected by local Spanish officials.[82] Pensacola surrendered on 7 November, after the small British force there withdrew, destroying Fort San Carlos, which guarded the mouth to the harbor.[83]

Alerted to the British build-up, and to the news that it was intended for New Orleans, Jackson (who had initially thought that the British were aiming for Mobile) then rapidly marched to the city, arriving there on 1 December. This was a key step as the loyalty of the city's population, much of which was used to French or Spanish rather than American rule, was unsettled (giving rise to British hopes[84]), while there was a lack of troops and matériel there.

In the absence of Pakenham's delayed forces, Alexander Cochrane resolved to seize the initiative. On 14 December, his gunboats and barges destroyed the American gunboats under Thomas ap Catesby Jones on Lake Borgne to the east of New Orleans. This battle greatly increased the vulnerability of New Orleans, as the British did not now need to sail up the Mississippi River from its delta and, instead, were now able to land and establish a forward position close to the city. However, unsure of the strength of New Orleans' defenses, Cochrane decided to wait for Pakenham, repeating the caution he had shown off Baltimore three months earlier.

American attempts on 23–24 December to regain the initiative by attacking the forces the British had already landed were checked, but they demonstrated American strength, which further convinced Cochrane to wait for Pakenham (who was delayed by contrary winds), and to land artillery and construct batteries rather than moving forward. Arsène Lacarrière Latour, a French engineer in American service, argued that these American attempts were "the saving of Louisiana," as they led the British not to advance on New Orleans while it was unprepared.[85]

Pakenham arrived on Christmas Day, but Jackson, meanwhile, had been building up his defenses. The young Thomas Wentworth Buller (1792–1852), a British naval officer and later a commander in the navy, wrote to his uncle from HMS *Bedford* off "Chandeleur Isles" [Chandler Island]:

> All hands here are earnestly employed in the siege of New Orleans; the place seems naturally unfavorable to our operations, almost the whole country consisting of one impassable morass, and the line of battle ships not having water enough to get within eighty miles of the landing place. The boats crews and West India regiments have suffered a little from the severity of the weather on our first arrival, but the landing has been effected in a place which seems to have been unknown or deemed impracticable by the enemy. The boats proceeded seven miles up a creek so narrow as for the most part to preclude the use of oars, and sheltered by reeds which in this country grow to a great height. Half the army disembarked undiscovered within nine miles of the town. The next night they were surprised by the enemy who dropped some ships down the river which opened a destructive fire upon their flank while General Jackson attacked in front. The darkness of the night created considerable confusion, but the enemy were repulsed with loss: The advance of our army has been retarded by a ship and schooner which completely commanded the only road to the town. Those obstacles are now removed but the enemy in the mean time have strongly entrenched themselves in our front. We are now employed transporting boats across a neck of land into the Mississippi to flank the enemy's lines; a reinforcement under General Pakenham has arrived and the army are sanguine in their expectations of overcoming the difficulties which oppose them. There is only a fortnight's provisions I believe remaining in the fleet . . . so that we have starvation in our rear, and consequently, I think the strongest incitement to proceed.[86]

On 28 December 1814, the British delivered a series of probing attacks aimed at gaining intelligence, but they were beaten off, with British columns checked by American firepower. Instead of appreciating the highly disadvantageous nature of the axis of advance on which the British forces were placed and altering plans, Pakenham resolved to persevere with the position he had taken over. Each side brought up artillery, but the improved American defenses helped Jackson repel another attack on 1 January 1815. This result owed something to the inability of the British artillery to suppress the American guns. Thanks to the availability of naval guns, the British had more cannon —twenty-two to the American fifteen—and knocked out three American cannon, losing one of their own; but they lacked sufficient ammunition, in large part due to the problems of bringing up enough from the fleet. Bowlby wrote of the period prior to 8 January, "We were being frequently marched up close to the enemy's breastworks and then retiring. The enemy were entrenched in strong fieldworks on a small isthmus between the swamps and the river."[87]

The American success provided an opportunity for the arrival of reinforcements, mostly twenty-five hundred militia from Kentucky, although there was an unwillingness on the part of many to serve and many of those who did were poorly equipped. The reinforcements, nevertheless, indicated the range of American commitment which the war helped give rise to. Brigadier General John Adair, the commander of the Kentucky troops, had been at the Battle of the Thames the previous year. Jackson's forces also included two battalions of "free men of color," i.e., not slaves. In contrast, due to the deficiencies of their plans, which unrealistically underestimated the problems of ensuring Native American cooperation, and also to Jackson's success, the British were backed by only a few Creeks and Seminoles. Thus, they did not receive the Native American support they had hoped for, while the Choctaws played a major role in helping Jackson. In the words of a critical modern account: "Pakenham was the agent of an anachronistic imperial order sent to make war against Americans with native allies who were in fact no longer capable of sustaining coalitions with Europeans. Jackson, the herald of a new empire, understood native peoples as at best expendable allies and at worst barbarous enemies."[88]

The British had also failed to win over the Baratarian pirates, while the Spanish and French population had not rebelled. More specifically in military terms, there was no equivalent to the decisiveness and speed of the British operations against Copenhagen in 1807, but then Copenhagen's coastal position made it more vulnerable, while the terrain was also very different. Reports from the British army published in the English press on 28 January 1815 noted the strain of operations:

> Ever since the 13th [of] December, when the army began to move from the ships, the fatigue of disembarking and bringing up artillery and supplies from such a distance has been incessant, and, I must add, that owing to the exertions of the navy, the army has never wanted provisions. The labor and fatigue of the seamen and soldiers were particularly conspicuous on the night of the 7th inst. when fifty boats were dragged through a canal into the Mississippi.

On 8 January 1815, having built up his strength, Pakenham launched what he saw as the decisive attack on the American position. Although Pakenham sent up the signal rocket before the British troops on the west (other) bank of the Mississippi were ready, they seized the American covering position on this bank. The weak defense of this position led to subsequent recriminations among the Americans.[89] In contrast, the British had no success on the main front. There, they were organized in four columns, but key units had not taken their positions before the advance was launched, and the sugarcane bundles and ladders designed to allow the troops to cross the canals were not brought to the fore. This later led to the court-martial and cashiering of Lieutenant Colonel Thomas Mullins.[90] Moreover, the main column was directed against what was the strongest part of the American defenses in the mistaken belief that it was the weakest. American defensive firepower, from cannon and guns, was formidable, and the British attack, in tightly packed formations, moving forward over the cane stubble on a narrow front, provided a good target. Harry Coles suggested that this was "Bunker Hill re-enacted on swampy Southern soil," but although the advancing British outside Boston in 1775 had also taken heavy losses, they had at least driven the Americans from their position.[91]

Not so in 1815. Whereas the twenty-six British cannon focused on the American artillery, the latter fired on the British infantry, causing heavy casualties with their grape and canister shot. Neither of the British advances were successful. Instead of pressing home the attack, the British infantry slackened, losing impetus and the initiative, and increasing their vulnerability to American fire, both cannon and infantry. One regiment, the 44th, broke and fled. Having galloped up to stop the rout, Pakenham was shot and his horse killed. He was in the act of mounting his aide-de-camp's horse when he was shot again, this time through the spine. The wound proved fatal, and as he lay dying he proclaimed that the battle was lost "from want of courage." British officers struck wavering troops with the flat of their swords, but to no effect,[92] although doggedness led other troops to stand under fire rather than to flee. Bowlby's account brought together the initial confusion and the decimating American firepower:

> The 44th Regiment being ordered to carry fascines and ladders across the ditch and breastwork, but missed finding them in the dark. They were sent back to bring them, and when they again came up the men were quite exhausted. Passing to the front it now being daylight, the enemy opened a tremendous fire, they threw down the fascines and ladders and rushed through the regiment in the rear throwing them into confusion. Generals Pakenham and Gibbs being killed the army retired. In this engagement I received a shot wound in the head striking over the right eye which left me insensible on the ground. There were a few riflemen to protect the wounded, and the enemy not having come out from their works, in half an hour I was able to rise and walk off the field.[93]

Joseph Hutchison of the 7th Royal Fusiliers recorded the strength of American firepower. He was in a force under Lieutenant Colonel Benny that attacked the redoubt on the Mississippi on the right of the American front line on the east bank of the river:

> After marching a short distance on a pretty good road by the river side we quitted it and remained in column covered by the 43rd company in extended order until a rocket which had been the arranged signal was let off upon which we gained the road and marched rapidly forward, still covered by the skirmishers.
>
> But we had scarcely advanced one hundred yards when it became suddenly broad daylight and we were saluted by two field pieces filled with grape shot. The troops on the road who had escaped the fire inclined to the left and got on the banks of the Mississippi and dashed on in double time and got into

the Redoubt without further opposition. After remaining in the Redoubt a short time during which Colonel Benny was killed, finding no support was coming and our men being killed I who was the senior officer in the Redoubt gave orders to retire—which was done, but before we could get out of range of the guns of the enemy they fired another round of grape and committed great destruction. On assembling the troops when out of fire, only fifteen men were found service-able out of 85 of which the company was composed one hour before. I received seven shots through my clothes and cape.

The battalion which had acted in line as the reserve in the attack of the morning, had approached near the works and been so long detained in covering the retreat of the attacking column that it was deemed more advisable to remain lying down where they were than retiring for half a mile across a perfect flat exposed to the fire of the whole American lines, and continued in that disagreeable situation until dark at night, a period of twelve or fourteen hours very much exposed and cost many men.[94]

The British suffered two thousand casualties, over forty per cent of the attacking force, including 484 prisoners, while the Americans suffered only seventy-one casualties.[95]

Pakenham's replacement, Major General John Lambert, in dis-patches of 10 January that were printed in the *London Gazette* of 11 March, argued that a delay in the attack was crucial in its failure. He reported that the delay was due to a fall in the river, that this affected the arrival of the boats intended to help cover the attack on the Amer-ican artillery on the other bank of the Mississippi, and that, as a result, four or five hours were lost. Thus, the attack was launched after it became light, which helped the aim of the defenders. Lambert continued: "As they advanced, a continued and most galling fire was opened from every part of the line, and from the battery on the right bank." He claimed that the death of the commanders, Pakenham and Major General Sir Samuel Gibbs, and "the preparations to act in crossing the ditch not being so forward as they ought to have been . . . caused a wavering in the column, which in such a situation became irreparable" and therefore led to the troops falling back. The author of the *Annual Register* was more pithy, writing of "an enterprise which appears to have been undertaken with more courage than judgment."[96] In a counterfactual essay, Thomas Fleming has suggested that Wellington, supported by stronger naval forces, would have enfiladed the barricades from the river, forcing the defenders to go down to defeat in the open.[97]

The British remained in an exposed position for ten days before retreating. In doing so they abandoned some of their cannon, but the Americans did not use the opportunity to harry the retreating forces. A secondary British attack on Fort St. Philip near the mouth of the Mississippi in January, which would have enabled the British to sail up the river and support the defeated forces near New Orleans, also failed. This attack underlined the deficiencies of naval bombardments when against a well-defended position. From 9 to 18 January, the British poured a lot of shot into the fort, but without inflicting many casualties, and the American garrison was able to return fire.

Lambert, more successfully, went on farther east to capture the inadequately manned Fort Bowyer, which protected the entrance to Mobile Bay. Having landed on 7 February, the British besieged the fort, which surrendered on the 11th, the day on which the British battery was completed. Bowlby noted that "as soon as the guns were ready to open [fire] upon [the fort] it surrendered having little strength towards the land side where we had our battery, though strong on the side of the sea."[98] Hutchison presented a somewhat idyllic account: "For want of amusement, we, by the assistance of the Navy, built of the pines and the old sails of the men of war a theatre and while besieging Mobile Fort acted plays, the officers once a week and the soldiers twice."[99]

News of the Peace of Ghent, however, prevented Lambert from proceeding against the city of Mobile, which would have proved an important base both on the Gulf of Mexico and for links with Native Americans. The peace also brought to an end Lieutenant Colonel Edward Nicolls' talk of marching from Fort Apalachicola with a force of blacks and Native Americans towards Charleston to link up there with a British amphibious force.[100] Instead, Nicolls faced pressure from the Americans to return slaves that had sought shelter from American or Spanish rule. He responded defiantly, replying to Benjamin Hawkins that they had been sent "to the British colonies where they are received as free settlers and land given them."[101] Cockburn rejected similar pressure.[102]

News of the battle of New Orleans also affected the possibility of new negotiations, for, as the Treaty of Ghent did not provide for peace until it had been ratified, the British government had to consider not only the prospect of the war continuing, but also the possibility of fresh talks and different terms if they were victorious at New Orleans. However, the government would not have pressed for the acquisition of the city had the Americans ratified the treaty. Although the British attack failed, the American leaders knew how close they had come to disaster. They realized that, had British troops taken the city, it would have been difficult to dislodge them short of accepting British terms, and that whoever controlled New Orleans ultimately controlled all the states of the Ohio and Mississippi valleys.

Indeed, the strategic significance of New Orleans helps also explain why Florida was so important, as any power that controlled one of the many fine ports on that coast (Biloxi, Mobile, Pensacola, Apalachicola, even Tampa) would have a good base from which either to blockade the mouth of the Mississippi or to mount an attack on New Orleans. In contrast, without a Gulf Coast port mounting a sustained attack on New Orleans would have been a lot more difficult. Militarily, had such a port been held, it would have been possible to continue despite one failed attack. The British could have withdrawn to Mobile and regrouped for another effort, as they had done in Halifax in 1776 after failure at Boston before attacking New York. Or, possibly, there would have been no need for an amphibious assault. A squadron in Mobile would have been just as effective at shutting down the port of New Orleans and throttling the trans-Appalachian west as a direct attack, and a whole lot less costly. Thus, New Orleans was the key to the West, Florida the key to New Orleans, and the commercial-political sense of threat that had led America to war in 1812 might have recurred, albeit in a different form.

The possibility that the Americans might not ratify the treaty also opened up other prospects. Colonel Thomas Browne sought to capitalize on his experience. He had served during the War of Independence as commander of the East Florida Rangers, a Loyalist provincial unit that had been successful in mounted raids in Georgia, and had also been responsible for links with Southern Native Americans. Browne informed Liverpool that, if war continued, it would be necessary to send "a very powerful force" to secure the British position in the Floridas and Louisiana, unless the ministry turned to him and provided him with a regiment of light troops as well as military stores and clothing so that he could exploit his links with the Native Americans.[103] Such projectors exist in all wars, but it is instructive to see the focus of their suggestions.

Due to the battle of New Orleans, however, the fighting ended with a strong impression of British failure. For the Americans, this was a welcome compensation to their setbacks in Canada and the Chesapeake. *Niles' Weekly Register* was able to claim on 4 March 1815 that "the war was finished in a blaze of glory." The victory, indeed, helped take Jackson to the presidency in 1829.

## CONCLUSIONS

Although the composition of Jackson's force was very different to the American armies on the Canadian border, they shared a greater familiarity with campaigning and combat than their predecessors in 1812. This familiarity contributed significantly to American combat success in 1814–15, a success which was an important compensation for the hardship of the war. A sample of the enlisted troops indicates that, during the course of the conflict, 3.2 percent were killed or wounded in battle, 8.2 percent died of accident or disease, 2.6 percent were taken prisoner, and 12.7 percent deserted.[104]

The results of combat in 1814–15 were not generally as spectacular as at New Orleans or Fort McHenry, but the other American achievements were possibly more impressive. The success in taking on British regulars on the Niagara front in July 1814—at Chippawa and Lundy's Lane—indicated a growing battlefield capability, even if this American campaign was not operationally significant. The defense of Plattsburg was not pushed to the same extent as the Niagara campaign, but American land forces there had held fast in the face of a formidable and numerically superior British force, and this was important to the peace talks. Pushed onto the defensive, the Americans had thwarted British offensives, and this contributed greatly to the postwar myth that they had won the war.[105]

# 6

## CONSEQUENCES

"The terms of this instrument [the peace treaty] are undoubtedly
not such as our country expected at the commencement of the war.
Judged of however by the actual condition of things, so far as is
known to us, they cannot be pronounced very unfavorable. We lose
no territory, I think no honor. . . . Judged of by another standard, the
pretensions of the enemy at the opening of the negotiation, the
conditions of the peace certainly reflect no dishonor on us."

Henry Clay, American peace commissioner in Ghent,
25 December 1814.[1]

W hile Pakenham and his men were dying outside New Orleans,
peace had already been negotiated. This chapter considers the
consequences of the war in three sections, first the peace, second, the
aftermath in Anglo-American relations and, third, the results for
America's geopolitical position.

### THE PEACE

Peace talks had begun at Ghent in Belgium on 8 August 1814 as the
result of the USA insisting on a neutral site for the negotiations. At
the same time, the choice of Ghent rather than Gothenburg in Sweden, which was the original intended location,[2] was a coup for the
British. With Napoleon's defeat, it was garrisoned by British troops

and also close enough to London for ministers to direct negotiations and, in the case of Robert, Viscount Castlereagh, the foreign secretary, to visit as it lay on the route from the Channel ports to the European peace negotiations at Vienna.

In the discussions at Ghent, the British initially demanded an international frontier between the United States and Native Americans. The British proposed that the latter were to have an independent state in the Old Northwest, with neither the British nor the Americans able to buy land from the Native Americans, a measure intended to give the state a degree of stability. The British wanted the border agreed under the 1795 Treaty of Greenville (see Chapter 1) as the frontier for the new state. In short, the British were to fulfill a debt of honor to their Native American allies, who had helped preserve Canada,[3] not least by diverting American strength from farther east. Moreover, the establishment of this state would protect Canada,—at least much of Upper Canada—and weaken the USA. The idea, however, was unacceptable to the latter, not least because many Americans lived in the region, while such a state would also have been a barrier to American expansion farther west. Self-interest alone, however, was not the key to British policy. A sense of obligation was also important, not least in contrasting the government with former administrations.

The exchanges between the commissioners on 9 August 1814 were particularly instructive. John Quincy Adams complained that such a state, and such a boundary to American expansion, was "never contemplated by them as being in dispute—no European power had ever considered the Indian nations as Great Britain appears now to consider them," while Henry Clay "stated in strong terms his sense of the extreme difficulty of any article being framed on the subject which would be acceded to by the American government." In contrast, the British commissioners claimed that "the general views of Great Britain were to procure to the Allies a peace as permanent as that procured for themselves and to re-establish the Indian nations as a sort of barrier between the two states to prevent their future collision."[4]

Castlereagh, who visited Ghent that month, pointed out that the issue created problems[5] as "it was not intended to preclude the Americans from conquering the Indians who might be at war with them and acquiring territory by conquest as a restriction of this nature would expose them to invasion from the Indians." Henry Goulburn, one of the British commissioners, a MP and the under secretary for war and the colonies, was opposed, however, to accepting conquests in such circumstances as he feared that they would enable the Americans to push up to the Canadian frontier. Instead, he insisted on the need to maintain a barrier between Canada and the USA.[6]

The British also pressed for the removal of American warships and forts from the Great Lakes, although they wanted to be able to keep theirs there. Reflecting a sense of vulnerability driven home by the recent war, this difference was seen as a way to protect Canada, rather than as the basis for any attack on the Americans. Frontier adjustments were also demanded by the British, as was the freedom to navigate the Mississippi. Such navigation would not only offer economic benefits, but would also ensure a means to further British contact with the Native Americans, and thus underline Britain's role in the interior of the continent. Indeed, filled with foreboding, Richard Rush suggested that the British government sought to confine the USA beyond the Appalachians, repeating the French plans that had led to the Seven Years' War: "If England can exclude us from the Indian country; if she can get the Lakes, with fortifications on their southern banks; if she can get New Orleans . . . with the right to navigate the Mississippi, where will be the difference between her plans and those of France in 1752?"[7]

The frontier adjustments discussed included the British acquisition of eastern Maine, which would have guaranteed overland links between Québec and New Brunswick and provided strategic depth to the British position in both;[8] a strip along the Niagara River, in order to strengthen the British position on that critical front and on Lakes Erie and Ontario; Fort Mackinac and the nearby territory, in order to protect the British route through the Great Lakes, strengthen links with the Native Americans, and facilitate British penetration south of the Great Lakes; and a frontier line to the west of the Great Lakes that ran due west from Lake Superior at its westernmost point, rather than from the lake at a point further north to the Lake of the Woods, the route in fact taken. Extrapolated westward to the Pacific, such a frontier parallel would have given Britain part of the future states of Minnesota and Idaho, most of North Dakota and Montana, and the future state of Washington in its entirety. There was also mention of a border along the Missouri, as well as one to prevent Americans from challenging the British positions on the Columbia River, and even of a border along 45°N,[9] which runs through Minneapolis-St. Paul and serves as the Montana-Wyoming state line.

The Americans rejected these proposals and, in turn, their demands included the return of wartime territorial losses, such as Forts Mackinac, Fort Niagara, and Fort Astoria on the Columbia River; and the return of, or full payment for, all black slaves who had gained freedom as a result of British operations. Given the importance the Americans at the start of the war attached to neutral rights and impressment, it was not surprising that they wished to discuss them, as well as a commercial treaty.

The American delegation also rejected the demand for an American Indian barrier state. This was, in turn, to be abandoned by the British ministry. Henry, 3rd Earl Bathurst, secretary for war and the colonies, a minister committed to a strong British position in the colonies, complained, indeed, about a lack of support on this issue from within the British government. In September 1814, he protested that the leading minister, Robert Banks, 2nd Earl of Liverpool, the first lord of the treasury, more familiarly known as the prime minister,

> proposes to be satisfied with a simple provision of peace with the Indians. I propose security for a time at least, that the lands they now occupy should not be under the pretence of sale, (which has been much abused) taken from them. I suggest not to begin a negotiation upon our boundaries in Canada, until we know (what might be a sine qua non) whether they will admit an article providing for peace at least with the Indians. As far as peace for the Indians goes, there can be no difference of opinion. We are bound not only in honor but in policy to include them. They would never forgive us, if we deserted them: and they would be most formidable enemies to our new settlements in Upper Canada by crossing the River St Clair, laying waste to everything, and returning back to their own country, where we must not follow them, if it be considered the territory of the United States . . . we must have an article providing for the peace and security of the Indian Nation.[10]

Liverpool, however, was concerned about what he saw as the bigger picture. As he pointed out to Bathurst on 15 September, Liverpool was worried that the problems posed by the conflict would increase, and he wanted the war over.[11] For Liverpool, this was an aspect of the demobilization after the Napoleonic Wars that he saw as crucial in order to stabilize society and address unprecedented levels of national debt. Concern about popular radicalism in fact was frequently expressed to and by ministers.[12] There was also a determination to end wartime taxation. Income tax, introduced in 1799, was to be repealed in 1816. This repeal would not have been easy if the War of 1812 had broadened out. In part in response to financial needs, the army underwent significant cuts following the end of hostilities in Europe in 1814.

Indeed, the ministry was so keen on peace that, had the British won the struggle for New Orleans in January 1815, they would not have pressed for the retention of Louisiana as long as the Americans ratified the peace treaty. Whatever earlier British interest in acquiring New Orleans, Liverpool wanted the war over, did not seek territory on the Gulf Coast, and regarded New Orleans as a position rendered dangerous by disease.[13] There was also an awareness of political pressures within Britain, pressures that encouraged an end to the uncertainty of the war. Although without any direct reference to the USA, Castlereagh observed on 18 December 1814 that "the opposition are harassing, especially upon points of foreign politics. Lord Liverpool expects that this game will be pushed with increased vigor after the holidays,"[14] in other words in January.

Underlining the need to see Anglo-American relations in the wider international context, this policy of restraint and compromise was in line with the British stance at the Congress of Vienna of 1814–15 that settled the post-Napoleonic European order. Alongside a successful British determination to retain some strategic wartime gains, such as Cape Town, Malta, and Mauritius, there was a willingness to return even more territory, including Curacao, Guadeloupe, Martinique, Pondicherry, Réunion, Surinam, and the Dutch East Indies. A sense of imperial sufficiency was important in this, as was a view that only so much was necessary in order to ensure colonial and maritime security, and imperial predominance. Attitudes toward the USA readily fitted into this world view, and this indicates the limitations of treating them separately.

Nevertheless, there were also variations within this general approach. Bathurst was keener than Liverpool to drive a hard bargain with the USA. A former president of the Board of Trade (from 1807 to

1812), Bathurst was well aware of commercial and maritime rivalry between Britain and the USA. He was also committed to the development of Britain's imperial position, and more so than Liverpool, Castlereagh, and Wellington, who were more concerned with domestic and European goals. To safeguard Canada, and to show that Britain had been successful, Bathurst was keen on territorial gains for Britain. Failures at Baltimore and Plattsburg in 1814 led him to take a more moderate stance, but he still wanted a minimum of *uti possidetis*, the confirmation of what each power currently held. This would have left Britain with eastern Maine and Forts Niagara and Mackinac, and the Americans with Fort Amherstburg. In early 1815, this list would have been expanded to include the British retention of Fort Bowyer on Mobile Point.

In October 1814, the British proposed a peace based on *uti possidetis*, but, in the event, they did not persist in this claim. Earlier, however, the British would have pressed for frontier changes had their advance along Lake Champlain been more successful in 1814, and this course was urged on them for "the future security of Canada."[15] John Quincy Adams, president from 1825 to 1829, however, rejected the advice of his fellow commissioners that the USA yield on the Maine border, and the British government was ready to abandon such schemes. Reports of American defensive successes on Lake Champlain and at Baltimore influenced the discussions at Ghent, although Clay, one of the commissioners, struck a pessimistic note on 17 October: "It appears that by the unfortunate failure of Chauncey to co-operate with Brown the campaign [on the Niagara Front] is lost; and we are compelled everywhere to act upon the defensive."[16]

In turn, British newspaper readers were informed that British peace terms had alienated much American opinion, weakened the Federalists, and led to a rallying to the war in the USA.[17] In the event, neither side was willing to wait for news of the operations round New Orleans. Clay was concerned that, if Britain was successful there or at Mobile, it would be difficult to ensure the return of eastern Maine.[18] This was not the case, but reflected American anxieties about British power and intentions. In waiting for news, there was also the problem that initial reports would probably be contradictory, unreliable, and unclear. This was illustrated by accounts of the state of the conflict round Fort Erie.[19]

When his advice was sought in November 1814, Wellington was

at the Congress of Vienna, which was an indication of his political importance. He prided himself on his crusty realism and did not suggest that victory could readily be won even if he was in command. Instead, Wellington emphasized the cost to Britain of any war of conquest in North America, the difficulty of achieving more without control of the Great Lakes, and the extent to which the British lacked the basis for pushing the Americans hard in the negotiations:

> There are troops enough there for the defense of Canada for ever, and even for the accomplishment of any reasonable offensive plan that could be formed from the Canadian frontier. I am quite sure that all the American armies of which I have ever read would not beat out of a field of battle the [British] troops that went from Bordeaux [in France] last summer, if common precautions and care were taken of them. That which appears to me to be wanting [to Britain] in America is not a general, or general officers and troops, but a naval superiority on the lakes. Till that superiority is acquired it is impossible, according to my notion, to maintain an army in such a situation as to keep the enemy out of the whole frontier, much less to make any conquest from the enemy, which, with those superior means, might, with reasonable hopes of success, be undertaken. . . . I think the whole history of the war proves its truth.[20]

Wellington's advice influenced the ministry, not least encouraging it to discard the demands for territory, demands that he did not believe justified. Indeed, Wellington allegedly sent a letter to Albert Gallatin, of the American commissioners, assuring him that he had brought his weight to bear to ensure peace. Moreover, the possibility of a resumption of war in Europe encouraged the British to speed the peace. Alexander I of Russia was peremptory about territorial arrangements,[21] but Britain, France, and Austria opposed Russo-Prussian pressure for the Prussian annexation of Saxony. On 3 January 1815, they concluded a Triple Alliance agreeing to oppose, if necessary by force, Prussian ambitions in Saxony and those of Russia in Poland. Such a confrontation, and, still more, conflict, required the end of any transoceanic diversion of British strength, as this would be seen as weakening Britain however much it did in practice. The troubling situation on the Continent gave the Americans a key diplomatic advantage, not that they could claim any credit for it; and it is striking how little the USA featured in the correspondence between the key British ministers, let alone European leaders and diplomats.

From the French perspective, the cooperation of the French foreign minister, Talleyrand, with Austria and Britain was designed to replace the alliance that had defeated Napoleon by a new diplomatic order in which France could have greater influence. The USA was not a viable alternative then, or earlier, for France, and this underlined the mistaken nature of confident American assumptions about their place in the international order.

Given his views already outlined, it was not surprising that, in November 1814, Wellington urged the signing of peace with the USA without insisting on the *uti possidetis*.[22] His view was crucial, as Wellington was seen by Liverpool as the most appropriate commander in North America.[23] In response to the duke's advice, Liverpool decided that it was inappropriate to continue the war in order to win territory or to secure gains already made.

A peace treaty was indeed signed at Ghent on 24 December 1814. That the battle of New Orleans occurred after the treaty was signed often attracts comment, but fighting on after peace had been signed was not a unique event. Indeed, in 1814 Wellington and an Anglo-Spanish army fought a major battle with the French at Toulouse in southern France on 10 April, with seventy-seven hundred casualties out of the ninety-two thousand troops taking part, although Napoleon had already agreed to abdicate on 6 April. In the southwest, the French also mounted a successful sortie from Bayonne against British besiegers on 14 April. In 1815, fighting continued after Napoleon had abdicated following his defeat at Waterloo.

Hostilities in the War of 1812 did not only continue into 1815 because the news of peace had not yet reached North America. The time it took the news to arrive was a point that was often to be remarked upon, but the continuation of fighting in these circumstances was not surprising. Aside from the problems posed by the slowness of communications, the treaty, crucially, was not to come into effect until it had been ratified by both sides. This was a measure insisted on by the British because they feared that the USA would not accept the terms, but would seek to renegotiate them. There was concern that the treaty would not be ratified. In 1794, there were suggestions that the Jay Treaty be renegotiated; indeed it was ratified only by a vote of 20 to 10. Moreover, the Senate negotiated with Britain in 1806.

Britain ratified the treaty once the terms had reached London, but the British did not know that the Americans would necessarily ratify the treaty, and thus had to be aware that conflict might continue. American politics were perceived in Britain as volatile, and, from the British perspective, the American decision in 1812 to fight on despite the British repeal of the Orders in Council was not an encouraging precedent. Had the USA refused to ratify, then operations would have continued and Britain might have offered the terms to New England as a separate peace, which would have been divisive. The terms essentially confirmed the prewar *status quo*,[24] which, however, meant that impressments of sailors by the British, the cause of so much dispute, and in June 1813 described by Richard Rush as "the only point,"[25] were not mentioned. Territorial gains were to be returned, including Fort Amherstburg, which had been captured in September 1813 by the Americans.

News of the Treaty of Ghent arrived in New York on 11 February 1815 and in Washington on 13 February 1815, and the Senate felt able to accept the terms unanimously, by a vote of 35 to 0, on 16 February. The House of Commons did not display this majority. Richard Rush observed of the peace, "It comes, indeed, at a most happy point of time for our interests and our fame."[26] Madison ratified the treaty, and the instruments of ratification were exchanged in Washington on 17 February. This made the treaty binding on both sides. The war came to an official close at 11:00 PM.

Madison was quick to announce victory, and thus claim credit. Proclaiming the treaty, he informed Congress on 18 February that the war had been "signalized by the most brilliant successes." Madison followed on 4 March with a proclamation calling for a day of thanksgiving in which he declared that God had "reared" the USA "into the strength and endowed them with the resources which have enabled them to assert their national rights and to enhance their national character."[27]

The fact that the Senate ratified the treaty unanimously indicated how far the hopes of the War Hawks had not been realized, a point that was made by Federalist critics. The cost of the war and the public debt arising from it was a factor. In turn, limited goals, which reflected the fact that they had not sought the conflict, had greatly helped the

British secure peace. On their part, this was no war of reconquest. There was no drive to regain the USA, in contrast to the Spanish attempts made in Latin America after the Napoleonic Wars; but these Spanish attempts interacted with a civil war between revolutionaries and royalists, and there was no equivalent in the USA. Nor was there any equivalent there to the ethnic character of the struggle in Latin America, with the revolution, largely mestizo (mixed race) in support, seen as a threat to the creoles as well as to Spanish authority.

Ratification was not the sole issue in causing delay. The news of the peace also took a long time to reach warships on distant stations. On 23 March the American 18-gun sloop *Hornet* captured the British 18-gun brig *Penguin*. The damaged *Penguin* was scuttled and the *Hornet* then sailed for the Cape of Good Hope in company with the 18-gun sloop *Peacock*. They were chased by the ship of the line *Cornwallis* and separated, the *Hornet* throwing most of her guns over the side and sailing back to the USA. The *Peacock* rounded the Cape and captured four valuable ships of the British East India Company before the last clash of the war occurred in the East Indies on 30 June 1815. Then, the *Peacock* captured the outgunned (14-gun) British East India Company brig *Nautilus*. The claim by the latter that peace had been signed was regarded by the *Peacock* as a ruse.

## The War in Comparison

Claiming victory ensured that the Americans could ignore or shelve difficult issues. In practice, aside from repeated disappointment and failure in the field, the War of 1812 had led to a serious crisis in American government. An unwillingness to bear the cost of the conflict, which in part reflected not only political divisions but also the serious limitations of American capital markets, had left the Treasury with insufficient money. As a result, as in the War of Independence, government paper bore a significant discount, while its own contractors rejected Treasury notes, and the Treasury found it difficult to manage the national debt.

These fiscal problems meant that, irrespective of political hopes and claims, large-scale offensive operations by the Americans were no longer a serious prospect. Instead, had the war continued, with the British able to mount renewed amphibious assaults, most of the American forces probably would have been largely focused on defending their own areas from attack. Such a regionalization of the war was, in part, anyway the product of the nature of communications and of the British attack, which American forces were unable to contain. The British challenge entailed not only amphibious attacks and the threat of attacks, but also the impact of blockade on coastal trade. However, this regionalization was pushed further by the crisis in American public finances. Finances demonstrated the gap between ends and means that was also more generally true of the American war effort, for example the militia; although this gap was even more readily apparent in the case of both sides (royalists and rebels) in Latin America.

Such comparisons are valuable, not least for the differences they highlight. Looking at the war in comparison with the contemporary Napoleonic conflict in Europe is most pertinent, if at all, at the tactical level, in particular with reference to similarities in weaponry and engagements. The search for comparison is less pertinent at the operational and strategic levels, in which contrasts between circumstances in North America and Europe readily emerge. This is especially the case with the crucial role of coalition warfare in Europe, which lacked a North American counterpart—although it is also important to note the diversity of European warfare in this period, both in terms of conflict and of scale. Nevertheless, even at the tactical level, there were important differences in scale between the War of 1812 and the mainstream of Napoleonic campaigning. These differences in scale were not simply a matter of contrasts in the number of troops. In addition, although cannon played a key role in battles in North America, notably at Lundy's Lane, both sides there also lacked the quantity of artillery that was increasingly apparent on the European battlefield. Moreover, as the British showed at Bladensburg, artillery could be overcome by an infantry advance. Providing, moving, and supporting artillery was especially difficult on the Canadian frontier and in the swampy terrain near New Orleans, and this posed particular challenges for combined arms operations.

Moreover, command and control requirements were different in North America. The role of the militia and of American Indians also contributed heavily to distinctive characteristics of the fighting there. It was not surprising that subsequent American interest in Napoleonic warfare, which was prominent at West Point, led to no comparable searching of the War of 1812 for examples of Napoleonic-style campaigning. Instead, the focus at West Point was on campaigns in Europe, most prominently with the central use of Jomini's work.

Alongside the stress on problems, it is instructive to note that in the War of 1812, as also in the War of Independence and later in the Civil War, there were important improvements in American performance during the conflict. These reflected the natural trajectory of a force, much of which comprised a large number of civilian officers and men rapidly thrown into war. More specifically, the Americans learned to respond both to their opponents and to the nature of their own military system, while officers and men also gained combat and maneuver experience. The net result was that the Americans fought better in 1814–15 than in 1812–13, not least in standing up to British regulars. The battle of Chippawa is particularly indicative in this respect, even if the defeat of American militia at Bladensburg and Hampden in 1814 showed the continued weakness of inexperienced militia. The overall improvement in American fighting capability fed through into the overall result of the war. It helps to explain why the terms of the peace were the *status quo ante bellum*, and indeed why the Americans under Jackson were able to force Native American tribes still farther south and west.

This American achievement, both in fighting capability and in terms of thwarting British hopes, cannot be discussed simply in terms of success at Baltimore and victory at New Orleans, important as they were. Instead, earlier, alongside defeats and setbacks, British tactical and, sometimes, operational success, where they occurred, did not translate into strategic triumph. Alongside the issue of the aggregate result of campaigning, and the particular consequences of key operations, this British failure owed much to the grand strategic situation, including the difficulty of "defeating" the USA in the normal sense. The extent to which British public opinion and government finances were affected by the Napoleonic Wars, limiting the wish to continue operations after 1814, was also an important aspect of this situation, as was the British desire to resume trade. The War of 1812 indeed occurred when Britain was already very war-weary.

Moreover, capable American tactical and operational performance, at least on the defensive, were also important. American failure outside Washington and in Maine in 1814 was therefore unrepresentative. Partly as a result of this capable performance, American deficiencies at every level of war led not to disaster, but to stalemate. This was an impressive result against the world's leading military power, for, if Britain was war-weary, it also had an experienced military.

The effectiveness of the British in distant operations, indeed, was to be demonstrated anew in the Maratha war of 1817–18 in India, although these campaigns were not waged at the expense of the British taxpayer, nor did they depend upon British manpower. Victories at Kirkee, Sitabaldi, Mahidpur, Koregaon, and Satara reflected the extent to which the British were proficient in warmaking on the Subcontinent and also the high tempo of conflict. These battles were hard-fought. Mahidpur, on 21 December 1817, showed that New Orleans did not prove that the British could not achieve triumphs in attack. Instead, with cavalry support, the infantry under Brigadier General Sir John Malcolm advanced under heavy fire from the Maratha artillery. The Maratha infantry mostly retreated, but the gunners continued to fire until bayoneted beside their cannon, as was also the case with Barney's gunners at Bladensburg. Like the successful British naval attack on Algiers in 1816, this Anglo-Maratha war indicated that war-weariness and financial problems did not prevent the British from mounting successful operations. This capability encourages a re-examination of the British decision to bring the War of 1812 to a close, but the situation and the context, both military and political, were very different in the various cases. The Algiers expedition, for example, was a short-term naval operation that did not involve any landing of troops and that matched established conventions of British power projection. The navy was readily able to fulfill the commitment. Against Algiers, Admiral, Lord Exmouth, commanded a fleet of five ships of the line and sixteen other warships, as well as the support of a Dutch frigate squadron. The successful bombardment of the port was very different, in course and impact, to the failure of the naval operation against Baltimore in 1814, although the British also took considerable casualties at Algiers. In 1815, the Americans blockaded Algiers to force the surrender of American sailors, but the expedition, although also successful, was on a much smaller scale.[28]

Britain could pursue the Anglo-Maratha war of 1817–18 with Indian resources, both military and financial. In contrast, there was no local support on this scale for Britain in North America. Canada and the West Indies could not offer comparably large military forces, particularly for a sustained offensive, and the Native Americans were not able to provide a significant offensive force. This contrast under-

lines the extent to which the strength and capability of a major imperial power have to be considered in specific spheres rather than simply as an overall or aggregate issue.

In terms of the goals it sought in 1812, the USA, which had, after all,
started the war, also lost it.[29] Indeed, the claim often made that the
Vietnam War was the first to be lost by the USA needs rethinking in
this light. This rethinking also opens up a new way to consider the
use of the Vietnam War in early American discussion of Gulf War II.[30]

Nevertheless, it has also been argued that there was victory for
both sides in the War of 1812, as the conflict led not only to the British
retention of Canada, but also to a major strategic accomplishment for
the USA: the defeat of the Native Americans and the breaking of their
link with the British.[31] The breaking of this link was crucial, as it was
part of a withdrawal of British power and concern from the interior of
much of North America, a withdrawal that was to play a key element
in the geopolitics of Native American power.[32] Spain, and still less its
successor, Mexico, were not strong enough to organize and support
Native American resistance to the expansion of the USA,[33] and only
Britain could play the role.

More specifically, the war played a decisive role in destroying the
Southeastern (Old Southwest) and Northwestern Native American
confederacies. The Creeks were devastated by the conflict that in part
was an aspect of the War of 1812, while the Iroquois were also hit hard.[34]
The devastating nature of American operations against the Native
Americans was captured by a letter of September 1812 to Madison from
Richard Mentor Johnson, the major of a battalion of mounted Kentucky
volunteers, as well as a member of the House of Representatives. Writing from Fort Wayne, Johnson noted: "I have just returned from the
expedition to the Elkhart village upon the River of that name, which
village we destroyed. Tomorrow we commence an expedition composed of mounted men, the object of which is to drive the savages from
our limits and destroy all we can find. We have conquered the Miamis
as enemies. The evidence of their hostility is complete."[35]

Two months later, Harrison sent John Campbell to destroy the
Miami villages on the Mississiniwa River, but the mission was ended
after a Miami attack in mid December.

After the defeat and death of Tecumseh at the Battle of the Thames, many of the northwestern Native Americans signed an armistice with Harrison on 14 October 1813 and, the following July, at Greenville, pledged loyalty to the USA. This was a major drawback for the British. As a result of the agreement with Harrison, Naiwash, an Ottawa chief, complained about a lack of unity and action at a meeting of the remains of Tecumseh's confederation held on 6 October 1814 at Dundas, Upper Canada: "Since our great chief Tecumseh has been killed, we do not listen to one another, we do not rise together, we hurt ourselves by it."[36] The Peace of Ghent obliged the Americans to restore the Native Americans to their prewar situation and to negotiate treaties with the tribes, but there was no British guarantee that their position would be maintained.[37]

The Native Americans east of the Mississippi had been greatly weakened in the war, which helped ensure that the European Americans encountered only localized resistance to their expansion over the following decades. The Native Americans made peace with the USA, the Potawatomi for example at Portage des Sioux on 18 July 1815. The American position was defined with the construction and rebuilding of forts such as Fort Crawford at Prairie du Chien,[38] while Indiana became a state in 1816, Illinois in 1818, and Missouri in 1821. Subsequent opponents east of the Mississippi were beaten. Black Hawk of the Sauks, an ally of the British during the war, who was disillusioned with their abandonment of the Native Americans in 1815, was defeated by the Americans in the Black Hawk War in Illinois and Wisconsin in 1832. Significantly, looking back to an earlier alignment, Black Hawk had visited Fort Simcoe in Canada on a number of occasions after the War of 1812 and his supporters were known as the "British Band,"[39] but the British ceased giving presents and links were broken, part of a more general process that greatly eased the American strategic position.[40]

The War of 1812 led, on the frontier, to squatters claiming Native American lands,[41] and, in already-settled territories, it strengthened anti–Native American attitudes in the USA, not least because politicians who had played a prominent role in the conflict, such as Andrew Jackson, rose to power. The Native Americans were not to be part of the new USA, except on terms that destroyed their cultural integrity. Even those who had helped the European Americans suffered, such as the Choctaws, who lost their land under treaties of 1816 and 1830.[42]

The rise of Jackson looked toward the American aggression shown in the First Seminole War in Florida in 1817–18.[43] Indeed, although during the War of 1812 the scene of struggle in the Southeast had in part shifted from Florida to Alabama, the Creek War there suggested some of the continuities in American expansionism, from the efforts under Madison to seize the Floridas (some of which, such as that in March 1812, were unsanctioned by the government[44]), to operations after 1815 along that frontier. This activity, rather than failure in Canada, helps situate the War of 1812 firmly in the course of American territorial expansionism, not least because the conflict encouraged support from the government for the acquisition of Florida.[45]

Thus, the War of 1812 was crucial to the course of US-Spanish relations. It enabled the USA to consolidate its pre-1812 gains and to add more along the Gulf Coast east of the Pearl River. The conquest of Mobile in 1813 (the sole American territorial gain during the war) was particularly important, not least in making Spain fearful of further American steps, which helped make Spanish officials in Pensacola and St. Augustine more amenable to American wishes in 1814 than they would otherwise have been. This accommodation was important to British and Native American options, notably the failure of the British to maintain a position in Pensacola. The American position in the hinterland was consolidated when Mississippi and Alabama became states in 1817 and 1819 respectively.

The combination of the two, of American success to the south with failure to the north, helped ensure that American migration would flow west and not north. Given the unwelcome cold of Canada, this might appear a surprising remark, but, in terms of the communications options in the late-1810s, there was a lot to be said for Americans settling north of Lakes Erie and Ontario, from which it was possible to trade back into America or down the St. Lawrence in the summer.

Black slaves were scarcely full participants either in the new USA, and it is unsurprising that about four thousand fled from the USA with the British at the close of the war. The British refused to accept the American argument that they were obliged to return them as property. Instead, using the argument of the jurist Sir William Blackstone, and of the judge, Lord Mansfield, in the Somersett case of 1772, that slavery could not be enforced in Britain (which was popularly interpreted as to mean that it did not exist there), British commanders argued that slaves who had reached the shelter of British units and ships were thereby free. This argument was also employed in the case of slaves from Spanish Florida who had taken shelter with the British. There were demands for their return, both from the owners and from the Spanish authorities, but British officers proved unhelpful. The crosscurrents of British governmental views toward slaves were captured, nevertheless, by Bathurst (who, as secretary for the colonies, was responsible for British slave colonies such as Jamaica) in issuing instructions to Colonel Sir Thomas Sidney Beckwith when he campaigned in the Chesapeake in 1813:

> You will on no account give encouragement to any disposition which may be manifested by the Negroes to rise against their Masters. The Humanity which ever influences His Royal Highness [the Prince Regent, later George IV] must make Him anxious to protest against a system of Warfare which must be attended by the atrocities inseparable from commotions of such a description. If any individual Negroes shall in the course of your operations have given you assistance, which may expose them to the vengeance of their Masters after your retreat, you are at liberty on their earnest desire to take them away with you. You are authorized to enlist them in any of the Black Corps if they are willing to enlist; but you must distinctly understand that you are in no case to take slaves away as slaves, but as free persons whom the public become bound to maintain. This circumstance as well as the difficulty of transport, will make you necessarily cautious how you contract engagements of this nature, which it may be difficult for you to fulfill.[46]

Later that year, Captain Barrie, then on blockade duty in Lynnhaven Bay, noted the opportunities:

> The Slaves continue to come off by every opportunity and I have now upwards of 120 men, women and children on board. I shall send about 50 of them to Bermuda. . . . Amongst the Slaves are several very intelligent fellows who are willing to act as local guides should their Services be required in that way, and if their assertions be true, there is no doubt but the Blacks of Virginia and Maryland would cheerfully take up Arms and join us against the Americans. Several Flags of

Truce have been off to make application for their Slaves, but not a single black would return to his former owner.[47]

During the war, as conflict moved southward and the British took the offensive, their willingness to receive and arm escaped slaves became more apparent and, indeed, aroused American anger. Cochrane's interest in raising slave support became more pronounced as the war came to a close. It was a pale equivalent of the increased reliance on Loyalists from 1778 in the War of Independence,[48] but is, nevertheless, instructive for what it suggests about a possible new order.

Some blacks, however, fought against the British, notably in the crews of boats on the Great Lakes and at the battle of New Orleans, providing possibly more than 10 percent of Jackson's manpower there.[49] In that campaign, Jackson also benefited from the support of the Baratarian pirates who were based on the coastal islands of Louisiana. An effort was made to accommodate them in the new America, and they were pardoned by Madison. However, some preferred to return to piracy and smuggling, now based on Galveston, and indeed several were hanged in New Orleans in 1819.[50]

Whereas, from the British conquest of French Canada in 1760 until the outbreak of the War of Independence in 1775, there had been no effective rivalry among the non-indigenous powers in North America, the situation had changed thereafter because the Americans failed to expel the British from Canada. As a result, there were two strong states in North America, which was a major constraint on American power as it ensured that America's North American opponents could look to Britain. However, for Britain the unwanted fact and unsuccessful character of the War of 1812 encouraged a new relationship between the two states. Postwar conciliation of the USA was seen in the speedy abandonment of British-held positions in lands agreed to belong to the USA, as well as in the rapid negotiation of a commercial convention, in the agreement to demilitarize the Great Lakes, in the British willingness to note at least the implications of the Monroe Doctrine for Latin America, and in the partial settlement of frontier disputes. This new position contrasted greatly with the more difficult situation after the War of Independence.

What this position meant in practice was frequently unattractive. At the close of the War of 1812, a significant number of runaway slaves remained at Prospect Bluff on the Apalachicola River in West Florida, where Edward Nicolls, a British officer, had constructed what he christened Fort Apalachicola, but which was known as Fort Negro by the Americans. Nicolls argued that article nine in the Peace of Ghent stating that lands taken from Native Americans during the war would be returned to them as part of the peace meant that the Treaty of Fort Jackson at the expense of the Creeks was invalid.[51] Nicolls also pressed for the Americans to heed Native American interests.[52] The Americans, however, insisted that the article only referred to Native Americans still at war at the time of the Peace of Ghent (which excluded the Creeks who had signed the Treaty of Fort Jackson), and claimed that the Creek chiefs linked to Nicolls were unrepresentative.[53] Nicolls' position was not formally taken by the British government. Without authority, Nicolls negotiated an alliance treaty between Britain and the Creeks and travelled to London with Josiah Francis, a Creek leader, only to find the British government unwilling to listen to either of them or to heed the treaty. Concerned about the runaway slaves, an unsanctioned American army and navy expedition under Colonel Duncan Clinch attacked and destroyed the fort on 27 July 1816. They found it mounting ten cannon and with thirty-two hundred firearms in the arsenal. An American shot ignited the powder magazine, destroying the fort and killing about 270 of the defenders. The blacks captured were enslaved.[54] Despite reports the previous year that the British would intervene in Florida,[55] they did not act.

## ANGLO-AMERICAN RELATIONS

The Treaty of Ghent had provided for the adjustment of boundary disputes between Canada and the USA by joint commissions. In 1818, a convention recognized American fishing rights off Labrador and Newfoundland, agreed to the evacuation of the British garrison on Moose Island, and extended the boundary along the 49th parallel, from the Lake of the Woods to the Rockies. Moreover, the Oregon Territory to the west was, it was agreed, to be jointly administered by Britain and America for ten years, structuring the USA claim to a Pacific border, which had not been insisted upon at the time of the Louisiana Purchase. Neither Britain nor the USA used the unsettled state of the border in 1815 as an excuse to attempt a wider revisionism nor, indeed, to reopen hostilities. This convention was extended indefinitely in 1827 and, in practice, until the Oregon Boundary Treaty of 1846.[56]

The 1818 Convention excluded Russia (in Alaska) and Spain, and its successor Mexico. These were the other two powers that bordered the Oregon Territory. Spain recognized the convention in 1819. Until that point, Spain refused to recognize a western boundary to the Louisiana Purchase. It had not been a party to the 1818 Convention, Britain claiming that Spain had no standing in the matter anyway because it had effectively surrendered title with Nootka Sound in 1790. Spain protested against Anglo-American presumptions, but might made right. In the 1819 Transcontinental Treaty (also called the Adams-Onis Treaty after the negotiators), Spain recognized the 1818 Convention as well as selling Florida to the USA. Jackson had invaded Florida in 1818 and Spain had no power to push him out and no ally to back it. The status of Texas, however, became a point of contention. Southern Democrats would charge Adams with having given away Texas in 1819, leading to talk of its "re-annexation" in 1845 as the lost and now restored part of the Louisiana Purchase. Given that the War of 1812 had demonstrated British military capability in the coastal parts of the region, with the arrival of HMS *Racoon* at Fort Astoria in December 1813, the American presence in the Oregon Territory after 1815 reflected the value to the USA of good relations with Britain as well as the willingness of Britain, in its search for good relations, to move beyond the military situation.

On the British side, Robert, Viscount Castlereagh, foreign secretary from 1812 to 1822, who, with Liverpool and Bathurst, practically decided all foreign policy and colonial questions, argued that patience, tact, and altered circumstances might produce solutions to disputes, both with the USA and more generally. In addition to the 1818 Convention, the Commercial Convention of 3 July 1815 sought to settle trade issues on the basis of reciprocity of tariffs, while the Rush-Bagot Agreement of April 1817 limited naval armaments on the Great Lakes to those necessary for preventing smuggling.[57] There had been talk at Ghent of America opening the navigation of the Mississippi to Britain in return for access to the inshore fisheries off Newfoundland,[58] but this was not pursued, and both treaty and convention were silent on the fisheries.[59] The war had left the Americans in a dire financial situation, which made them vulnerable; but, after the war, the American government was able to borrow the necessary money from British banks.

At the same time, there were also continuing tensions between Britain and the USA. As envoy in London from 1817 to 1825, Richard Rush complained about his failure to win concessions over impressments or trade to the West Indies, and he was convinced of British hostility to the USA, a hostility that he regarded as widely held and not restricted to the Tory government.[60] Tensions became more acute in the 1830s, with the disputed Maine frontier leading in 1838 to the bloodless "Aroostook War" between Maine, which had become a state in 1820, and the colony of New Brunswick (which was part of Canada); and, in 1839, to American planning for war. Political concern about relations was more sustained, with Democratic expansionists seeing Britain as a threat.

The prospect of war throws interesting light on the War of 1812. Despite the political-economic problems of the Panic of 1837 in America, the American and British commanders considered the logistical situation in 1837–39 much better for the Americans than in 1812: with the Erie Canal and new roads, there was much more infrastructure available, which would have aided the deployment of American power against Canada. Indeed, the War of 1812 had led to a major development in the American economy, in part because of the stop of imports from Britain, a stop that reflected wartime disruption, legal prohibition, and a crisis in American liquidity that reflected the collapse of America's exports. The shift of resources to American manufacturing then laid the foundation for rapid growth after 1815.[61]

Nevertheless, British strengths in 1837 are also an instructive comment on the War of 1812. The Royal Navy remained the most powerful in the world, and the unsuccessful insurrection of 1837–1908 in Canada (which was backed by American filibusters)[62] led to a significant increase in the British garrison which the navy was well able to convoy across the Atlantic. The nature of British military power that had posed such a challenge to the Americans during the War of 1812 remained significant in 1837–39: the interconnected nature of British military strength and the role of the Royal Navy was shown with the navy moving troops within British North America—from Halifax to Saint John, New Brunswick, and Québec—and also there from the West Indies, Gibraltar (units en route home from Corfu), and the British Isles.

Warships moreover carried specie for the commissariat. The vessels used as troopships included large warships.[63]

Furthermore, British success in the War of 1812 had ensured an increase in the Canadian population, which served as the basis for Loyalist support. This helped counteract concern about the extent of French Canadian backing for British rule, not least the possibility of active resistance, on the part of French Canadians[64] and also from American settlers. In 1815, Henry, Viscount Sidmouth, the home secretary, had received a suggestion from Colonel Stephenson that the government stabilize the situation in Canada by introducing a form of military feudalism:

> I have understood that your Lordship is sensible of the hostile spirit which prevails in America against this country and that political rivalship which keeps it alive, and that your Lordship is anxious to guard our Canadian provinces against surprise, as the Americans will not fail to strengthen their frontier and build vessels of force on the Lakes. I conceive the most economical mode would be to disband some of the young regiments that may now be in America and, to induce the officers to settle there, to grant lands according to their rank to be held of the Crown by feudal service for themselves and heirs. You would thus have an effective and formidable militia that could be brought into immediate active service without the expense of recruiting, and commanded by officers of some experience. I think it would be politic to engage as many officers to settle as you could from any regiments as the mode of conducting war in that country is different from the tactics of Europe and requires local knowledge and experience.[65]

In practice, the British government relied on encouraging large-scale emigration to Canada, although this proved more difficult than had been anticipated. Army veterans were settled on the frontier in both Lower and Upper Canada after 1815. Alongside American settlers in Upper Canada, in 1815–30, the majority of British emigrants went to Canada and, partly as a result, the population of Upper Canada rose from 60,000 in 1811 to 150,000 by 1824. Loyalists played a major role in suppressing an insurrection in Canada in 1837–38 that arose from anger about land tenure, and Wellington, then commander in chief of the army, pressed, in the 1840s, the importance of "a well organized and well disciplined militia" for the defense of Canada.[66]

Continued American concern about the British, and, in particular, the strength of their fleet, led in turn to a program of coastal fortification. New York harbor, for example, was strengthened with Fort Hamilton from 1825 and Fort Wadsworth from 1847. The capture of Pensacola was followed by major fortifications there which were intended to control the anchorage; and, after gaining San Francisco in 1846 during the Mexican-American War, a fortress was built to control the narrows at the entrance to the bay. It survives under the southern ramp to the Golden Gate Bridge. West Point focused on the education of engineering officers for such positions.

American concern also led Brigadier General Edmund Gaines to press the federal government, in the 1830s and 1840s, to build a rail system capable of rapidly moving militia from the interior to the coasts. Gaines himself had been badly injured while commanding the defense of Fort Erie in 1814. He was typical of the importance of the War of 1812 for the development of a key generation of commanders. In turn, rumors of American invasion preparations, for example from New York in late 1845, were followed carefully in Britain, where there was also concern about the position on the Great Lakes, not least in response to the number of American steamships plying the Great Lakes. The eventual location of the capital of the United Province of Canada (Québec and Ontario), formed in 1841, at inland Ottawa was a defensive measure to overcome the apparent vulnerability of Toronto, Kingston, and Montréal to American attack. Earlier, Wellington, as master general of the ordnance from 1818 to 1827, had supported building not only forts but also the Rideau canal system so as to be able to move troops from Montréal to Kingston away from the frontier. This capability was designed to reduce the vulnerability of Canada to American attack, and reflected the level of concern about the latter.

American willingness to act against the Canadian rebels in 1837–1908, however, played a major role in reassuring the British, which was an aspect of a more general lack of American enthusiasm after the War of 1812, whether in policy or in public culture, for war with Britain. This caution was linked to a widespread willingness to accept the restraints entailed by principles and notions of international law, and to a search for agreement. In 1816, Jefferson wrote to a sympathetic British correspondent:

Both [Britain and the USA] ought to wish for peace and cordial friendship; we [USA] because you do us more harm than any other nation; and you [Britain], because we can do you more good than any other. Our growth is now so well established by regular enumerations through a course of 40 years, and the same grounds of continuance so likely to endure for a much longer period, that, speaking in round numbers, we may safely all ourselves be 20 millions in 20 years, and 40 millions in 40 years. . . . Of what importance then to you must such a nation be, whether as friends or foes."[67]

Despite imperial rivalry and crises,[68] there was a clearly discernible trend in Anglo-American relations after the War of 1812 to resort to arbitration, in large part because war was now recognized as too problematic. The resulting peace meant neutralizing the northern frontier of the USA. By reducing tension with Britain, this neutralization helped prepare the way for American territorial expansion in Florida, to the west and, eventually, overseas. Thus, Britain made it possible for Americans to see the possibility of their country becoming a great nation. At the same time, however, exaggerated notions of a continued British threat stoked the fires of American nationalism, and among Democrats and Whigs alike, although with radically different assessments of risk. Indeed, the difficulties the USA encountered in the War of 1812 shaped an entire generation of policy-making. For another thirty years, until 1845, the USA effectively gave up serious western expansion. The main reason for this uncharacteristic hesitation was a fear of being roughly handled by Britain if it took umbrage at America's acquisitive ways.

Drawing on the stimulus of the War of 1812, anglophobia remained important,[69] and it was encouraged by fresh sources of suspicion. Thus, anxiety about British political and commercial plans included unfounded concern about British meddling in Texas.[70] James Polk was able to campaign successfully for the presidency in 1844 on the platform "fifty-four forty or fight" as a solution for the Oregon issue. In the event, Polk was willing to settle for the 49th parallel without British Columbia and Vancouver Island.[71] "Manifest Destiny" could only provide so much. Many of the American politicians of the period had served in the War of 1812. William Henry Harrison did well in the presidential contest in 1836 and won in 1840, only to die in 1841, while

Zachary Taylor was elected in 1848, dying in 1850. Winfield Scott won a nomination in 1852, only to be defeated. This pattern was also very apparent at the level of governors and congressmen.

Earlier, aside from settling the frontier to the Rockies in 1818, the British were willing not to flout the Monroe Doctrine, although, given the respective naval strength of the two powers, the Americans were in no position to thwart British intervention in Latin America. Indeed, the doctrine implicitly depended on the British navy to deter the use of French and Spanish naval power. In 1839, frontier disputes between Maine and Canada over land and timber cutting seemed about to lead to war, and the governor of Maine called up the militia, but, helped by British restraint, Winfield Scott kept the peace.[72] Moreover, the Anglo-American Ashburton-Webster Treaty of 1842 settled disputes over the Maine, New Hampshire, and Minnesota boundaries. British policy toward the USA from 1840 to 1864, especially that of George, 4th Earl of Lord Aberdeen, the foreign secretary from 1841 to 1846, and prime minister from 1852 to 1855, has been described in terms of appeasement.[73]

Allowing for the serious Anglo-American disputes, again mainly over neutral rights, stemming from the American Civil War (1861–65), the so-called North American Question in fact had been settled by the War of 1812. Partly due to the lessons of that war, a fresh conflict in the 1860s was anyway less likely. Moreover, trade and financial links were important structural factors encouraging not only Anglo-American coexistence but also a sense of mutual interest,[74] although that was compatible with a feeling of British superiority to American public culture.[75] During the Civil War, relations were tense as the British government expressed sympathy for the Confederacy, and there was anger about commercial disruption and the Union blockade, which hit British trade links.[76] There was also much concern among British policymakers and observers about the Union threat to Canada.[77] In the resulting atmosphere of crisis, the British fleet in North American and Caribbean waters was strengthened. However, opinion within Britain was divided over recognition of the Confederacy,[78] there were powerful voices for caution, and, to Confederate disappointment, the controversial building of Confederate warships by British shipyards was banned in 1863, and war between Britain and the Union was avoided. In March 1863, the French envoy in Washington suggested to his British counterpart that the two powers bring the war to a close by recognising the Confederacy, but the British envoy retorted that Britain was against interfering by force.[79]

Had it occurred, British entry would have transformed the situation at sea. American naval strength should not be exaggerated, as the Union's ironclad warships, although in part intended to resist possible British intervention, were not really suited for distant service on the high seas. Moreover, Union ships would also have been inferior in battle conditions, because their naval ordnance had too low a muzzle velocity to be effective against British armor, while Union armor was inferior because the Americans lacked the technology to roll thick iron plates.[80] Building lots of warships was not enough. The Union fleet would probably have been badly battered in any war, although the Union's monitors acted, from 1862, as a deterrent against British pressure,[81] while the fast wooden screw steamers authorized by Congress in 1864 would have been a threat to British trade, and, indeed, led to the British building fast unarmored iron-hulled warships in response.

The rapid demobilization of the Union fleet after the war improved the British position. There was to be no conflict between the two powers over Canada or over American colonial ambitions, because the Americans chose not to use their military strength for expansionist ends, other than against Native Americans. Instead, Anglo-American differences were settled by the Treaty of Washington of 1871, which permitted a reduction in the British military presence, with garrisons in Canada restricted to the naval bases of Esquimalt on Vancouver Island and Halifax, both important coaling stations for the navy.

## THE DEVELOPMENT OF THE USA

Crises in Anglo-American relations, including the War of 1812, were too brief and limited to lead to the sweeping political and governmental changes in the USA that the protracted character of the French Revolutionary and Napoleonic Wars (1792–1815) led to in Europe, most obviously for France but also for its opponents. Prior to the War of 1812, there had been a measure of American integration through economic growth and better communications, although far less than was to follow the conflict. Despite this integration, the state/regional focus of loyalties and identities had been shown during the war to be a challenge for American political coherence and military effectiveness. For example, aside from competing views over means and goals during the war, there were divisions over the peace. At Ghent, Adams and Clay clashed not only personally but also over regional interests, especially the opening of the Mississippi to British navigation and the issue of American fishing off Newfoundland.

Nevertheless, nothing was done to alter the situation constitutionally. The Federalists offered an agenda for governmental change designed to deal with the protracted crisis that arose from American vulnerability and international tension, but, during the war, as earlier, the crisis never became sufficiently severe to lead to a major reconfiguration of government. Moreover, the Federalists lost the politics of the war. New England was "identified with Old England" and accused of prolonging the war,[82] although another legacy of the war, and one in which the region was to have more lasting impact, was a mobilization of anti-slavery and anti-Southern sentiment in New England.[83]

Federalist opposition to the war led to a convention at Hartford from 15 December 1814 to 5 January 1815, with delegates attending from Connecticut, Massachusetts, New Hampshire, Rhode Island, and Vermont. This convention proposed amendments to the Constitution, including one-term presidencies, as well as the individual states being responsible for their own defense and receiving taxes accordingly. Although this idea had been advanced when the Constitution was being formulated, it was now, however, colored in the public eye by extremist talk of secession by New England.[84] Indeed, James Monroe, the secretary of war, authorized Peter Porter to employ volunteers he had raised in New York to deal with disturbances in New England if they occurred, which looked back to the use of Republican mobs against Federalist newspapers in Baltimore, Norristown, and Savannah.

Talk of secession was, as Jefferson later noted,[85] an encouragement to the government's wish for a prudent peace, but it also seriously compromised the Federalists, helping Monroe to win the 1816 and 1820 presidential elections, the first by 183 to 34 electoral votes. This result signalled the end of the Federalists as a national force. Dying out before the war, they had had a resurgence during it, before their final collapse. In 1820, Monroe's margin over John Quincy Adams, another

Democratic-Republican, was 231 to 1. These victories ensured not only a continuity in Jeffersonian Democratic-Republican government, but also in control by the group that had waged the recent war, a complaint made at Hartford. Moreover, the war, in which about six hundred thousand Americans served (three-quarters in the militia[86]), led to an emergent sense of euphoria and nationalistic pride and shaped it to a particular nationalist agenda.

This sense of euphoria and pride may, in part, have been a case of relief, consciously or subliminally, at having survived conflict with Britain; but the euphoria and pride also pointed straight toward the notion of a "Manifest Destiny" for the USA, however much this was out of line with the actual results of the war. Militarism and myths were linked, with the war focusing and strengthening an American nationalism that, earlier, had not been particularly conspicuous. In September 1813, Richard Rush responded to Perry's victory on Lake Erie by claiming that "victory will do more than anything else can, towards reconciling the country to this just war."[87] Although not true at the time, the glow of hindsight was to vindicate this view. A harsh recent conclusion, indeed, is that the conflict "glorified the resort to arms, sanctified the nation's military heroes," and led to "enhanced chauvinism" and "ambitious jingoism."[88] War songs registered this mood,[89] a mood which encouraged a tendency to ignore the more troubled experience of veterans who had suffered the often inglorious reality of the struggle.[90] Pottery, much in fact made in Staffordshire in England, also celebrated an American victory.[91]

This triumphalism was also seen in Britain, although there it was directed against France, and not the USA. In his "Ode for the Day of General Thanksgiving" for victory, held on 18 January 1816, the poet William Wordsworth urged "this favored nation" to "be conscious of thy moving spirit . . . thy protecting care."[92]

At the same time, the weaknesses that the conflict exposed in the federal government made Americans more receptive to the idea of a larger central government, and this receptiveness was a key aspect of the extent to which the long-term effects of the war were more noticeable on the USA than on Britain. The receptiveness to a larger central government was especially seen in the realms of economic development (Henry Clay's American System, with increased expenditure for internal improvements and the creation of a Second National Bank) and foreign policy (John Quincy Adams' aggressive

agenda as epitomized by the Oregon settlement, the American acquisition of Florida, and the Monroe Doctrine). These two strands
were linked because economic development of the interior was seen
as a way to strengthen America.

Indeed, the war had shown that a strong reliance on foreign trade
was dangerous, both because it might lead to conflict and as it would
make America vulnerable during this conflict. As a result, there was a
revival of what can be seen as the Hamiltonian system of a large
internal market able to ensure national self-sufficiency, a system advanced through the tariffs of 1816, 1820, and 1824. In power, the
Democratic-Republicans adopted a number of Federalist views and
programs—the Bank of the United States (chartered in 1816), tariff
protection, a federal program of internal improvements, a standing
army, and, after 1812, an oceanic navy and a general staff (created in
1813).[93] Madison proposed a new national bank and internal improvements in his final annual message, delivered on 5 December 1815,
while the retired Jefferson changed tack on the need for the federal
government to strengthen the American state. The enhanced transport routes that were crucial to the program of internal improvements led to greater pressure on the Native Americans.[94]

The process of postwar reform and revival in response to wartime
problems and a sense of crisis had also been seen in Britain as a consequence of the War of Independence. This process had encompassed
both the military and civil society. The War of 1812 indeed was followed in the USA by anxiety about another conflict, most likely with
Britain, that might be less fortunate,[95] and a conviction, as a result,
that America required a stronger military. Already, in August 1813,
Rush had observed "Machiavelli says war ought to be the only study
of a prince. We shall indeed be taught, by terrible experience, that it
must henceforth be more the study of our republic."[96] Although there
was a postwar demobilization, with the army cut from its official
authorized size of 62,674 men (troop strength was actually lower),
there was nonetheless a determination not to return to the prewar
situation. The core of the wartime staff system was retained, with a
new reform leadership instigating new procedures for efficiency and
accountability, and a de facto acceptance of the regular army as the
true first line of land defense. On 3 March 1815, Congress voted for a
new peacetime establishment of 12,383 troops (as opposed to the
3,284 in 1807). In 1816, it followed by voting $1 million per annum for

eight years to construct a navy, including nine 74-gun ships of the line. This was not a force able to beat Britain, but it would have increased the difficulty of any naval conflict with the USA. Moreover, the Fortification Board, established by Congress in 1814 in order to survey America's frontiers and draw up a plan for their protection, was continued, becoming the country's military agency responsible for planning national security.[97] The War of 1812 indeed led to the launching of a systematic program of seacoast fortification that long remained the centerpiece of American defense policy and of the professional development of the army officer corps.

The legacy of the War of 1812 in the USA was also seen in the working through of personnel issues. For example, in 1815 Madison nominated Henry Dearborn as secretary of war, the post he had held from 1801 to 1809, but Federalist focus on his failures as senior major general in 1812–13 led Madison to withdraw the nomination. Instead, William Crawford, a supporter of the annexation of Florida, who had been minister to France from 1813 to 1815, was appointed that August to a post he had himself turned down in early 1813.

Dearborn himself had predicted in October 1812 that "we shall ultimately overcome all difficulties and show the world that although we make a clumsy beginning, we are nevertheless capable of prosecuting a war with vigor and effect. Perhaps it is best, all things considered, that we should find it difficult to commence war. We might otherwise be too ready to engage in wars."[98] Subsequent nineteenth-century conflicts—the Second Seminole War (1835–42), the Mexican-American War (1846–48), and the Civil War (1861–65)— were to reveal that the problems of beginning wars successfully had not been overcome by the USA (until, at least at sea, in the brief war with Spain in 1898); but, in each case, as in the two World Wars, success was finally achieved.

It was not only foreign war that had helped define the American state by 1815. Internal struggles were also significant, although largely as a result of their absence. The key episodes were Shays' Rebellion in Massachusetts in 1786–77 and the Whiskey Rebellion in Pennsylvania in 1794. In the former, which involved the state government of Massachusetts, not the confederal government, heavily debt-ridden farmers rebelled in order to stop the confiscation of their property to pay debts and taxes they could not meet. The rebellion was put down in early 1787 when about fifteen hundred rebellious

regulators, armed with pitchforks and other weapons of limited effectiveness, dispersed after a forty-four hundred-strong volunteer militia force under Benjamin Lincoln opened fire, including with cannon.
A bold advance by Lincoln ten days later surprised and disrupted an
attempt to regroup, effectively ending the rebellion.

In contrast, the Whiskey Rebellion involved a federal military
response, which led to criticism of the use of force against citizens by
the Democratic-Republicans and influenced their behavior in office
after 1801. Moreover, the potential of military exigencies for authoritarian politics was shown, during the War of 1815, by Jackson when
he approved the hanging of seven militiamen for desertion or disobe-
dience, and, after the departure of the British from New Orleans,
continued to insist on martial law, ordered the deportation of French-
speaking residents, jailed a critical newspaper editor, and arrested
Dominick Augustin Hall, a federal judge.[99]

Nevertheless, compared to the serious and persistent civil violence throughout Latin America that followed independence—both
sustained separatism and bitter struggles for political control within
individual states—the situation in the USA was relatively peaceful.
Indeed any reading of the history of Colombia or Mexico, Argentina,
or Peru serves as a salutary comparison to the political history of the
USA. Although smaller, these states also had serious sectional and
constitutional divisions, as well as differences over ideology, and,
furthermore, major problems over how to control generals and other
military leaders.[100] Unlike their American counterparts, presidents
in Latin America were not apt to give up power.

Crises in the USA, in contrast, were resolved without much violence. Thus, Vermont separatism, which dated back to the beginning
of the American Revolution, did not, despite an upsurge in the late
1780s, lead to significant problems, and, in 1791, Vermont joined the
union as the fourteenth state: it was not conquered. This level of
comparative success can be seen as arising from the political culture
and dispersed governmental power of the USA, although contingent
factors were also important. The failure of Shays' and the Whiskey
rebellions ensured that there was no pressure for a strong federal force
capable of enforcing government power; nor a divisive "balkaniza-
tion" akin to that which affected Mexico, where local militias and
caudillos (strongmen) enjoyed great power in the 1820s. A similar
process was also seen in Argentina and Brazil. In the USA, in con-

trast, political differences were institutionalized in a federal system of shared sovereignty which made it easier to express interests and manage disputes short of conflict. Moreover, the locally prominent operated through the political system and did not defy or seek to overthrow it in the fashion of Latin American *caudillos*.

The American system of shared sovereignty broke down in the Civil War, with tragic consequences for individual families including those which had played a prominent role in the War of 1812. Thus, at Gettysburg in 1863, Brigadier General Lewis Armistead was fatally wounded while fighting for the Confederacy. His uncle, Major George Armistead, had served in the American army from 1799 until his death in 1818, commanding at Fort McHenry from 1813.

GEOPOLITICS

Externally, the key definition of the USA from 1775 was the winning and sustaining of independence, but in circumstances that did not lead to the creation of a significant military able to give effect to bold expansionist plans. Instead, thanks in part to the limitations of the military, considerable difficulties were encountered in taking war to the Native Americans and, even more, as the War of 1812 showed, the British in Canada; while, against the British elsewhere, only defensive successes could be achieved by the Americans: Lake Champlain, Fort McHenry and, to a certain extent, Fort Erie, all in 1814, and New Orleans in 1815.

Alongside developments within the USA, the conflict that defined American liberty and empire was, ironically, the longstanding one in which America's role was marginal or nonexistent: that between Britain and France, a perspective that qualifies American exceptionalism or, at least, triumphalism. It was this conflict that ensured that the French were unable to maintain their positions in North America, losing Canada in 1760, and feeling it necessary to sell vulnerable Louisiana in 1803 after they had regained it from Spain only three years earlier. Similarly, it was the resumption of war between Britain and France in 1803 that doomed the French attempt to reconquer its key Caribbean colony, Saint-Domingue/Haiti. In the face of British naval power, Napoleon's western strategy, his hope of an empire that would include Louisiana, Florida, Cayenne, Martinique, and Guadeloupe, was foolish, which was why he sold off Louisiana at a bargain price. The

Americans, in contrast, did not have the naval capability to consider the option of wrecking Napoleon's strategy.

War between Britain and France did not only affect French policy towards the USA. It also ensured that Britain could devote only part of its attention to war with the USA in 1778–83 and, even more, 1812–14, and, more generally, lessened the chances for British pressure on the USA on other occasions. Indeed, prefiguring the attempt to exert military pressure on the USA once Napoleon had fallen in 1814, the British had only been able to make a major effort to regain North America (including Canada) in 1776–77 because they were not yet then at war with France. This point was amply recognized at the time and helped make French entry into the War of Independence a crucial goal for the Americans. Indeed, French entry in 1778 ensured that the conflict became a world war. In military, strategic, and political terms, France's alliance provided force, range, and options that the Americans on their own could not readily deploy. Politically, this included a representation in international power politics that the rebels could not obtain on their own. Crucially, French entry into the war in 1778 also cleared the hurdle to that of Spain, for the Spanish government had been worried about supporting the rebels, but it was persuaded to do so by its ally France. Spanish entry in 1779, in turn, made a major difference to the arithmetic of naval strength: France and Spain combined then had a larger fleet than Britain. In the War of 1812, in contrast, there was no comparable support for the USA. Spain was allied with Britain, while France was heavily committed in Europe.

Conversely, the lancing of Anglo-American tensions in the War of 1812 ensured that the Spaniards could not turn to Britain to resist American territorial demands in 1818–19, and this greatly eased American geopolitical concerns in the Gulf region. The war had allowed the USA to consolidate its earlier gains and to add new territory along the Gulf Coast east of the Pearl River. With Ferdinand VII's return to power in 1814, Spain believed that, supported by the British, they could restore all that they had lost in North America since the return of Louisiana to France in 1800. The Madison and Monroe administrations, indeed, initially worried that the British might support such claims or, at least, frustrate their efforts to negotiate for East Florida. But the British ministry was as unwilling to risk a new Anglo-American war as the American government was, and this left Spain on its own hook and fatally so when Jackson attacked.[101]

Just as the British, in 1765–1848, benefited in India from fighting rival powers separately, particularly Mysore, the Marathas, the Gurkhas, the Afghans, and the Sikhs, and, indeed, at times, allying with one against the other; so the same for the Americans and their opponents. Between 1775 and 1848, the USA, like the British in India, did not fight its major opponents simultaneously. Instead, sequential conflict played a role in American success, whereas in the Atlantic sphere, Britain faced conflict with both France and America in 1812–14. This challenge to British power was particularly important because the role of European naval power ensured that America was not protected from the power politics of the Western world, as might be imagined, by distance or by the wide moat of the Atlantic Ocean. Indeed, it was easier for Britain, France, or Spain to intervene in the New World than in Eastern Europe. Mexico discovered this with the French in 1861–77, although that intervention culminated in French failure, while in 1865–66 Spain used naval power to put pressure on Peru, Bolivia, and Chile.

The possibility of European power projection ensured that America had to act within the international system. In part, the very rhetoric of standing outside this system and being different to the other powers was an expression of American aspirations to do so and of anger about not being able to fulfill them, rather than being a description of America's true circumstances. Moreover, participation in the international system[102] helped set the parameters and sometimes the contents of American domestic history as well. The War of 1812 is therefore important in part because of the might-have-beens, not least the impact on the USA had Britain sustained its attack and, indeed, been more successful. The war is more directly important because of its geopolitical consequences. Alongside these consequences in terms of American failure, in the shape of the repeated inability to end the British presence in Canada or to force Britain to accept the American interpretation of its maritime rights, there were important successes, not least the rupturing of Anglo–Native American cooperation, the marked weakening of Native American opposition, and the blocking or defeat of British attacks. By the end of the war, the geopolitics of North America had been transformed, and America's position as an independent power had been consolidated.

# 7

# CONCLUSIONS

"Fifty years hence, twenty years hence, ten years hence, the
victories which we have gained, and the greater ones which I trust
we will gain, will be celebrated in orations, in histories, in songs, in
the epick, with the pencil, neither as democratic or federal
victories, but as American, as national triumphs and the sources of
our national glory. Of the thousands in England who can still shout
at the names of Cressey [Crécy, 1346], Agincourt [1415], Blenheim
[1704], Ramillies [1706], how many are there who recollect, or, if
they recollect, care anything about the causes of the wars in which
such names become illustrious in their annals. And yet, no doubt
at all each of them had their peace party. I am anticipating the time
when the grandchildren of Henry Clay and Josiah Quincey, will all
be exulting in this war, which their different grandfathers strove so
patriotically the one to bring about, the other to oppose."

Richard Rush to John Adams, 1813.[1]

"I wish you joy of being released from the millstone of an American
war."

Robert, Viscount Castlereagh, British Foreign Secretary, 1815.[2]

The central theme of this book has been an attempt to locate the
War of 1812 in its international context, diplomatic, military,
and economic. This context is important not only in describing and
explaining what occurred, but also in providing a comparative frame-

work for considering the relative capability of combatants, as well as in evaluating the consequences of decisions and the significance of events, in both the short and long terms. At the time, there had been no hesitation in using such a context. Thus, in late January 1815, a British visitor who saw Napoleon on the island of Elba to which he had been exiled, recorded his host as saying that

> peace with America should have been made sooner, as it would have given us [Britain] greater influence in the Congress. The Americans, he observed, wanted a ten years war to make them a nation: at present they had no noblesse—a set of *marchands*. That we should in the course of time lose Canada; and of what great importance was it to England, with her immense possessions? That America would one day probably rival our navy; an attempt he had made, but failed.[3]

As so often, Napoleon was only perceptive up to a point, if not glib, while his instructive social snobbery toward the USA reflected his failure to appreciate economic factors. Moreover, it is not clear that an earlier peace with America would have made Britain more influential at the Congress of Vienna. Napoleon's comments on future Anglo-American naval rivalry, however, were instructive. Indeed, imprisoned after his defeat at Waterloo in 1815 on the distant South Atlantic island of St. Helena, a British colony, Napoleon was to return to the theme of future competition between Britain and the USA. In 1816, reflecting his sense of Britain, France, and USA as constituting a competitive system, Napoleon told Lieutenant Colonel Mark Wilks, the governor of St. Helena, "Your [British] coal gives you an advantage we cannot possess in France. But the high price of all articles of prime necessity is a great disadvantage in the export of your manufactures . . . your manufacturers are emigrating fast to America . . . In a century or perhaps half a century more: it will give a new character to the affairs of the world. It has thriven upon our follies."[4]

Part of the great interest in Anglo-American relations between 1783 and 1945 was that there was rivalry, but that, after 1815, there was no conflict. Instead, one great power succeeded another without a war between them. The reasons for this are varied, but some can be seen as stemming from the War of 1812. The failure of both powers to achieve their goals and vindicate fully their martial reputation and image encouraged in each a measure of prudence and restraint that was to be important. Although plans for war continued to be drawn up for over a century,[5] the Americans learned in 1812–14 that Canada could not be conquered. Because of poor leadership, political decentralization, logistical problems, environmental factors, and the strength of the resistance, the USA was unable to launch a successful offensive against Canada. The realization that Canada could not be conquered greatly eased subsequent relations with Britain. Failure in Canada also spared the Americans from the problems of acting there as an occupying power. In turn, Britain was distracted throughout most of the war by events in Europe and elsewhere, and thus unable to bring its military strength to bear. The outcome was a standoff that initiated a long-term willingness by both powers to settle their mutual grievances short of war. Less honorably, a learned restraint included on the British part the abandonment of the Native Americans, which was destructive for the latter but helpful to America's westward expansion.

On the strategic level, Britain and the USA had experienced in the War of 1812 the grave difficulty of inflicting sufficient damage on the other to force them to peace. Operationally, they had discovered the problems of offensives, problems that owed much to the interplay between logistical limitations and the difficulties of building up and sustaining a powerful strike force. Tactically, the importance of defensive firepower had been underlined, most dramatically at New Orleans; but also the possibilities of successful attacks.

The War of 1812 enjoyed some prominence in the USA during the late nineteenth century, a period of American assertion as a great power and of Anglo-American naval and imperial competition. Challenging earlier British studies by William James and Edward Brenton, both Theodore Roosevelt and Alfred Thayer Mahan published books on the naval dimension of the war, a dimension that could be presented both as heroic and as demonstrating the need for American naval strength.[6] Furthermore, in the aftermath of the traumatic Civil War, the War of 1812, by then a distant episode, was also a less divisive episode in American military history, and thus worthy of commemoration, although, in the shadow of the Civil War and the Wars of German Unification, the War of 1812 was also no longer of such relevance for strategic thought for land warfare.

In the early twentieth century, the centenary of the war led to commemorative celebrations. American, Canadian, and British Peace Centenary Commissions were established and money raised to leave a permanent memorial. The British committee launched an appeal in 1913 for £60 thousand to erect a memorial in Westminster Abbey, to purchase "Sulgrave Manor, Northants[Northamptonshire], the ancestral home of the Washington family, as a place of pilgrimage for the Americans in England, and as a fruitful symbol of the kinship of the two peoples," and to found a chair of Anglo-American history in British universities as well to endow school prizes. A ceremony for commemorating, on 5 January 1915, the anniversary of the Treat of Ghent, could not be held due to the German occupation of the Belgian city, but the so-called Watson Chair was established in 1919 and in 1921 a bronze statue of George Washington, a gift of the state of Virginia, was erected in Trafalger Square. That same year Sulgrave Manor, now fully restored, was opened and dedicated. The Marquess of Cambridge, presiding over the dedication ceremony, declared: "We want this house to be . . . a center from which sentiments of friendship and goodwill forever radiate; and these sentiments we believe to be the greatest security for world peace." The interwar years of assertive American isolationism proved an appropriate backdrop for celebration of a different type, not least with the swashbuckling Hollywood film *The Buccaneer* (1938), which focused on Jean Lafitte and his role in the battle of New Orleans. Stamps were also an aspect of commemoration. In 1936–37, the U.S. Post Office issued five stamps each for the army and the navy. The two-cent army stamp featured Jackson and Scott, and the two-cent navy featured Decatur and MacDonough. In 1947, the USS *Constitution* was honored on a stamp for helping the USA to become a naval power in the War of 1812, while in 1948 there was an issue honoring Francis Scott Key.[7]

With the creation in 1941 of an Anglo-American alliance as the key plank of American (and British) foreign policy,[8] the War of 1812 rapidly receded from attention. Even so, a second version of *The Buccaneer* appeared in 1958, and in 1965 a commemorative stamp marked the 150th anniversary of the Battle of New Orleans. Although a celebration of victory, the stamp featured a reproduction of the Battle of New Orleans Sesquicentennial medal. Designed by New Orleans sculptress Angela Gregory, the medal emphasized 150 years of unbroken peace between America and Britain.[9]

When, moreover, Patrick O'Brian's novel of British naval fortitude and success, *The Far Side of the World* (1984) was filmed in

Hollywood as *Master and Commander: The Far Side of the World* (2003), the setting was changed from 1812 to 1805 and the enemy was switched from the Americans to the French. In the film, a shared Anglo-American world view was projected.[10] The war, however, left an echo in the greater strength and superior construction of the French frigate, which was based on the condition of American ships. In contrast, in Anthony Price's novel *The Old Vengeful* (1982), the War of 1812 was referred to by the hero, Paul Mitchell, as Britain being stabbed in the back while engaged in a life and death struggle with France. Subsequently in the book, it was argued that the Royal Navy was overstretched in 1812 and that Britain was losing the war with Napoleon at that juncture.[11]

Recent references vary. Writing in the aftermath of the attacks on September 11, 2001, John Lewis Gaddis, a prominent historian with links to the Bush administration, saw a precedent in the burning of Washington in 1814, claiming that this was a surprise attack which led to an emphasis on preemption as a means to ensure security: "The pattern set by this now barely remembered violation of homeland security is one that has persisted ever since: that for the United States, safety comes from enlarging, rather than from contracting, its sphere of responsibilities."[12] The First Seminole War of 1817–18 was presented by Gaddis as the first consequence of this policy of preemption. His argument, however, was mistaken, not least because British operations in the Chesapeake were scarcely a surprise, indeed looked back to the War of Independence, while the First Seminole War looked back to earlier American expansionism in the Southeast, not only prior to the War of 1812 but also during the war prior to the burning of Washington. In 1814, there was a theme of reciprocity in British action, and the Americans indeed had burned freely in Canada, notably at York in April 1813 and Newark in December 1813; but this was not the case in 2001.

At a different level of reference, the London newspaper the *Guardian* in March 2008 printed a reflection by Michael Tomasky: "Who knew the Treaty of Ghent would factor into this election? The pact that ended the war of 1812 between us Yanks and those sneaky British aggressors kept Michigan as part of the United States. And now Michigan may be poised to settle between Barack Obama and Hillary Clinton."[13]

The war has largely faded from memory in the USA and, even more, Britain;[14] although far less so in Canada. Indeed, the conflict recently has been termed utterly absurd by a British academic.[15] There is an old American parenting joke in which the family is driving in Idaho or another state in the West. The children in the back want to know what a monument they are passing is for and the parents reply "It is for the War of 1812." The joke refers to parental ignorance, as there were no 1812 battles in Idaho or nearby, but the parents can rely on the War of 1812 being so unknown that their reply will not be queried. Those members of the American public who know of the conflict tend not to appreciate how poorly the war was conducted and how disastrous it nearly was for them.

Aside from the war's importance to the history of North America, which is a theme of this book, it is also instructive for what it suggests about the unpredictabilities, indeed perils, of what in hindsight can appear as a limited war lacking in searing trauma. In practice, such warfare requires skillful management, and puts a premium on political and military leadership, and on public maturity. The American and British failure to understand the views, interests, and capability of the other came, at the time, with serious cost. It was fortunate that, thereafter, *revanche* played little role in the lexicon of either power. This was important to the development of the nineteenth-century world and to the eventual transition from British to American power.

A postscript can be added from a very different perspective. My visit to the Gulf Coast in 2007 underlined my interest in events at Fort Apalachicola, or, as it was also known, Fort Negro or the Negro Fort.[16] Like most fortified positions of those years on the Gulf Coast, for example the early fortifications at Pensacola, this is no more, and the site is a subject for the archaeologist rather than the historian. Yet, the muddy reaches of the river also conjure up a very different world, one in which Native Americans and blacks could maintain or seek their independence, autonomy, or freedom. This outcome was not to be. From a variety of motives, the American government and prominent interest groups were to support the idea of a free black state or federation of states in Africa, but freedom for blacks was only acceptable at a distance from America.[17] In contrast, the nearby example of Fort Apalachicola was totally unacceptable. It was attacked and destroyed in 1816, and the Native Americans and blacks were subjugated. Yet Apalachicola, and the aspirations of Nicolls and Cochrane[18] for Britain to take a role in a new order, serve as a reminder of the variety of views that war could throw to the fore.

# Notes

## ABBREVIATIONS

| | |
|---|---|
| AE | Paris, Ministère des Relations Extérieures |
| Auburn | Auburn, University Library, Frank Owsley donation, Accession No 82-08XX. |
| BL. Add. | London, British Library, Department of Manuscripts, Additional Manuscripts |
| Clay | J. F. Hopkins, ed. *The Papers of Henry Clay*. Vol. 1, *The Rising Statesman, 1797–1814*. Lexington, Kentucky, 1959. |
| CP | Correspondance Politique |
| DRO | Exeter, Devon Record Office |
| FO | Foreign Office papers |
| Madison | J. C. A. Stagg, ed. *The Papers of James Madison.* Charlottesville, VA. |
| NA | London, National Archives |
| NAM | London, National Army Museum |
| *Naval War of 1812* | W. S. Dudley, ed. *The Naval War of 1812: A Documentary History*. Washington, 1985. |
| Penn. Hist. Soc. | Philadelphia, Historical Society of Pennsylvania |

## PREFACE

1. The song was recorded live in Seattle at *Sketchfest*.

2. Topping the *Billboard* "Hot 100," Johnny Horton won the 1959 Grammy Award for Best Country and Western Performance for his recording of this song. The song details the battle from the perspective of an American

fighting alongside Andrew Jackson against British forces, but the tone is lighthearted.

3. Jefferson to Sir John Sinclair, 31 July 1816, Exeter, Devon CRO. 152M/C1816/OF30.

4. The immediate assaults on Washington and New Orleans were overland, but the forces had been transported by sea.

5. NAM. 1968-07-339-1, 14.

6. NAM. 2001-09-36-1.

## INTRODUCTION

1. For example, P. Young and J. Lawford, eds., *History of the British Army* (London, 1970); D. Chandler and I. F. W. Beckett, eds., *The Oxford Illustrated History of the British Army* (Oxford, 1994). J. Latimer, *1812: War with America* (Cambridge, MA, 2007) is an effective study from the British perspective, and is particularly strong on the operational dimension.

2. For a crucial historiographical essay, D. R. Hickey, "The War of 1812: Still a Forgotten Conflict?" *Journal of Military History* 65 (2001): 741–69.

3. R. S. Quimby, *The U.S. Army in the War of 1812: An Operational and Command Study* (East Lansing, MI, 1997), vii.

4. J. Lynn, "The Embattled Future of Academic Military History," *Journal of Military History* 61 (1997): 777–89; V. Hanson, "The Dilemma of the Contemporary Military Historian," in *Reconstructing History*, eds. E. Fox-Genovese and E. Lasch-Quinn (London, 1999), 189–201.

5. For successful accounts of high quality, R. F. Weigley, *The American Way of War: A History of United States Military Strategy and Policy* (Bloomington, IN, 1973); D. Higginbotham, "The Early American Way of War: Reconnaissance and Appraisal," in *War and Society in Revolutionary America*, ed. D. Higginbotham (Columbia, SC, 1988), 260–312; W. E. Lee, "Early American Ways of War: A New Reconnaissance, 1600–1815," *Historical Journal* 44 (2001): 269–89; A. R. Lewis, *The American Culture of War* (New York, 2007), 1–36; B. M. Linn, *The Echo of Battle: The Army's Way of War* (Cambridge, MA, 2007), 3–4.

6. T. Abernethy, *The Burr Conspiracy* (New York, 1954).

7. J. J. Ripley, *Tarnished Warrior: Major General James Wilkinson* (New York, 1933).

8. L. G. Schwoerer, *"No Standing Armies!": The Antiarmy Ideology in Seventheenth-Century England* (Baltimore, MD, 1974).

9. S. Brumwell, *Redcoats: The British Soldier and War in the Americas, 1755–1763* (Cambridge, MA, 2002).

10. This is known in Britain as the Seven Years' War, and is dated 1756 to 1763.

11. F. Anderson, *A People's Army: Massachusetts Soldiers and Society in the Seven Years' War* (Chapel Hill, NC, 1984).

12. L. D. Cress, *Citizens in Arms: The Army and Militia in American Society to the War of 1812* (Chapel Hill, NC, 1982).

13. For an excellent study of the American side, J. C. A. Stagg, *Mr. Madison's War: Politics, Diplomacy and Warfare in the Early American Republic, 1783–1830* (Princeton, NJ, 1983).

## CHAPTER 1. PATHS TO WAR

1. This story is apocryphal.

2. J. Black, *America as a Military Power: From the American Revolution to the Civil War* (Westport, CT, 2002).

3. S. Cornell, *A Well Regulated Militia: The Founding Fathers and the Origins of Gun Control in America* (Oxford, 2006).

4. W. B. Skelton, "Officers and Politicians: The Origins of Army Politics in the United States before the Civil War," *Armed Forces and Society* 6 (Fall, 1979): 34–35; W. Robinson, *American Forts: Architectural Form and Function* (Urbana, IL, 1977); E. R. Lewis, *Seacoast Fortifications of the United States* (Annapolis, MD, 1979); J. W. Moore, *The Fortifications Board, 1816–1828 and the Definition of National Security* (Charleston, SC, 1980); R. S. Browning, *Two if by Sea: The Development of American Coastal Defense Policy* (Westport, CT, 1980); R. S. Gilmore, *Guarding America's Front Door: Harbor Forts in the Defense of NY City* (Brooklyn, NY, 1983).

5. D. Higginbotham, "The Early American Way of War: Reconnaissance and Appraisal," in *War and Society in Revolutionary America*, ed. D. Higginbotham (Columbia, SC): 290–91; J. Resch, *Suffering Soldiers: Revolutionary War Veterans, Moral Sentiment, and Political Culture in the Early Republic* (Amherst, MA, 2000), 38.

6. M. Cunliffe, *Soldiers and Civilians: The Martial Spirit in America, 1775–1865* (Boston, 1968; 2nd ed., NY, 1973); C. Royster, *A Revolutionary People at War: the Continental Army and American Character, 1775–1783* (New York, 1979).

7. R. H. Kohn, *Eagle and Sword: The Federalists and the Creation of the Military Establishment in America, 1783–1802* (New York, 1975).

8. F. C. Leiner, *Millions for Defense: The Subscription Warships of 1798* (Annapolis, MD, 1999).

9. Miranda to Castlereagh, 10 June 1807, BL. Loan 57/107 fol. 165.

10. L. S. Kaplan, *Alexander Hamilton: Ambivalent Anglophile* (Wilmington, DE, 2002).

11. T. J. Crackel, *Mr. Jefferson's Army: Political and Social Reform of the Military Establishment, 1801–1809* (New York, 1989).

12. W. B. Skelton, "The Commanding Generals and the Question of Civil Control in the Antebellum U.S. Army," in *The Vistas of American Military History, 1800–1898*, ed. B. H. Reid and J. G. Dawson (Abingdon, 2007), 18.

13. Rush to Adams, 2 Aug. 1813, Penn. Hist. Soc. AM. 1352.

14. G. A. Smith, "A Means to an End: Gunboats and Thomas Jefferson's Theory of Defense," *American Neptune* 55 (1994): 111–21.

15. S. C. Tucker, *The Jeffersonian Gunboat Navy* (Columbus, SC, 1993).

16. W. S. Cormack, *Revolution and Political Conflict in the French Navy, 1789–1794* (Cambridge, 1995).

17. John Adams to John Jay, Secretary of State, 2 June 1785, *The Works of John Adams*, ed. C. F. Adams (Boston, 1853), 8:255–57.

18. P. L. Ford, ed., *The Autobiography of Thomas Jefferson 1743–1790*

(New York, 1914), 94; C. R. Ritcheson, "The Fragile Memory: Thomas Jefferson at the Court of George III," in *Eighteenth-Century Life*, vol. 6, pts. 2–3 (1981), 1–16.

19. M. R. Shulman, *Navalism and the Emergence of American Sea Power, 1882–1893* (Annapolis, MD, 1995).

20. N. Onuf, *Federal Union, Modern World: The Law of Nations in an Age of Revolutions, 1776–1814* (Madison, WI, 1993).

21. J. Klaits and M. Haltzel, eds., *The Global Ramifications of the French Revolution* (Cambridge, MA, 1994), 53.

22. A. G. Condon, *The Envy of the American States: The Loyalist Dream for New Brunswick* (Frederickton, New Brunswick, 1984); N. MacKinnon, *This Unfriendly Soil: The Loyalist Experience in Nova Scotia, 1783–1791* (Kingston, 1986). Neither New Brunswick nor Nova Scotia was part of Canada. They along with Lower and Upper Canada were encompassed within British North America. Canada, however, is employed in this book in the present geographical sense.

23. C. R. Ritcheson, *Aftermath of Revolution: British Policy toward the United States, 1783–1795* (Dallas, 1969).

24. Thornton to Burges, 11 July 1794, NA. FO. 5/6 fol. 342.

25. R. A. Burchell, *The End of Anglo-America: Historical Essays in the Study of Cultural Divergence* (Manchester, 1991); Jay to Webster, 31 May 1813, in *The Correspondence and Public Papers of John Jay*, ed. H. P. Johnston (New York, 1893), 4:373. There has also been an emphasis on continuities, e.g., debate in *Historically Speaking* 6, no. 4 (Mar.–Ap. 2005): 19–22.

26. P. P. Hill, *French Perceptions of the Early American Republic 1783–1793* Philadelphia, 1988); J. Meyer, "Les Difficultés du commerce franco-american vues de Nantes, 1776–1790," *French Historical Studies* 11 (1979): 159–83; Fohlem, "The Commercial Failure of France in America," in *Two Hundred Years of Franco-American Relations*, eds. N. L. Roelker and C. K. Warner (Worcester, MA, 1983), 93–119.

27. AE. CP. Etats Unis 35, fol 135.

28. Hawkesbury to William, Lord Grenville, Foreign Secretary, 17 Oct. 1794, BL. Add. 38310 fol. 122.

29. Hawkesbury to Charles Bond, 4 Jan. 1790, BL. Add. 38310 fol. 148.

30. Liverpool to William Ludlam, 17 June 1797, BL. Add. 38310 fol. 197.

31. AE. CP. Etats Unis 35 fol. 188.

32. Beckwith's reports, NA. FO. 4/12; H. C. Syrett, ed., *The Papers of Alexander Hamilton* (New York, 1963), 7:70–74; J. P. Boyd, *Number 7: Alexander Hamilton's Secret Attempt to Control American Foreign Policy* (Princeton, NJ, 1964), 4–13.

33. Hammond to Grenville, 1 Nov. 1791, BL. Add., vol. 58939.

34. Johnston, ed., *Jay*, 4:360, 363–404.

35. A. DeConde, *The Quasi-War: The Politics and Diplomacy of the Undeclared War with France, 1797–1801* (New York, 1966).

36. Liverpool to Phenias Bond, 23 May 1798, BL. Add. 38310 fol. 221.

37. Oxford, Bodleian Library, Department of Western Manuscripts, Bland Burges papers, vol. 21.

38. B. Perkins, *The First Rapprochement: England and the United States, 1795–1805* (Philadelphia, 1955).

39. S. C. Tucker and F. T. Reuter, *Injured Honor: The "Chesapeake"-"Leopard" Affair, June 27, 1807* (Annapolis, MD, 1996).

40. F. Crouzet, "Wars, Blockade and Economic Change in Europe, 1792–1815," *Journal of Economic History* 24 (1964): 570.

41. Robert, Viscount Castlereagh, Secretary of War, to William, 3rd Duke of Portland, Prime Minister, 26 Oct. 1807, BL. Add. 49177 fol. 58.

42. R. Pares, *Colonial Blockade and Neutral Rights, 1739–1763* (Oxford, 1938); I. de Madariaga, *Britain, Russia and the Armed Neutrality of 1780* (London, 1962); A. C. Carter, *Neutrality or Commitment: the Evolution of Dutch Foreign Policy, 1667–1795* (London, 1975).

43. O. Feldbaeck, *Denmark and the Armed Neutrality, 1800–1801* (Copenhagen, 1980).

44. A. Burton, "British Evangelicals, Economic Warfare and the Abolition of the Atlantic Slave Trade, 1794–1810," *Anglican and Episcopal History* 65 (1996): 197–225, esp. 223.

45. B. Spivak, *Jefferson's English Crisis: Commerce, Embargo and the Republican Revolution* (Charlottesville, VA, 1979).

46. Jefferson to Joel Barlow, 14 Aug. 1805, BL. Add. 39908 fol. 13.

47. H. Heaton, "Non-Importation, 1806–1812," *Journal of Economic History* 1 (1941): 178–98.

48. Liverpool to Dudley Ryder, Vice-President of the Board of Trade, 29 May 1797, BL. Add. 38310 fol. 194.

49. J. Villiers and P. Carey, eds., *The British in Java 1811–1816: a Javanese Account* (Oxford, 1992).

50. R. D. Edmunds, "'A Watchful Safeguard to Our Habitations': Black Hoof and the Loyal Shawnees," in *Native Americans and the Early Republic*, eds. F. E. Hoxie et al. (Charlottesville, VA, 1999), 162–99.

51. M. Duffy, *Soldiers, Sugar and Seapower: The British Expeditions to the West Indies and the War against Revolutionary France* (Oxford, 1987).

52. D. L. Flores, ed., *Jefferson and Southwestern Exploration: The Freeman and Custis Accounts of the Red River Expedition of 1806* (Norman, OK, 1984).

53. L. S. Kaplan, "France and Madison's Decision for War, 1812," *Mississippi Valley Historical Review* 50 (1964): 652–71.

54. Threlkeld to John Fisher, 1 Mar. 1817, DRO. 1148M/19/9.

55. C. L. Egan, *Neither Peace Nor War: 1803–1812* (Baton Rouge, 1993); C. Jörgensen, *The Anglo-Swedish Alliance against Napoleonic France* (New York, 2004).

56. R. Glover, "The French Fleet, 1807–1814: Britain's Problem and Madison's Opportunity," *Journal of Modern History* 39 (1967): 249–51.

57. Melville to Popham, 4 Aug. 1812, BL. Loan 57/108. 114.

58. P. W. Schroeder, *The Transformation of European Politics, 1763–1848* (Oxford, 1994), 435–40, quote 440.

59. B. Hilton, *A Mad, Bad, and Dangerous People? England 1783–1846* (Oxford, 2006), 220.

60. Smith to William Pinkney, Minister in London, 22 May 1810, *Documents Accompanying the Message of the President* (Washington, DC, 1810), copy in BL. Add. 49178 fol. 3.

61. B. Perkins, *Prologue to War: England and the United States, 1805–1812* (Berkeley, California, 1961), 55.

62. *Annual Register* 54 (1812), 420–503; P. Coquille, *Napoleon and England, 1803–1810* (London, 1904), 270–71.

63. L. E. Davis and S. L. Engerman, *Naval Blockades in Peace and War: An Economic History Since 1750* (New York, 2006).

64. BL. Add. 49990 fol. 25.

65. BL. Add. 49990 fols 17–20.

66. J. D. Richardson, ed., *Messages and Papers of the Presidents, 1789–1898* (Washington, DC, 1896–98), 1:499–505.

67. R. H. Brown, *The Republic in Peril: 1812* (New York, 1964).

68. H. W. Fritz, "The War Hawks of 1812," *Capitol Studies* 5 (Spring 1977): 25–42.

69. R. L. Hatzenbuehler and R. L. Ivie, "Justifying the War of 1812: Toward a Model of Congressional Behaviour in Early War Crises," *Social Science History* 4 (1980): 453–77; *Congress Declares War* (Kent, OH, 1983); M. F. Wehtje, "Opposition in Virginia to the War of 1812," *Virginia Magazine of History and Biography* 77 (1970): 67–72.

70. L. R. Johnson, "The Suspense Was Hell: The Senate Vote for War in 1812," *Indiana Magazine of History* 65 (1969): 247–67.

71. B. H. Tolley, "The Liverpool Campaign against the Order in Council and the War of 1812," in *Liverpool and Merseyside: Essays in the Economic and Social History of the Port and its Hinterland*, ed. J. R. Harris (1969); D. Moss, "Birmingham and the Campaigns against the Orders-in-Council and East India Company Charter, 1812–13," *Canadian Journal of History* 11 (1976): 173–88.

72. I would like to thank Huw Davies for letting me read a copy of his unpublished paper "British Imperial Intelligence and Strategic Direction, 1798–1842."

73. Robert, Viscount Castlereagh, Foreign Secretary, to Lords of the Admiralty, 6, 12 Aug., John Croker, Secretary to the Admiralty, to Warren, 7 Aug. 1812, NA. ADM 1/4222, 2/1735.

74. S. T. Jackson, "Impressment and Anglo-American Discord, 1787–1818," (PhD dissertation, University of MI, 1976).

75. I. T. Kelsay, *Joseph Brant, 1743–1807: Man of Two Worlds* (Syracuse, NY, 1984); W. Sword, *President Washington's Indian War: The Struggle for the Old Northwest, 1790–1795* (Norman, OK, 1985).

76. P. J. Marshall, "Britain Without America—A Second Empire?" in *The Oxford History of the British Empire*, in *The Eighteenth Century*, ed. P. J. Marshall (Oxford, 1998), 2:579.

77. T. Fulford, *Romantic Indians: Native Americans, British Literature, and Transatlantic Culture, 1756–1830* (Oxford, 2006).

78. R. D. Edmunds, "Tecumseh, the Shawnee Prophet, and American History: A Reassessment," *Western Historical Quarterly* 14 (1983): 261–76; R. White, *The Middle Ground: Indians, Empires, and Republics in the Great*

*Lakes Region, 1650–1815* (Cambridge, 1991); G. E. Dowd, *A Spirited Resistance: The North American Indian Struggle for Unity, 1745–1815* (Baltimore, 1992); J. Sugden, *Tecumseh: A Life* (New York, 1997).

79. S. Warren, *The Shawnees and Their Neighbors, 1795–1870* (Urbana, IL, 2005).

80. K. DuVal, *The Native Ground: Indians and Colonists in the Heart of the Continent* (Philadelphia, 2006).

81. BL. Add. 49990 fols 59–60.

82. R. M. Owens, "Jeffersonian Benevolence on the Ground: The Indian Land Cession Treaties of William Henry Harrison," *Journal of the Early Republic* 22 (2002): 434.

83. G. E. Dowd, "Thinking and Believing: Nativism and Unity in the Ages of Pontiac and Tecumseh," *American Indian Quarterly* 16 (1992): 324–26. Then deserted, the village of Prophet's Town was destroyed by the Kentucky militia under Samuel Hopkins in November 1812.

84. *Clay*, 1:642.

85. Jefferson to Adams, 11 June 1812, L. J. Cappon, ed., *The Adams-Jefferson Letters* (Chapel Hill, NC, 1959), 308.

86. W. R. Barlow, "The Coming of the War of 1812 in Michigan Territory," *Michigan Territory* 53 (1969): 91–107.

87. R. Kagan, *Dangerous Nation: America and the World, 1600–1898* (London, 2006), 145.

88. For a report of September 1814 to the British government on American views on these lines, BL. Add. 38259 fols 93–94.

## CHAPTER 2. THE AMERICANS ATTACK, 1812

1. J. B. Hattendorf, *England in the War of the Spanish Succession: A Study of the English View and Conduct of Grand Strategy, 1701–1712* (New York, 1987); N. A. M. Rodger, "The Idea of Naval Strategy in Britain in the Eighteenth and Nineteenth Centuries," in *The Development of British Naval Thinking*, ed. G. Till (Abingdon, 2006), 19–33.

2. A. Taylor, "A Northern Revolution of 1800? Upper Canada and Thomas Jefferson," in *The Revolution of 1800: Democracy, Race, and the New Republic*, eds. J. Horn, J. E. Lewis and P. S. Onuf (Charlottesville, VA, 2002), 383–409.

3. R. Horsman, "Western War Aims, 1811–1812," *Indiana Magazine of History* 53 (1957): 1–18; Barlow, *Michigan Territory* 53:91–107.

4. *Clay*, 1:842.

5. W. Gray, *Soldiers of the King: The Upper Canadian Militia, 1812–1815* (Erin, Ontario, 1995).

6. R. Glover, *Peninsular Preparation: The Reform of the British Army 1795–1809* (Cambridge, 1963); A. J. Guy, ed., *The Road to Waterloo: The British Army and the Struggle against Revolutionary and Napoleonic France, 1793–1815* (London, 1992).

7. H. Davies, "The Influence of Intelligence on Wellington's Art of Command," *Intelligence and National Security* 22 (2007): 641.

8. K. B. Linch, "The Recruitment of the British Army, 1807–15," (PhD

dissertation, Leeds., 2001); Z. Moore, "Army Recruitment and the Uncertainties of the British 'Fiscal-Military' State, 1793–1815" (PhD thesis, London, 2006).

9. R. Middleton, ed., *Amherst and the Conquest of Canada* (Stroud, 2003).

10. Rush to John Adams, 25 Sept. 1813, Penn. Hist. Soc., AM. 1352.

11. A. Blumberg, "A Rather Unsuitable Crew: American General Officers and the Start of the War of 1812," *Journal of the War of 1812* (Winter 2001): 6–8; D. E. Graves, "The Hard School of War: A Collective Biography of the General Officers of the United States Army in the War of 1812, pt. 1, "The Class of War," *The War of 1812 Magazine* 2 (2006).

12. J. Kimball, "The Fog and Friction of Frontier War: The Role of Logistics in American Offensive Failure during the War of 1812," *Old Northwest* 5 (Winter 1979): 323–43.

13. "An Ohio Volunteer," *The Capitulation* (Chillicothe, 1812), in *War on the Detroit,* ed. M. M. Quaife (Chicago, 1940), 209.

14. *Madison,* 5:627.

15. *Madison,* 5:279.

16. *Madison,* 5:311.

17. *Madison,* 5:277.

18. *Madison,* 5:411.

19. R. S. Quimby, *The U.S. Army in the War of 1812: An Operational and Command Study* (East Lansing, MI, 1997); C. E. Skeen, *Citizen Soldiers in the War of 1812* (Lexington, KY, 1999).

20. M. Pitcavage, "Ropes of Sand: Territorial Militias, 1801–1812," *Journal of the Early Republic* 13 (1993): 481–500.

21. *Madison,* 5:344.

22. *Clay,* 1:723.

23. J. C. A. Stagg, "Between Black Rock and a Hard Place: Peter B. Porter's Plan for an American Invasion of Canada in 1812," *Journal of the Early Republic* 19 (1999): 385–422.

24. R. Horsman, "On to Canada: Manifest Destiny and the United States Strategy in the War of 1812," *Massachusetts Historical Review* 13 (1987): 1–24; *Clay,* 1: 674, 720.

25. Lord, "The Mohawk/Oneida Corridor: The Geography of the Inland Navigation across New York," in *The Sixty Years' War for the Great Lakes, 1754–1814,* ed. D. C. Skaggs and L. L. Nelson (East Lansing, MI, 2001), 275–90.

26. R. Holmes, *Redcoat: The British Soldier in the Age of Horse and Musket* (London, 2002)

27. C. Fredriksen, *Green Coats and Glory: The United States Regiment of Riflemen, 1808–1821* (Youngstown, NY, 2000); D. R. Hickey, *Don't Give Up the Ship!: Myths of the War of 1812* (Urbana, IL) 240–42.

28. *The Journal of Major John Norton* (1816), 308.

29. G. Satterfield, *Princes, Posts and Partisans: The Army of Louis XIV and Partisan Warfare in the Netherlands, 1673–1678* (Leiden, 2003); J. Ewald, *Treatise on Partisan Warfare,* eds. R. A. Selig and D. C. Skaggs (Westport, CT, 1991).

30. J. Grenier, *The First Way of War: American War Making on the Frontier, 1607–1814* (Cambridge, 2005), 43–52, and *On the Far Reaches of Empire: Anglo-Americans' Fifty Years' War on the Nova Scotia Frontier, 1710–1760* (Vancouver, 2006); M. M. Mintz, *Seeds of Empire: The American Revolutionary Conquest of the Iroquois* (New York, 1999).

31. W. Murray, "Does Military Culture Matter?", *Orbis* 43 (1999): 27–42; W. E. Lee, "Early American Ways of War: A New Reconnaissance, 1600–1815," *Historical Journal* 44 (2001): 269–89.

32. G. Chet, *Conquering the American Wilderness: The Triumph of European Warfare in the Colonial Northeast* (Amherst, MA, 2003).

33. D. Gates, *The British Light Infantry Arm c. 1790–1815: Its Creation, Training, and Operational Role* (London, 1987).

34. *Madison*, 7:211.

35. J. M. Hitsman, "Sir George Prevost's Conduct of the Canadian War of 1812," *Canadian Historical Association Report* (1962): 34–43.

36. NAM. 1968-07-339-1, 4.

37. NAM. 1968-07-339-1, 5.

38. *Madison*, 5:440.

39. T. Tackle to Bathurst, 24 Nov. 1812, BL. Loan 57/21 no. 105.

40. R. S. Allen, *His Majesty's Indian Allies: British Indian Policy in the Defence of Canada, 1774–1815* (Toronto, 1992).

41. Francis Gore, memorandum in Bathurst papers, 4 Aug. 1812, BL. Loan 57/21 no. 87.

42. C. A. Bayly, *Imperial Meridian: The British Empire and the World, 1780–1830* (Harlow, 1989).

43. NAM. 1968-07-339-1, 7–8.

44. C. Duffy, *Borodino and the War of 1812* (London, 1972); A. Mikaberidze, *The Battle of Borodino* (Barnsley, 2007).

45. *Madison*, 5:287.

46. *Madison*, 5:328.

47. R. Malcomson, " 'It Remains Only to Fight': The Battle of Queenston Heights, 13 October 1812," in *Fighting for Canada: Seven Battles, 1758–1945*, ed. D. E. Graves (Toronto, 2000), 89–130, and *A Very Brilliant Affair: The Battle of Queenston Heights, 1812* (Annapolis, MD, 2003). Canadian scholars have been particularly effective in their treatment of campaigning along the frontier. See, in particular, J. M. Hitsman, *The Incredible War of 1812: A Military History*, updated by D. E. Graves (Toronto, 1965); G. F. G. Stanley, *The War of 1812: Land Operations* (Toronto, 1983); D. E. Graves, "The War of 1812 Along the St. Lawrence Border and the Lake Ontario Littoral: A Canadian Perspective," in *A Shared Heritage: The Historical Legacy of Sacket's Harbor*, ed. J. M. Saltzgaber, (Ithaca, NY, 1993).

48. NA, Colonial Office Papers 42/148, 17–19.

49. N. Thompson, *Earl Bathurst and the British Empire* (Barnsley, 1999), 62.

50. R. C. Stuart, "Special Interests and National Authority in Foreign Policy: American-British Provincial Links during the Embargo and the War of 1812," *Diplomatic History* 8 (1984): 311–28.

51. John Adams to Jefferson, 28 June 1812, Cappon, *The Adams-Jeffer-*

son *Letters* (Chapel Hill, NC, 1959), 311; Rush to Adams, 18 July 1812, Penn. Hist. Soc., AM. 1352.

52. *Clay*, 1:727.

53. S. E. Siry, *DeWitt Clinton and American Political Economy: Sectionalism, Politics, and Republican Ideology, 1787–1828* (New York, 1990).

54. Egan, *Neither Peace Nor War*, 184.

55. *Madison*, 5:364, 344.

56. A. Peskin, *Winfield Scott and the Profession of Arms* (Kent, OH, 2003), 20.

57. Edinburgh, National Archives, GD16 34/359/11.

58. *Madison*, 5:441.

59. J. Stevenson, *Popular Disturbances in England, 1700–1870* (London, 1971), 155–61.

60. R. Muir, *Salamanca, 1812* (New Haven, CT, 2001).

61. J. P. LeDonne, "Geopolitics, Logistics, and Grain: Russia's Ambitions in the Black Sea Basin, 1737–1834," *International History Review* 28 (2006): 22–26.

62. *Madison*, 5:364–65.

## CHAPTER 3. THE ATTACK RENEWED, 1813

1. *Clay*, 1:751.

2. Wellington to Bathurst, 10 Feb. 1813, J. Gurwood, ed., *The Dispatches of Field Marshal, the Duke of Wellington* (London, 1838), 108; N. Thompson, *Earl Bathurst and the British Empire* (Barnsley, 1999), 63.

3. R. Malcomson, "Unturned Stones in War of 1812 Studies," *War of 1812 Magazine* 4 (2006).

4. C. D. Hall, *British Strategy in the Napoleonic War, 1803–15* (Manchester, 1992), 198–99; J. Dull, *The French Navy and American Independence: A Study of Arms and Diplomacy, 1774–1787* (Princeton, NJ, 1975).

5. R. Muir, *Britain and the Defeat of Napoleon, 1807–1815* (New Haven, CT, 1996), 258.

6. Harrison to John Symmes, 30 Nov. 1812, BL. Add. 39908 fol. 35.

7. *Clay*, 1:729.

8. *Clay*, 1:769–71.

9. NAM. 1968-07-339-1, 13.

10. A. D. Gaff, *Bayonets in the Wilderness: Anthony Wayne's Legion in the Old Northwest* (Norman, OK, 2004).

11. I am most grateful to Naomi Nelson, Assistant Director of the Manuscript, Archives, and Rare Book Library of Emory University, which has a copy of this rare work, for providing information and photocopies.

12. Brock to Prevost, 17 Aug. 1812, in *Documents Relating to the Invasion of Canada and the Surrender of Detroit, 1812*, ed. E. A. Cruickshank (Ottawa, 1912), 157.

13. NAM. 1968-07-339-1, 8–11.

14. R. D. Hurt, *The Ohio Frontier: Crucible of the Old Northwest, 1720–1830* (Bloomington, IN, 1996), 337.

15. L. L. Nelson, *Men of Patriotism, Courage and Enterprise: Fort Meigs in the War of 1812* (Canton, OH, 1986).

16. NAM. 1968-03-339-1, 17.

17. B. Bowlus, "A 'Signal Victory': The Battle for Fort Stephenson, August 1–2 1813," *Northwest Ohio Quarterly* 63 (1991): 43–57.

18. George to Prevost, 22 Oct. 1811, NA. CO. 42/23.

19. S. Antal, *A Wampum Denied: Procter's War of 1812* (Carleton, 1997), and "The Western Theatre in the War of 1812," *The War of 1812 Magazine* 6 (2007).

20. Selkirk to Bathurst, 21 Ap. 1813, BL. Bathurst Loan 57/7.

21. R. Malcomson, *Capital in Flames: The American Attack on York, 1813* (Annapolis, 2008); G. F. G. Stanley, *Battle in the Dark: Stoney Creek, 6 June 1813* (Toronto, 1991).

22. D. E. Graves, "'As long as the powder burnt, to kill and scalp' . . . ," *The War of 1812 Magazine* 1 (2006).

23. P. Wilder, *The Battle of Sacket's Harbor* (Baltimore, MD, 1994).

24. R. Malcomson, *Lords of the Lake: The Naval War on Lake Ontario* (Toronto, 1998), 181–211.

25. Ibid.

26. Bathurst to Robert, 2nd Viscount Melville, First Lord of the Admiralty, 24 July 1813, BL. Loan 57/107 fol. 209.

27. C. O. Paullin, ed., *The Battle of Lake Erie* (Cleveland, 1918); D. C. Skaggs and W. J. Welsh, eds., *War on the Great Lakes: Essays Commemorating the 175th Anniversary of the Battle of Lake Erie* (Kent, OH, 1991); G. T. Altoff and D. C. Skaggs, *A Signal Victory: The Lake Erie Campaign, 1812–1813* (Annapolis, MD, 1997); D. C. Skaggs, *Oliver Hazard Perry: Honor, Courage, and Patriotism in the Early U.S. Navy* (Annapolis, MD, 2006).

28. *Clay*, 1:846.

29. M. A. Palmer, "A Failure of Command, Control, and Communications: Oliver Hazard Perry and the Battle of Lake Erie," *Journal of Erie Studies* 17 (1988): 7–26.

30. O. Connelly, *Blundering to Glory: Napoleon's Military Campaigns*, 2nd ed. (Wilmington, DE, 1999).

31. A. C. Quisenberry, *Kentucky in the War of 1812* (Frankfort, KY, 1915).

32. NAM. 1968-07-339-1, 21–22.

33. D. R. Hickey, *The War of 1812: A Short History* (Urbana, IL, 1995), 108.

34. A. Starkey, *European and Native American Warfare, 1675–1815* (London, 1998), 159–63.

35. S. Antal, *A Wampun Denied*, 356.

36. J. R. Grodzinski, "Command Structure and Appointments in Upper Canada, 1812 to 1814," *The War of 1812 Magazine* 1 (2006).

37. J. Richardson, *The Letters of Veritas* (Montréal, 1815); H. Procter, "A Canadian Campaign," *London Quarterly Review* 27 (Ap., July 1822).

38. D. M. Griffin, "Forging an 1812 General: The Early Life of Sir Gordon Drummond," *Ontario History* 98 (1996): 297–313.

39. Robert Smith, Secretary of State, to David Holmes, Governor of Mississippi Territory, 15 Nov. 1810, in *Documents Accompanying the Message of the President* (Washington, DC, 1810), 150.

40. E. H. Gould, "Entangled Histories, Entangled Worlds: The English-Speaking Atlantic as a Spanish Periphery," *American Historical Review* (2007): 781.

41. J. G. Cusick, *The Other War of 1812: The Patriot War and the American Invasion of Spanish East Florida* (Gainesvill, FA,2003).

42. Hawkins to David Mitchell, Governor of Georgia, 7 July 1813, Auburn.

43. G. A. Waselkov, *A Conquering Spirit: Fort Mims and the Redstick War of 1813–1814* (Tuscaloosa, AL, 2006).

44. F. B. Johnson to Henry Dundas, Secretary for War, 1796, Edinburgh National Archives, GD 51 1/521.

45. *The Journal of John Norton* (1816).

46. C. Benn, "Iroquois Warfare, 1812–1814," in *War along the Niagara*, ed. R. A. Bowler (Youngstown, NY, 1991), 61–76, and *The Iroquois in the War of 1812* (Toronto, 1998).

47. G. F. G. Stanley, *The War Of 1812: Land Operations* (Ottawa, 1983), 417–18.

48. D. Chandler, *Atlas of Military Strategy: The Art, Theory and Practice of War, 1618–1878* (London, 1980), 116–17.

49. R. S. Quimby, *The U.S. Army in the War of 1812: An Operational and Command Study* (East Lansing, MI, 1997), 343.

50. D. E. Graves, *Field of Glory: The Battle of Crysler's Farm, 1813* (Toronto, 1999).

51. *Clay*, 1:839–40.

52. NAM. 1968-07-339-1, 25–30.

53. General Returns, Canada, 1813, NA. WO. 17/1517.

54. *Naval War of 1812*, 2:325.

55. W. Napier, *The Life and Opinions of General Sir Charles James Napier*, 4 vols. (London, 1857), 1:217, 229; J. D. Richardson, *Defense of Craney Island on the 22nd of June, 1813* (Richmond, VA, 1849).

56. *Naval War of 1812*, 2:342.

57. *Naval War of 1812*, 2:342, cf. 345.

58. J. W. Pratt, *Expansionists of 1812* (New York, 1949), 270; R. Fabel, "The Laws of War in the 1812 Conflict," *Journal of American Studies* 14 (1980): 199–218.

59. *Clay*, 1:842.

60. F. A. Golder, "The Russian Offer of Mediation in the War of 1812," *Political Science Quarterly* 31 (1916): 360–91.

61. *Madison*, 5:646.

62. Wellington to Sir Henry Wellesley, 23 May 1813, Gurwood, *Dispatches of . . . Wellington*, (London, 1838), 10:395.

63. Dudley, *Naval War of 1812*, 2:162, 356.

64. B. Perkins, *The Creation of a Republican Empire, 1776–1865* (Cambridge, 1993), 137.

65. C. K. Webster, ed., *British Diplomacy 1813–1815: Select Documents Dealing with the Reconstruction of Europe* (London, 1921), 112.

66. M. Leggiere, "From Berlin to Leipzig: Napoleon's Gamble in North Germany, 1813," *Journal of Military History* 67 (2003): 39–84.

67. D. Smith, *1813 Leipzig: Napoleon and the Battle of the Nations* (Mechanicsburg, PA, 2001).

68. Ex inf. Michael Leggiere. Email of 20 May 2008.

69. *Naval War of 1812*, 2: 328.

70. *Naval War of 1812*, 2:345.

71. S. Watts, *The Republic Reborn. War and the Making of Liberal America, 1790–1820* (Baltimore, 1987), 281.

72. I would like to thank Harvey Sicherman for giving me a copy of his paper "Stephen Girard: Globalist and Navalist" and for discussing Girard with me.

73. BL. Add. 38259 fols 91–93.

74. *Clay*, 1: 630; M. B. Pound, *Benjamin Hawkins: Indian Agent* (Athens, Georgia, 1951).

75. *Clay*, 1: 693–94.

76. Rush to Madison, 4 Sept. 1812, Penn. Hist. Soc. Am. 13520; Clay, 1:750.

77. *Madison*, 5:xxiii.

78. G. F. G. Stanley, *Canada Invaded: 1775–1776* (Toronto, 1977).

## CHAPTER 4. THE WAR AT SEA

1. T. C. Hansard, *The Parliamentary Debates from the Year 1803 to the Present Times*, vol. 24 (1813), cols 580–84.

2. M. L. S. Kitzen, *Tripoli and the United States at War: A History of American Relations with the Barbary States, 1785–1805* (Jefferson, NC, 1993); G. A. Smith, "To Effect a Peace through the Medium of War": Jefferson and the Circumstances of Force in the Mediterranean," *Consortium on Revolutionary Europe 1750–1850: Selected Papers* (Tallahassee, FA, 1996), 155–60.

3. J. B. Hattendorf, "The American Navy in the World of Franklin and Jefferson, 1775–1826," *War and Society* 2 (1990); S. Tucker, *The Jeffersonian Gunboat Navy* (Columbia, SC, 1993); G. A. Smith, *"For the Purposes of Defense": The Politics of the Jeffersonian Gunboat Program* (Newark, DE, 1995).

4. C. Symonds, *Navalists and Antinavalists: The Naval Policy Debate in the United States, 1785–1827* (Newark, DE, 1980).

5. P. J. Kastor, "Toward the Maritime War Only": The Question of Naval Mobilization, 1811–1812," *Journal of Military History* 61 (1997): 455–80.

6. J. H. Schroeder, *Commodore John Rodgers: Paragon of the Early American Navy* (Gainesville, FA, 2006).

7. J. C. A. Stagg, "James Madison and the Coercion of Great Britain: Canada, the West Indies, and the War of 1812," *William and Mary Quarterly* 38, 3rd ser. (1981): 32–34.

8. G. S. Graham, *Sea Power and British North America, 1783–1820* (Cambridge, MA, 1941), 142–50.

9. S. Willis, *Fighting at Sea in the Eighteenth Century: The Art of Sailing Warfare* (Woodbridge, 2008), 5–6.

10. T. G. Martin, *A Most Fortunate Ship: A Narrative History of Old Ironsides,* 2nd ed. (Annapolis, MD, 1997).

11. For advice to the British government to send large frigates to American waters, James Abernethy to Liverpool, 2 Aug. 1812, BL. Add. 38249 fol. 8.

12. T. G. Martin, "*Constitution*'s Winning Captains," in *New Interpretations in Naval History,* eds. R. W. Love, et al. (Annapolis, MD, 2001), 98–104.

13. *Clay,* 1:751.

14. B. J. Lohnes, "British Naval Problems at Halifax during the War of 1812," *Mariner's Mirror* 59 (1973): 317–33.

15. *Hansard's Parliamentary Debates,* 24:643.

16. Peter Le Fevre, "Sir John Borlase Warren," in *British Admirals of the Napoleonic Wars: The Contemporaries of Nelson,* eds. R. Harding and Le Fevre, (2005), 240.

17. *Naval War of 1812,* 2:183.

18. *Naval War of 1812,* 1:508–509, 649–51.

19. *Naval War of 1812,* 2:11.

20. D. Syrett, "The role of the Royal Navy in the Napoleonic Wars After Trafalgar, 1805–1814," *Naval War College Review* (1977): 71–84; K. McCranie, *Admiral Lord Keith and the Naval War Against Napoleon* (Gainesville, FA, 2006).

21. W. L. Clowes, *The Royal Navy,* (London, 1900), 5:9.

22. *Naval War of 1812,* 2:14.

23. *Naval War of 1812,* 2:78.

24. W. G. Dudley, *Splintering the Wooden Wall: the British Blockade of the United States, 1812–1815* (Annapolis, MD, 2003).

25. *Naval War of 1812,* 2:308.

26. Papers of Admiral Sir Henry Hotham, Hull, University Library, DDHO/7/71.

27. T. Roosevelt, *The Naval War of 1812* (New York, 1882; Annapolis, MD, 1987), 358–64; W. M. P. Dunne, "The United States Frigate *President*: The Victor or the Vanquished," in *New Interpretations,* ed. Love, 83–97; R. J. Allison, *Stephen Decatur: American Naval Hero, 1779–1820* (Amherst, MA, 2005).

28. H. F. Pullen, *The Shannon and the Chesapeake* (Toronto, 1970).

29. I. Dye, *The Fatal Cruise of the "Argus": Two Captains in the War of 1812* (Annapolis, MD, 2001).

30. C. Berube and J. A. Rodgaard, *A Call to the Sea: Captain Charles Stewart of the USS Constitution* (Dulles, VA, 2005).

31. W. H. Duffy, *Captain Blakeley and the Wasp: The Cruise of 1814* (Annapolis, 2001).

32. J. M. Sherwig, *Guineas and Gunpowder: British Foreign Aid in the Wars with France, 1793–1815* (Cambridge, MA, 1969).

33. G. K. Harrington, "The American Naval Challenge to the English East India Company during the War of 1812," in *New Interpretations in Naval History,* ed. J. Sweetman (Annapolis, MD, 1993), 129–52.

34. N. A. M. Rodger, *The Command of the Ocean: A Naval History of Britain, 1649–1815* (London, 2004), 570.

35. J. Glete, *Navies and Nations: Warships, Navies and State Building in Europe and America, 1500–1860* (Stockholm, 1993), 395.

36. W. F. Galpin, "The American Grain Trade to the Spanish Peninsula, 1810–1814," *American Historical Review* 28 (1923): 24–28; G. E. Watson, "The United States and the Peninsular War, 1808–12," *Historical Journal* 19 (1976): 871.

37. *Madison*, 5:646.

38. B. Gough, *Fighting Sail on Lake Huron and Georgian Bay: The War of 1812 and Its Aftermath* (Annapolis, MD, 2002).

39. R. Malcomson, "HMS *St Lawrence*: The Freshwater First-Rate," *Mariner's Mirror* 83 (1997): 419–33.

40. Malcomson, *Warships of the Great Lakes, 1754–1834* (London, 2001), 102, 118.

41. Wellington to Liverpool, 9 Nov. 1814, 2nd Duke of Wellington, ed., *Supplementary Despatches, Correspondence and Memoranda of Field Marshal Arthur Duke of Wellington* (London, 1862), 9:425.

42. Wellington to Sir George Murray, 22 Dec. 1814, Gurwood, *Dispatches of . . . Wellington*, 12:224.

43. *Clay*, 1:750.

44. *Madison*, 5:326.

45. Not one of the Great Lakes.

46. A. T. Mahan, *Sea Power in its Relations to the War of 1812*, 2 vols. (Boston, 1918), 1:v.

47. L. A. Norton, *Joshua Barney: Hero of the Revolution and 1812* (Annapolis, MD, 2000).

48. R. Malcomson, *Lords of the Lake: The Naval War on Lake Ontario, 1812–1814* (Annapolis, MD, 1998), 255.

49. J. A. Goldenberg, "The Royal Navy's Blockade in New England Waters, 1812–1815," *International History Review* 6 (1984): 424–39.

50. F. M. Kert, *Prize and Prejudice: Privateering and Naval Prize in Atlantic Canada in the War of 1812* (St. Johns, Newfoundland, 1997); A. Gutridge, "George Redmond Hulbert: Prize Agent at Halifax, Nova Scotia, 1812–14," *Mariner's Mirror* 87 (2001): 30–42.

51. Kert, "The Fortunes of War: Commercial Warfare and Maritime Risk in the War of 1812," *Northern Mariner* 8 (Oct. 1998): 1–16.

52. *Madison*, 5:339–41.

53. D. Hickey, "New England's Defense Problem and the Genesis of the Hartford Convention," *New England Quarterly* 50 (1977): 587–604.

54. C. J. Bartlett, "Gentlemen versus Democrats: Cultural Prejudice and Military Strategy in Britain in the War of 1812," *War in History* 1 (1994): 140–59.

55. J. T. de Kay, *The Battle of Stonington: Torpedoes, Submarines, and Rockets in the War of 1812* (Annapolis, MD, 1990).

56. T. J. Crackel, "The Battle of Queenston Heights, 13 October 1812," in *America's First Battles 1776–1965*, eds. C. E. Heller and W. A. Stofft (Lawrence, KS, 1986): 33.

57. *Naval War of 1812*, 2:185–86.

58. W. S. Coker, "The Last Battle of the War of 1812: New Orleans: No, Fort Bowyer!," *Alabama Historical Quarterly* 43 (1981): 42–63.

59. Cochrane to Major General John Lambert, 3 Feb. 1815, NA. WO. 1/143; R. Morriss, *Cockburn and the British Navy in Transition: Admiral Sir George Cockburn, 1772–1853* (Exeter, 1997), 83–120.

60. *Trewman's Exeter Flying-Post*, 2 Mar. 1815.

61. R. J. Miller, *Native America, Discovered and Conquered: Thomas Jefferson, Lewis and Clark, and Manifest Destiny* (Westport, CT, 2006).

62. B. Gough, *The Royal Navy and the Northwest Coast of America, 1810–1914: A Study of British Maritime Ascendancy* (Vancouver, 1971), 8–28; J. A. Hussey, ed., *The Voyage of the "Racoon"* (San Francisco, 1958).

63. *Naval War of 1812*, 2:162; D. W. Thomson, "Robert Fulton's Torpedo System in the War of 1812," *United States Naval Institute Proceedings* 68 (1942): 1206–17.

64. BL. Add. 71593 fol. 134; W. S. Hutcheon, *Robert Fulton, Pioneer of Undersea Warfare* (Annapolis, MD, 1981).

65. J. Clark, "The War of 1812: American Nationalism and Rhetorical Images of Britain," *War and Society* 12 (1994): 1–26; Bartlett, "Gentlemen versus Democrats." *War in History* 1 (1994): 140–59.

## CHAPTER 5. THE EMPIRE STRIKES BACK, 1814–15

1. J. H. Cooke, *A Narrative of Events in the South of France, and of the Attack on New Orleans, in 1814 and 1815* (London, 1835), 234.

2. Five days earlier, he abdicated in favor of his son, the King of Rome.

3. Rush to Adams, 17 June 1814, Penn. Hist. Soc. Am. 1352.

4. Colonel Torrens to Sir George Murray, 14 Ap. 1814, Wellington, *Supplementary Despatches*, (London, 1862), 9:58.

5. State of Divisions, 18 May 1814, Gurwood, *Dispatches of . . . Wellington*, 9:119.

6. J. K. Mahon, "British Command Decisions in the Northern Campaigns of the War of 1812," *Canadian Historical Review* 46 (1965): 219–37.

7. J. Black, *Parliament and Foreign Policy in the Eighteenth Century* (Cambridge, 2004), 3–4, 107.

8. *Clay*, 1:884.

9. W. B. Skelton, "High Army Leadership in the Era of the War of 1812: The Making and Remaking of the Officer Corps," *William and Mary Quarterly* 51, 3rd ser. (1994): 253–74.

10. J. Buckley, *William Clark. Indian Diplomat* (Norman, OK, 2008), 105.

11. B. Gough, *Fighting Sail on Lake Huron and Georgian Bay: the War of 1812 and its Aftermath* (Annapolis, MD, 2002), 93–94.

12. G. S. May, *War 1812: The United States and Great Britain at Mackinac, 1812–1815* (Mackinac, MI, 2004).

13. B. Gough, *Through Water, Ice and Fire: Schooner Nancy and the War of 1812* (Toronto, 2006).

14. L. Lépine, *Les Officers des Milice du Bas-Canada, 1812–1815* (Québec, 1996).

15. A. Taylor, "The Late Loyalists. Northern Reflections of the Early American Republic," *Journal of the Early Republic* 27 (2007): 30–31.

16. G. Sheppard, *Plunder, Profit, and Paroles: A Social History of the War of 1812 in Upper Canada* (Montréal, 1994).

17. J. Kimball, "The Battle of Chippawa: Infantry Tactics in the War of 1812," *Military Affairs* 31 (1967–68): 169–86; D. E. Graves, *Red Coats and Grey Jackets: The Battle of Chippawa, 5 July 1814* (Toronto, 1994); J. Morris, *Sword of the Border: Major General Jacob Brown, 1775–1828* (Kent, OH, 2000); R. V. Barbuto, *Niagara 1814: America Invades Canada* (Lawrence, KS, 2000).

18. D. E. Graves, "Field Artillery of the War of 1812: Equipment, Organization, Tactics, and Effectiveness," *Army Collecting* 30 (May 1992): 39–48.

19. D. E. Graves, *The Battle of Lundy's Lane* (Baltimore, 1993), 71.

20. D. E. Graves, ed., *Merry Hearts Make Light Days: The War of 1812 Journal of Lieutenant John Le Couteur* (Ottawa, 1993), 176.

21. G. E. Rothenberg, *The Art of Warfare in the Age of Napoleon* (Bloomington, IN, 1978), 123–24.

22. J. Whitehorne, *While Washington Burned: The Battle for Fort Erie, 1814* (Baltimore, 1992).

23. M. Pitcavage, " 'Burthened in Defence of Our Rights': Opposition to Military Service in Ohio during the War of 1812," *Ohio History* 104 (1995): 142–62.

24. G. Stott, *Great Evils: The War of 1812 in Southwestern Ontario* (Arkona, Ontario, 2001); S. A. Rammage, *The Militia Stood Alone: Malcolm's Mills, 6 November 1814* (Penticton, British Columbia, 2000).

25. London report of 6 Oct. 1814 in *Trewman's Exeter Flying-Post*, 13 Oct. 1814; D. C. Skaggs, *Thomas Macdonough: Master of Command in the Early U.S. Navy* (Annapolis, MD, 2003), 127–34.

26. D. E. Graves, " 'The Finest Army Ever to Campaign on American Soil'? The Organization, Strength, Composition, and Losses of British Land Forces During the Plattsburgh Campaign, September, 1814," *Journal of the War of 1812* 7 (2003): 6–13; A. S. Everest, *The War of 1812 in the Champlain Valley* (Syracuse, NY, 1981).

27. Wellington to Sir George Murray, 22 Dec. 1814, Gurwood, *Dispatches of . . . Wellington* (London, 1838), 12:224.

28. H. Lydenberg, ed., *Archibald Robertson: His Diaries and Sketches in America* (New York, 1930), 38.

29. N. A. M. Rodger, "The Idea of Naval Strategy in Britain in the Eighteenth and Nineteenth Centuries," in *The Development of British Naval Thinking*, ed. G. Till (London, 2006): 27.

30. C. T. George, *Terror on the Chesapeake: The War of 1812 on the Bay* (Shippensburg, PA, 2000).

31. The small American navy had two very similar ships named *Adams* and *John Adams* and they are sometimes confused.

32. B. J. Lohnes, "A New Look at the Invasion of Eastern Maine, 1814," *Maine Historical Quarterly* 15 (Summer 1975): 5–25.

33. Wellington to Liverpool, 9 Nov. 1814, Wellington, *Supplementary Despatches,* (London, 1862), 9:426.

34. Mores to Wellington, 15 May 1820, Southampton, University Library, Wellington papers, WP1/645/8.

35. B. Perrett, *The Real Hornblower: The Life of Admiral of the Fleet Sir James Alexander Gordon* (Annapolis, MD, 1997).

36. Mackesy, "Problems of an Amphibious Power: Britain against France, 1793–1815," *Naval War College Review* 30 (1978): 18–19.

37. NA. WO. 1/141, p. 36.

38. NA. WO. 1/141.

39. NAM. 2002-02-729-1; J. L. Sanford, "The Battle of North Point," *Maryland Historical Magazine* 24 (1929), 356–65.

40. Threlkeld to John Fisher, 1 Mar. 1817, DRO. 1148M/19/9.

41. *Naval War of 1812*, 3:207–208.

42. C. Hibbert, ed., *A Soldier of the Seventy-First* (London, 1975), 1–13; I. Fletcher, *The Waters of Oblivion: The British Invasion of the Rio de la Plata, 1806–1807* (Tunbridge Wells, 1991).

43. NAM. 2002-02-729-1.

44. William Kirke to his father, 13 Nov. 1814, Nottingham, Nottinghamshire Archives DD/MM/43.

45. Dolly Madison to Lucy Payne Washington, Todd, 23, 24 Aug. 1814, D. B. Mattern and H. C. Shulman, eds.,*The Selected Letters of Dolly Payne Madison* (Charlottesville, VA, 2003), 193–94.

46. E. Skeen, *John Armstrong Jr., 1758–1843: A Biography* (Syracuse, NY, 1981).

47. NA. WO. 1/141, pp. 31-5; A. S. Pitch, *The Burning of Washington: The British Invasion of 1814* (Annapolis, MD, 1998).

48. F. A. Cassell, "The Great Baltimore Riot of 1812," *Maryland Historical Magazine* 70 (1975): 241–59; D. R. Hickey, "The Darker Side of Democracy: The Baltimore Riots of 1812," *Maryland Historian* 7 (1976): 1–14.

49. F. W. Hopkins, *Tom Boyle, Master Privateer* (Cambridge, MA, 1976); J. R. Garitee, *The Republic's Private Navy: The American Privateering Business as Practiced by Baltimore during the War of 1812* (Middletown, CT, 1977); T. C. Gillmer, *Pride of Baltimore: the Story of the Baltimore Clippers, 1800–1990* (Camden, ME, 1992).

50. NA. WO. 1/141; NAM. 2002-02-729-1.

51. NA. WO. 1/141.

52. BL. Add. 59282 fol. 170, 59281 fols 88–97; B L. Bathurst Loan 57/108 fol. 327; F. Winter, *The First Golden Age of Rockets: Congreve and Hale Rockets of the Nineteenth Century* (Washington, DC, 1991).

53. S. Kroll, *By the Dawn's Early Light: The Story of the Star-Spangled Banner* (New York, 1994).

54. S. S. Sheads, *The Rockets' Red Glare: The Maritime Defense of Baltimore in 1814* (Centreville, MD, 1986) and *Guardian of the Star-Spangled Banner: Lt. Colonel George Armistead and the Fort McHenry Flag* (Baltimore, 1999); Sheads and M. T. Cole, *Fort McHenry and Baltimore's Harbor Defenses* (Charleston, SC, 2001).

55. NA. WO. 1/141; William Kirke to his father, 13 Nov. 1814, Nottingham, Nottinghamshire Archives, DD/MM/43.

56. T. Munch-Petersen, *Defying Napoleon: How Britain Bombarded Copenhagen and Seized the Danish Fleet in 1807* (Stroud, 2007).

57. NA. WO. 1/141, 75–84; J. Whitehorne, *The Battle for Baltimore, 1814* (Baltimore, 1997).

58. NAM. 2002-02-729-1.

59. *Trewman's Exeter Flying-Post*, 20 Oct. 1814.

60. J. Black, *What If? Counterfactualism in History* (London, 2008).

61. B. Vale, *Cochrane in the Pacific* (London, 2007).

62. John Harriott to Sidmouth, 7 May 1814, DRO. 152M/C1814/OF 13. For earlier British interest in threatening support for slaves, 152M/C1813/OF 3.

63. J. M. Hartley, "Russia in 1812. Part I: The French Presence in the *Gubernii* of Smolensk and Mogilev," *Jahrbücher für Geschichte Osteuropas* 38 (1990): 179–82.

64. *Clay*, 1:988–99.

65. *Clay*, 1:996.

66. J. S. Hare, "Military Punishments in the War of 1812," *Journal of the American Military Institute* 4 (1940): 225–39.

67. R. V. Barbuto, *Niagara 1814* (Lawrence, KS, 2000), 319–21.

68. J. M. Banner, *To the Hartford Convention: The Federalists and the Origins of Party Politics in Massachusetts, 1789–1815* (New York, 1970); R. Buel, *America on the Brink: How the Political Struggle over the War of 1812 Almost Destroyed the Young Republic* (New York, 2005); D. R. Hickey, "New England's Defense Problem and the Genesis of the Hartford Convention," *New England Quarterly* 50 (1977): 587–604; A. LaCroix, "A Singular and Awkward War: The Transatlantic Context of the Hartford Convention," *American Nineteenth Century History* 6 (2005): 3–32.

69. G. de Bertier de Sauvigny, "The American Press and the Fall of Napoleon in 1814," *Proceedings of the American Philosophical Society* 98 (1954): 337–76.

70. W. F. Galpin, The American Grain Trade to the Spanish Peninsula, 1810–1814," *American Historical Review* 28 (1923): 25, 40–44.

71. Melsup Hill to Liverpool, no date, received 22 Sept. 1812, BL. Add. 38249 fols 194–97; R. K. Murdock, "A British Report on West Florida and Louisiana, November 1812," *Florida Historical Quarterly* 43 (1964): 36–51; for his career, Statham-Drew, *James Stirling: Admiral and Founding Governor of Western Australia* (Perth, 2003); anon. undated memorandum, BL. Loan 57/6 no. 629.

72. Thompson, *Bathurst and British Empire*, 81.

73. T. Kanon, " 'A Slow Laborious Slaughter': The Battle of Horseshoe Bend," *Tennessee Historical Quarterly* 58 (1999): 2–15.

74. J. Grenier, *The First Way of War: American War-Making on the Frontier* (New York, 2005), 217.

75. F. L. Owsley, "The Role of the South in the British Grand Strategy in the War of 1812," *Tennessee Historical Quarterly* 31 (1972), 22–38; Hawkins to Mitchell, 20 Jan. 1813, Auburn.

76. NA. WO. 1/141, 21, 67.

77. Edward Nicolls to Jean Lafitte, 31 Aug. 1814, U.S. Congress, *American State Papers, I: Foreign Relations*, 6 vols. (Washington, D.C., 1832–59),

4:547; J. Sugden, "Jean Lafitte and the British Offer of 1814," *Louisiana History* 20 (1979): 159–67; W. C. Davies, *The Pirates Lafitte: The Treacherous World of the Corsairs of the Gulf* (New York, 2005).

78. NA. WO. 1/141, 63–67.

79. M. D. Childs, *The 1812 Aponte Rebellion in Cuba and the Struggle against Atlantic Slavery* (Chapel Hill, NC, 2006).

80. F. A. Cassell, "Slaves of the Chesapeake Bay Area and the War of 1812," *Journal of Negro History* 57 (1972): 144–55; C. T. George, "Mirage of Freedom: African Americans in the War of 1812," *Maryland Historical Magazine* 91 (1996): 426–50.

81. W. S. Brown, *The Amphibious Campaign for West Florida and Louisiana, 1814–1815: A Critical Review of Strategy and Tactics at New Orleans* (Tuscaloosa, AL, 1969).

82. I would like to thank John Clune and Margo Stringfield for lending me a copy of their forthcoming *Pensacola, 1559–1821* (Gainesville, FA, 2008).

83. John to James Innerarity, 10–11 Nov. 1814, Pensacola, University of West Florida, papers of Panton, Leslie and Co., no. 7437.

84. Nicolls to Cochrane, 27 July 1814, Edinburgh, National Library of Scotland, Ms. 2328.

85. A. J. Latour, *Historical Memoir of the War in West Florida and Louisiana in 1814–15*, ed. G. A. Smith, rev. ed. (Gainesville, FA, 1999), 83.

86. Buller to James Buller, DRO. 2065M/F6/10. The letter is dated 5 December 1815, which is obviously a mistake. The letter appears to have been written in some haste. The paper is watermarked 1813, which proves nothing. The postmark is 1815, but the letter has been re-directed from Crediton to London. If it was written in December 1814, it might not have reached Crediton until some time in January, at which time it could have received a later postmark. It is odd to date a letter the year after it was written, whereas to write the previous year in January was quite common. The probable explanation is that Buller wrote the letter on 5 January 1815 and got the month wrong.

87. NAM. 2002-02-729-1.

88. F. Anderson and A. Cayton, *The Dominion of War: Empire and Liberty in North America, 1500–2000* (New York, 2005), 234.

89. D. B. Morgan, "General David B. Morgan's Defense of the Conduct of the Louisiana Militia in the Battle of New Orleans," *Louisiana Historical Quarterly* 9 (1926): 16–29.

90. "Court-Martial Held at the Royal Barracks, Dublin, For the Trial of Brevet-Lieutenant Colonel Thomas Mullins," *Louisiana Historical Quarterly* 9 (1926): 33–110.

91. H. L. Coles, *The War of 1812* (Chicago, 1965), 267.

92. Smith, *Memoir*, 109.

93. NAM. 2002-02-729-1.

94. NAM. 2001-09-36-1.

95. Latimer, *1812*, 387.

96. R. V. Remini, *The Battle of New Orleans: Andrew Jackson and America's First Military Victory* (London, 2001); T. Pickles, *New Orleans*

*1815* (London, 1993); *Annual Register* 57 (1815): 123. For a map of operations before New Orleans in December 1814 to January 1815, Oxford, Bodleian Library, Ms. Maps. Misc. a.2 (S.C. 33091) fol. 8.

97. T. Fleming, "Napoleon's Invasion of North America," in *More What If?*, ed. R. Cowley (2001; 2003 edn, Basingstoke), 150.

98. NAM. 2002-02-729-1; Coker, "Last Battle," 42–63.

99. NAM. 2001-09-36-1.

100. Hawkins to Peter Early, Governor of Georgia, 20 Feb. 1815, Auburn.

101. Hawkins to Nicolls, 19 Mar., and reply, 28 Ap. 1815, Auburn.

102. Cockburn to Sebastian Kindelan, Governor of St. Augustine, 13, 22 Feb., to General Forbes, 26 Feb., and to Admiral Cochrane, 28 Feb., NA. WO. 1/144.

103. Browne to Liverpool, 29 Dec. 1814, BL. Add. 38260 fol. 408.

104. J. C. A. Stagg, "Enlisted Men in the United States Army, 1812–1815: A Preliminary Survey," *William and Mary Quarterly* 43, 3rd ser. (1986): 615–45.

105. Hickey, *War of 1812*, 219, 309.

## CHAPTER 6. CONSEQUENCES

1. *Clay*, 1:1007.

2. H. Koht, "Bernadotte and Swedish-American Relations, 1810–1814," *Journal of Modern History* 16 (1944): 265–85.

3. C. G. Calloway, *Crown and Calumet: British-Indian Relations, 1783–1815* (Norman, OK, 1987), 220–22.

4. Henry Goulburn to Bathurst, 9 Aug. 1814, BL. Loan 57/7 no. 779.

5. Castlereagh to Liverpool, 28 Aug. 1814, BL. Add. 38259 fols 43–44.

6. Goulburn to Bathurst, 21 Aug. 1814, BL. Loan 57/7 no. 786.

7. Rush to Adams, 23 Oct. 1814, Penn. Hist. Soc. Am. 1352.

8. Memorandum, 20 Aug. 1814, BL. Loan 57/21 no. 154.

9. Anon. memoranda in Bathurst papers, BL. Loan 57/21 nos 154–55; George Wyke to Liverpool, 5 Sept. 1814, BL. Add. 38259 fol. 118.

10. Bathurst to Henry, Viscount Sidmouth, 15 Sept. 1814, DRO. 152M/C1814/OF15.

11. Historical Manuscript Commission, *Report on the Manuscripts of Earl Bathurst* (London, 1923), 288–89.

12. Eg. from papers of Sidmouth, the Home Secretary, DRO. 152M C1815 OH, 3, 8.

13. J.A. Carr, "The Battle of New Orleans and the Treaty of Ghent," *Diplomatic History* 3 (1979), 273–82.

14. Castlereagh to Wellington, 18 Dec. 1814, BL. Add. 38360, fol. 396.

15. DRO. 152M/C1814/OF11.

16. *Clay*, 1:989.

17. 19 Nov., London report in *Trewman's Exeter Flying-Post*, 24 Nov. 1814.

18. *Clay*, 1:995.

19. *Trewman's Exeter Flying-Post*, 15 Dec. 1814.

20. Wellington to Liverpool, 9 Nov. 1814, Wellington, *Supplementary*

*Despatches*, 9:425; D. Mills, "The Duke of Wellington and the Peace Negotiations at Ghent in 1814," *Canadian Historical Review* 2 (1921): 19–32.

21. Castlereagh to Wellington, 21 Nov., Castlereagh to Liverpool, 25 Nov. 1814, BL. Add. 38260 fols 194, 220–21.

22. Wellington to Liverpool, 9 Nov. 1814, Wellington, *Supplementary Despatches*, 9:426.

23. Liverpool to Castlereagh, 4 Nov. 1814, Wellington, *Supplementary Despatches*, 9:405.

24. F. L. Engleman, *The Peace of Christmas Eve* (New York, 1962).

25. Rush to Adams, 29 June 1813, Penn. Hist. Soc. AM. 1352.

26. Rush to Madison, 15 Feb. 1815, Penn. Hist. Soc. Am. 13520.

27. J. D. Richardson, ed., *Messages and Papers of the Presidents, 1789–1998* (Washington, DC, 1896–98), 1:560–61.

28. F. C. Leiner, *The End of Barbary Terror: America's 1815 War Against the Pirates of North Africa* (Oxford, 2006).

29. Hickey, *War of 1812*.

30. J. Record, "The Use and Abuse of History: Munich, Vietnam and Iraq," *Survival* 49 (2007): 163–80. See, more generally, E. R. May, *"Lessons" of the Past: The Use and Misuse of History in American Foreign Policy* (New York, 1973).

31. W. B. Turner, *The War of 1812: The War that Both Sides Won* (Toronto, 1990).

32. D. P. Barr, ed., *The Boundaries between Us: Natives and Newcomers along the Frontiers of the Old Northwest Territory, 1750–1850* (Kent, OH, 2006); T. D. Willig, *Restoring the Chain of Friendship: British Policy and the Indians of the Great Lakes, 1783–1815* (Lincoln, NE, 2008).

33. P. G. Williams, S. C. Bolton, and J. M. Whayne, eds., *A Whole Country in Commotion: The Louisiana Purchase and the American Southwest* (Fayetteville, AR, 2005).

34. C. Benn, *The Iroquois in the War of 1812* (Toronto, 1998).

35. *Madison*, 5:332.

36. D. E. Graves, "In Their Own Words—Aboriginal Leaders and the War of 1812," *The War of 1812 Magazine* 2 (2006).

37. C. G. Calloway, "The End of an Era: British-Indian Relations in the Great Lakes Region after the War of 1812," *Massachusetts Historical Review* 12 (1986): 3–4.

38. F. P. Prucha, *The Sword of the Republic: The United States Army on the Frontier, 1783–1846* (Bloomington, IN, 1977), 123–28.

39. P. J. Jung, "The Black Hawk War Reconsidered: A New Interpretation of its Causes and Consequences," *Journal of the Indian Wars* 1 (1999): 31–69.

40. S. Watson, "Militarily Effective but Politically Contingent: Evaluating U.S. Army Pacification Efforts on the Northwestern Trans-Mississippi Frontier, 1820–1846," paper presented to the conference of the Society for Military History, 18 Ap. 2008.

41. Griffin, *American Leviathan. Empire, Nation, and Revolutionary Frontier* (New York, 2007), 258.

42. C. K. Reeves, *The Choctaw Before Removal* (Jackson, MS, 1985).

43. D. S. Heidler, "The Politics of National Aggression: Congress and the First Seminole War," *Journal of the Early Republic* 13 (1993): 501–30;

D. C. Skaggs, "The Sixty Years' War for the Great Lakes: An Overview," in *The Sixty Years" War for the Great Lakes, 1754–1814*, ed. Skaggs and L. L. Nelson (East Lansing, MI, 2001), 17.

44. J. G. C. Cusick, *The Other War of 1812: The Patriot War and the American Invasion of Spanish East Florida* (Gainesville, FA, 2003), 6.

45. R. Balufarb, "The Western Question: The Geopolitics of Latin American Independence," *American Historical Review* 112 (2007): 751.

46. *Naval War of 1812*, 2:325–26.

47. *Naval War of 1812*, 2:396.

48. C. J. Bartlett and G. A. Smith, "'A Species of Milito-Nautico-Guerilla-Plundering Warfare': Admiral Alexander Cochrane's Naval Campaign against the United States, 1814–1815," in *Britain and America Go to War. The Impact of War and Warfare in Anglo-America, 1754–1815*, ed. J. Flavell and S. Conway (Gainesville, FA, 2004), 187–90.

49. G. T. Altoff, *Amongst My Best Men: African-Americans and the War of 1812* (Put-in-Bay, OH, 1996).

50. R. C. Vogel, "Jean Lafitte, the Baratarians, and the Historical Geography of Piracy in the Gulf of Mexico," *Gulf Coast Historical Review* 5 (1990): 63–77.

51. Nicolls to Benjamin Hawkins, 28 Ap. 1815, Auburn.

52. Nicolls to Hawkins, 12 May 1815, NA. WO. 1/143.

53. Hawkins to Jackson, 26 May 1815, Auburn.

54. M. F. Boyd, "Events at Prospect Bluff on the Apalachicola River," *Florida Historical Quarterly* 16 (1937): 55–93; J. W. Covington, "The Negro Fort," *Gulf Coast Historical Review* 5 (1990): 79–91; S. C. Tucker, *The Jeffersonian Gunboat Navy* (Columbia, SC, 1993), 175.

55. Hawkins to Jackson, 8 Dec. 1815, Auburn.

56. J. Scafer, "The British Attitude to the Oregon Question, 1815–1846," *American Historical Review* 16 (1910–11): 273–99.

57. S. L. Falk, "Disarmament on the Great Lakes: Myth or Reality?," *United States Naval Institute Proceedings* 87 (1967): 69–73.

58. F. Bickley, *Historical Manuscripts Commission Report on the Manuscripts of the Earl of Bathhurst* (London, 1923), 316.

59. G. S. Graham, *Sea Power and British North America, 1783–1820: A Study in British Colonial Policy* (Cambridge, MA, 1941), 256.

60. Rush to Madison, 13 Dec. 1818, 15 Nov. 1820, Penn. Hist. Soc. Am. 13520.

61. J. F. Willis and M. L. Primack, *An Economic History of the United States*, 2nd ed. (Englewood Cliffs, NJ, 1989), 103–104.

62. D. E. Graves, *Guns Across the River: The Battle of the Windmill, 1838* (Toronto, 2001).

63. J. C. Arnell, "Trooping to the Canadas," *Mariner's Mirror* 53 (1967): 143–60.

64. L. Lépine, *Les Officiers des Milice du Bas-Canada, 1812–1815* (Québec, 1996).

65. Stephenson to Sidmouth, 29 Aug. 1815, DRO. 152M/C1815/OC1.

66. NA. WO. 6/86, 300–301.

67. Jefferson to Sir John Sinclair, 31 July 1816, DRO. 152M/C1816/OF30.

68. D. A. Campbell, *Unlikely Allies: America, Britain and the Victorian Beginnings of the Special Relationship* (London, 2007).

69. A. W. Robertson, " 'Look on This Picture . . . and on This!': Nationalism, Localism, and Partisan Images of Otherness in the United States, 1787–1820," *American Historical Review* 106 (2001): 1263–80.

70. S. W. Haynes, "Anglophobia and the Annexation of Texas: The Quest for National Security," in *Manifest Destiny and Empire: American Antebellum Expansionism,* ed. Haynes and C. Morris (College Station, TX, 1997), 115–45; E. D. Adams, *British Interests and Activities in Texas* (Gloucester, 1963).

71. F. Merk, *Albert Gallatin and the Oregon Problem: A Study in Anglo-American Diplomacy* (Cambridge, MA, 1950); K. Bourne, *Britain and the Balance of Power in North America, 1815–1908* (Berkeley, California, 1967); H. Jones and D. Rakestraw, *Prologue to Manifest Destiny: Anglo-American Relations in the 1840s* (Wilmington, DE, 1997).

72. F. M. Carroll, *A Good and Wise Measure: The Search for the Canadian-American Boundary, 1783–1842* (Toronto, 2001), 208–21.

73. G. L. Bernstein, "Special Relationship and Appeasement: Liberal Policy Towards America in the Age of Palmerston," *Historical Journal* 41 (1998): 727.

74. F. M. Leventhal and R. Quinault, ed., *Anglo-American Attitudes: From Revolution to Partnership* (Aldershot, 2000).

75. M. de Nie, "The London Press and the American Civil War," in *Anglo-American Media Interactions, 1850–2000,* ed. J. H. Wiener and M. Hampton (Basingstoke, 2007), 129–54.

76. H. Jones, *Union in Peril: The Crisis over British Intervention in the Civil War* (Chapel Hill, NC, 1992); K. Brauer, "British Mediation and the American Civil War: A Reconsideration," *Journal of Southern History* 38 (1972): 49–64.

77. J. J. and P. P. Barnes, eds., *The American Civil War Through British Eyes; Dispatches from British Diplomats,* 3 vols. (Kent, OH, 2003–2005).

78. R. J. M. Blackett, *Divided Hearts: Britain and the American Civil War* (Baton Rouge, LA, 2001).

79. NA. FO. 5/879 fols 52–7.

80. J. F. Beeler, *British Naval Policy in the Gladstone-Disraeli Era, 1866–1880* (Stanford, California, 1997), 199–200.

81. H. J. Fuller, *Clad in Iron. The American Civil War and the Challenge of British Naval Power* (Westport, CT, 2008), 282–85.

82. Rush to Adams, 21 Mar., 17 Ap. (quote) 1814, Penn. Hist. Soc. AM 1352; Hickey, *War of 1812,* 108.

83. M. Mason, *Slavery and Politics in the Early American Republic* (Chapel Hill, NC, 2006).

84. J. M. Banner, *To the Hartford Convention: The Federalists and the Origins of Party Politics in Massachusetts* (New York, 1970).

85. H. Adams, *History of the United States During the Administration of James Madison* (New York, 1986 [1889–91], 1122.

86. Hickey, *Don't Give Up the Ship!,* 297.

87. Rush to Adams, 25 Sept. 1813, Penn. Hist. Soc. AM. 1352.

88. K. J. Hagan and I. J. Bickerton, *Unintended Consequences: The United States at War* (London, 2007), 45, 47.

89. *American War Songs* (Philadelphia, 1925), 44–50.

90. M. A. Bellesiles, "Experiencing the War of 1812," in *Britain and America Go to War*, ed. Flavell and Conway, 205–40.

91. W. G. Keener, "The Price of Fame: Staffordshire Wins the War of 1812," *Timeline* (Ap.–May 1989): 29–33.

92. Lines 189–200.

93. W. A. McDougall, *Freedom Just Around The Corner: A New American History, 1585–1828* (New York, 2004), 420–21; D. C. Hendrickson, "Preemption, Unilateralism, and Hegemony: The American Tradition?," *Orbis* 50 (2006): 276–77.

94. R. Morriss, "Colonization, Conquest, and the Supply of Food and Transport: The Reorganisation of Logistics Management, 1780–1795," *War in History* 14 (2007): 310–24.

95. N. Onuf, *Nations, Markets, and War: Modern History and the American Civil War* (Charlottesville, VA, 2006), 240, 243, 247.

96. Rush to Adams, 2 Aug. 1813, Penn. Hist. Soc. AM. 1352.

97. J. W. Moore, *The Fortifications Board 1816–1828 and the Definition of National Security* (Charleston, SC, 1981); B. M. Linn, *The Echo of Battle: The Army's Way of War* (Cambridge, MA, 2007), 12–13.

98. *Madison*, 5:411.

99. J. Lurie, "Andrew Jackson, Martial Law, Civilian Control of the Military, and American Politics: An Intriguing Amalgam," *Military Law Review* 126 (1989): 133–45; W. H. Rehnquist, *All the Laws but One: Civil Liberties in Wartime* (New York, 1999), 69–70; M. Warshauer, *Andrew Jackson and the Politics of Martial Law: Nationalism, Civil Liberties, and Partisanship* (Knoxville, TN, 2006).

100. J. Lynch, *Caudillos in Spanish America, 1800–1850* (New York, 1992); M. A. Centeno, "War in Modern Latin America," in *War in the Modern World since 1815*, ed. J. Black (London, 2003), 149–64.

101. L. Langley, *Struggle for the American Mediterranean: United States-European Rivalry in the Gulf-Caribbean, 1776–1904* (Athens, Georgia, 1969); J. E. Lewis, *American Union and the Problem of Neighbourhood: The United States and the Collapse of the Spanish Empire* (Chapel Hill, NC, 1998).

102. E. H. Gould, "The Making of an Atlantic State System. Britain and the United States, 1795–1825," in *Britain and America Go to War: The Impact of War and Warfare in Anglo-America, 1754–1815*, ed. J. Flavell and S. Conway (Gainesville, FA, 2004), 260.

## CHAPTER 7. CONCLUSIONS

1. Rush to Adams, 25 Sept. 1813, Penn. Hist. Soc. AM. 1352.

2. Castlereagh to Liverpool, 2 Jan. 1815, Wellington, *Supplementary Despatches*, 9:523.

3. Ibid., 554.

4. BL. Add. 57315 fol. 39.

5. R. A. Preston, *The Defence of the Undefended Border: Planning for War in North America, 1867–1939* (Montréal, 1977).

6. M. R. Shulman, The Influence of History upon Sea Power: The Navalist Reinterpretation of the War of 1812," *Journal of Military History* 56 (1992): 183–206.

7. *Sunday Times*, 14 Oct. 1913; H. C. Smith, *Sulgrave Manor and the Washingtons* (London, 1933), 202–212; Wilentz, "The Buccaneer," in *Past Imperfect. History According to the Movies*, eds. M.C. Carnes, T. Mico, J. Miller-Monzon and D. Rubel (London, 1996), 110–15. For an accurate account, J. L. Grammond, *The Baratarians and the Battle of New Orleans* (Baton Rouge, 1961).

8. K. Burk, *Old World, New World: The Story of Britain and America* (London, 2007).

9. Philatelic Affairs Division, United States Postal Service, *United States Postage Stamps* (Washington, DC, 1972), 202.

10. J. Chapman, " 'This Ship is England': History, Politics and National Identity in *Master and Commander: The Far Side of the World* (2003)," in *The New Film History: Sources, Methods, Approaches*, eds. Chapman, M. Glancy and S. Harper (Basingstoke, 2007), 53–68, esp., 63.

11. A. Price, *The Old Vengeful* (London, 1982; 1984 edn), 111, 255, 231.

12. J. L. Gaddis, *Surprise, Security, and the American Experience* (Cambridge, MA, 2004), 12–13.

13. *Guardian*, 13 Mar. 2008, 22.

14. Paul Johnson, review of J. Latimer, *1812*, in *Literary Review* (Oct. 2007): 23.

15. B. Hilton, *A Mad, Bad, and Dangerous People? England 1783–1846* (Oxford, 2006), 231.

16. M. F. Boyd, "Events at Prospect Bluff on the Apalachiola River," *Florida Historical Quarterly* 16 (1937): 55–93; J. W. Covington, "The Negro Fort," *Gulf Coast Historical Review* 5 (1990): 79–91.

17. E. S. Vansickle, "A Transnational Vision for African Colonization: John H. B. Latrobe and the Future of Maryland in Liberia," *Journal of Transatlantic Studies* 1 (2003): 214–32. I would like to thank Eugene Vansickle for discussing this topic with me.

18. Cochrane to Rear Admiral Pultney Malcolm, 17 Feb. 1815, NA. WO. 1/143.

# Selected Further Reading

Albright, H. *New Orleans—The Battle of the Bayous.* New York, 1990.

Allen, R. S. *His Majesty's Indian Allies: British Indian Policy in Defense of Canada, 1774–1815.* Toronto, 1992.

Allison, R. J. *Stephen Decatur: American Naval Hero, 1779–1820.* Amherst, Massachusetts, 2005.

Altoff, G. T. *Amongst My Best Men: African-Americans and the War of 1812.* Put-in-Bay, Ohio, 1996.

Antal, S. *A Wampum Denied: Proctor's War of 1812.* Ottawa, 1997.

Barbuto, R. V. *Niagara, 1814: America Invades Canada.* Lawrence, Kansas, 2000.

Barnes, J. *Naval Actions of the War of 1812.* London, 1969.

Benn, C. *The Iroquois in the War of 1812.* Toronto, 1998.

Borneman, W. R. *1812: The War That Forged a Nation.* New York, 2004.

Bowler, R. A., ed. *War along the Niagara: Essays on the War of 1812 and Its Legacy.* Youngstown, New York, 1991.

——. *The War of 1812.* London, 1973.

Byron, G. *The War of 1812 on the Chesapeake Bay.* Baltimore, 1964.

Calloway, C. *Crown and Calumet: British-Indian Relations, 1783–1815.* Norman, Oklahoma, 1987.

Carroll, F. M. *A Good and Wise Measure: The Struggle for the Canadian-American Border, 1783–1842.* Toronto, 2001.

Coles, H. L. *The War of 1812.* Chicago, 1965.

Collins, G. *Guidebook to the Historic Sites of the War of 1812.* 2nd ed. Toronto, 2006.

Cress, L. D. *Citizens in Arms: The Army and Militia in American Society to the War of 1812.* Chapel Hill, North Carolina, 1982.

Dudley, W. G. *Splintering the Wooden Wall: The British Blockade of the United States, 1812–1815.* Annapolis, Maryland, 2003.

Elting, J. R. *Amateurs to Arms! A Military History of the War of 1812*. New York, 1995.

Fredriksen, J. C. *Free Trade and Sailors' Rights: a Bibliography of the War of 1812*. Westport, Connecticut, 1985.

——. *War of 1812: Eyewitness Accounts: An Annotated Bibliography*. Westport, Connecticut, 1997.

George, C. T. *Terror on the Chesapeake: The War of 1812 on the Bay*. Shippenburg, Pennsylvania, 2000.

Graves, D. E. *Field of Glory: The Battle of Crysler's Farm, 1813*. Toronto, 1999.

——. *Red Coats and Grey Jackets: The Battle of Chippawa, 1814*. Toronto, 1994.

—— *"Where Right and Glory Lead!" The Battle of Lundy's Lane, 1814*. Toronto, 1997.

Gough, B. M. *Fighting Sail on Lake Huron and Georgian Bay: The War of 1812 and Its Aftermath*. Annapolis, Maryland, 2002.

Heidler, D. S. and J. T. Heidler, eds, *Encyclopaedia of the War of 1812*. Santa Barbara, 1997.

Hickey, D. R. *The War of 1812: A Forgotten Conflict*. Urbana, Illinois, 1989.

——. *Don't Give Up the Ship! Myths of the War of 1812*. Urbana, Illinois, 2006.

Hitsman, J. M. *The Incredible War of 1812: A Military History*. Updated by D. E. Graves. Toronto, 1999.

Holland, J. W. *Andrew Jackson and the Creek War: Victory at the Horseshoe*. Tuscaloosa, Alabama, 1968.

Horsman, R. *The War of 1812*. London, 1969.

—— *The Causes of the War of 1812*. Philadelphia, 1962.

Langguth, A. J. *Union 1812: The Americans Who Fought the Second War of Independence*. London, 2006.

Latimer, J. *1812: War with America*. London, 2007.

Lemmon, S. M. *Frustrated Patriots: North Carolina and the War of 1812*. Chapel Hill, North Carolina, 1973.

Mahon, J. K. *The War of 1812*. Gainesville, Florida, 1972.

Malcomson, R. *Lords of the Lake: The Naval War on Lake Ontario, 1812–1814*. Annapolis, Maryland, 1998.

——. *A Very Brilliant Affair: The Battle of Queenston Heights, 1812*. Annapolis, Maryland, 2003.

Owlsey, F. L. *Struggle for the Gulf Borderlands: The Creek War and the Battle of New Orleans, 1812–1815*. Gainesville, Florida, 1981.

Pitch, A. S. *The Burning of Washington: The British Invasion of 1914*. Annapolis, Maryland, 1998.

Quimby, R. S. *The U.S. Army in the War of 1812: An Operational and Command Study*. East Lansing, Michigan, 1997.

Silverstone, S. A. *Divided Union: The Politics of War in the Early American Republic*. Ithaca, Cornell, 2004.

Smith, D. L. *The War of 1812: An Annotated Bibliography*. New York, 1985.

Stagg, J. C. A. *Mr. Madison's War: Politics, Diplomacy and Warfare in the Early American Republic, 1783–1830*. Princeton, New Jersey, 1983.

Stanley, G. F. G. *The War of 1812: Land Operations.* Toronto, 1983.

Sugden, J. *Tecumseh, a Life.* New York, 1997.

Turner, W. B. *British Generals in the War of 1812: High Command in the Canadas.* Montréal, 1999.

Whitehorne, J. A. *The Battle for Baltimore, 1814.* Baltimore, Maryland, 1997.

Willig, T. D. *Restoring the Chain of Friendship: British Policy and the Indians of the Great Lakes, 1783–1815.* Lincoln, Nebraska, 2008.

Zuehlke, M. *For Honour's Sake: The War of 1812 and the Brokering of an Uneasy Peace.* Toronto, 2006.

# Index

275